F
391   179615
.S48
M4

Msgr. Wm. Barry Memorial Library
Barry University
Miami, FL   33161

METZ

JOHN SELMAN,...

JOHN SELMAN

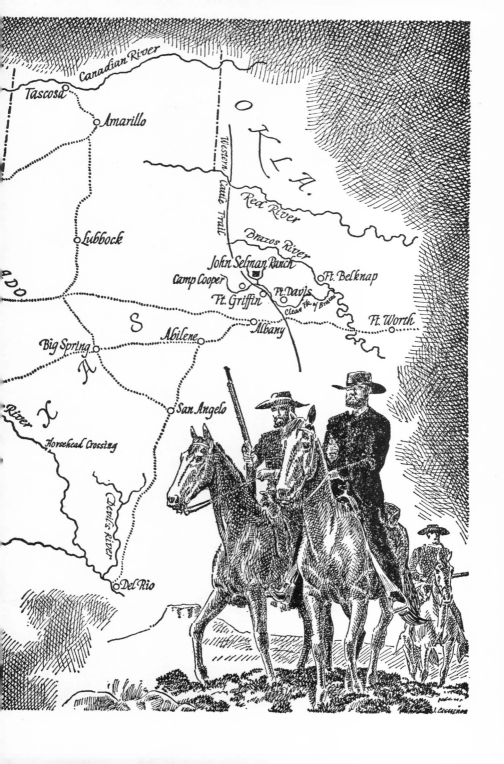

JOHN SELMAN, GUNFIGHTER

BY LEON CLAIRE METZ

Norman
University of Oklahoma Press

By Leon Claire Metz

The Shooters (El Paso, 1976)
Pat Garrett: Story of a Western Lawman (Norman, 1974)
Dallas Stoudenmire: El Paso Marshal (Austin, 1969; Norman, 1979)
John Selman: Texas Gunfighter (New York, 1966; second edition, *John Selman, Gunfighter,* Norman, 1980)

ISBN: 0-8061-1557-2

*This book is affectionately dedicated
to my father and mother.*

CONTENTS

LIST OF ILLUSTRATIONS

11

INTRODUCTION

SHOULD A prize ever be given for the least-written-about gunman in Western history, the award will almost certainly go to John Selman. Though everybody knows who he was, nobody knows anything about him. He is probably the only well known six-gun figure whose soul has not been repeatedly probed by a writer's pen. Others, such as Billy the Kid, John Wesley Hardin and Wild Bill Hickok, to name a few, have captured the fancy of numerous biographers and floated away on a torrent of words.

The reason for Selman's relative obscurity soon becomes apparent to a researcher. Unlike many other killers, he was not an exhibitionist. He did not want to become well known.

Selman's avoidance of the limelight, his shunning of publicity, his retreat to the shadows during moments of climactic activity, have all contributed to a researcher's nightmare. When the "old-timers" speak or write of the memories of their youth, the name John Selman usually pops up as an afterthought. People who actually knew him thought of this gunman only as a secondary character, one who merely took part in events and was not a prime mover. Yet, time after time, Selman appears in the blur of racing events, and when the total number of such appearances is added up, the idea begins to emerge that this man was far from being a mere extra in the cast of Western characters. Many a time it was his hand that manipulated events from behind the scene.

In spite of Selman's anonymity, or perhaps because of it, the usual fantastic hodge-podge of tales and folklore has developed about him. Frequently, he is accused of doing things he did not do, but more important, he is moved all the way up or all the way down in the moral scale and described as a heroic upholder of law and order or the blackest kind of a frontier villain. The fact is, he could be both. But when all the facts are in, he never seems to occupy any middle ground. He is either black or white and hardly ever dons a coat of gray.

Because so many people have such diverse opinions of Selman, it is hard for his biographer to come up with a single, straight account of any particular incident. Only occasionally is the evidence so complete and irrefutable that one story will suffice. Where controversy exists in the pages which follow, all the views which seem to have any merit will be presented.

From a historian's point of view John Selman is a hilltop emerging from heavy mist. The background is often obscure. It is not that events do not shape themselves around him; but the degree of his participation in these events is sometimes hard to determine—especially during the momentous years from 1860 to 1874. With the Southwest in chaos, the Civil War in full stride, Indian raids and white outlawry on the rise, John Selman barely emerges into focus.

Yet he was a dangerous man, a leader of outlaws, with many notches on his gun. The number of men who fell before his pistol may have been as few as twelve, but the total probably rises much higher than that—perhaps to twenty-five or thirty. Magazine writers have given him an arbitrary score of twenty, without citing evidence to back it up.

Some of Selman's killings can be documented, of course. The shooting of John Wesley Hardin is the most obvious example—in fact, this is the killing which gave him his claim to fame. And there are others, as the following pages will show, which bear the mark of John Selman's handiwork and so must lie in his smokehouse. Frequently, however, the killings in which he was involved occurred while he was in the company of others and it is impossible to say that he was completely and solely responsible. He certainly was an accessory, however, and must bear at least partial responsibility.

As an admitted member of the Fort Griffin Vigilance Committee, for instance, he participated in numerous lynchings, maybe as many as twenty. In one Fort Griffin shooting which was labeled "suicide," the victim should have had the name John Selman stamped on his forehead. In New Mexico, as well as in Texas, he participated in group killings. He and his party were charged by Governor Lew Wallace with the murder of four boys—brutal, senseless slaughters. And a number of other killings in that territory have been charged to Selman's prowess with a pistol.

With all this behind him, he drops out of sight for seven years. Supposedly he went to Mexico. No one knows exactly what happened during this period, but it is not likely that he laid down his weapon and became a man of peace.

Of course he was not all bad. At one time or another he showed considerable humanity and was even liked and admired. For several years he was the sole support of his widowed mother, three sisters and a brother. Although the records show that he was a deserter from the Confederate Army, the offense may not have been as serious as it seems. During the early part of his life there is evidence that he was an average, well liked, even popular frontiersman—a man who was respected by others and who appeared to have much good in him. Toward the end it was not unusual for a crowd of children to follow Selman through the streets of El Paso, and he had no objections to letting them ride on his horse or sit in his lap while he told them stories. His young friends, and even some adults, never knew him by any other name than Uncle John. The whole town turned out to pay its respects at his funeral.

John Selman was never convicted of any crime. Although he was called a rustler, a robber, a murderer, whenever he went to court witnesses had either moved or disappeared, the charges were dropped or he was acquitted. In Fort Griffin, when he was indicted for crimes, the citizens furnished a horse for his escape. Only once did he ever come close to a conviction and that was during his trial for killing John Wesley Hardin. He case ended in a hung jury and was never brought to court again, for Selman himself met death before another trial could be held.

Although Selman's bloody escapades are important enough to stand alone in history, his claim to fame is the killing of Hardin. There in the Acme saloon two men met in a still-controversial burst of gunfire. One died instantly. The other lived only a few months longer, whisky-soaked and unhappy, himself to die in a drunken encounter with another quick-shooting gunman.

The careers of both these dangerous men had pinched out long before and their reputations were basically all they had left. Selman—old, half blind, partially crippled—still dreamed of one final thunderous convulsion to cap his blood-stained career. Hardin, a middle-aged ex-gunfighter, had left his fiery youth in the prison where he had spent fifteen years, but he too looked back with some nostalgia on the days when he had terrified whole counties in southeast Texas, and he yearned to recapture the glory that now existed only in his imagination.

16

Hardin and Selman had much in common. Both had grown up with sound religous training—Hardin with probably a little more than Selman, since the senior Hardin was a Methodist preacher. Both had lived a raw, rough tumultuous life in lawless times. Both had seen their relatives and friends die violently and were hardened to scenes of blood and violence. Both had a weakness for women. And both were coldblooded killers to whom the life of a fellow human being meant next to nothing.

In one way Hardin was different, however: he had the impulse to write his memoirs and did so in the leisure time afforded him by a non-existent law practice in El Paso. His autobiography is still the best source of information about his life and the best indicator of what went on in his complicated and tormented inner world. One strange fact stands out. In telling of his past life he scarcely bothered to justify his offenses against society; in fact, he seemed to revel in them. Most of the defenses he presented for his acts seem to be little more than boyish boasting, and in episode after episode he regards himself as an instrument of destiny appointed to eliminate the bad men who opposed him.

Selman's motives are as obscure as Hardin's are obvious. His nature is an enigma so hard to penetrate that no biographer up to the present time has succeeded in getting more than a glimpse of the interior of a killer who may have outdone even Hardin in bloodletting. A sort of late-blooming dark angel, he gave almost no indication during the first thirty years of his life of a disposition to ride the hurricane of violence. Once aboard the storm, however, he never climbed off until the day he died.

1

THE DESERTION

ON APRIL 25, 1863, John Selman[1] deserted from the Confederate Army.[2] The day before, he was performing his duties in a soldierly manner. Now he was gone, riding a big horse and heading south.

His flight from the Confederate Gray was the first recorded footprint on a long, bloodstained trail which winds for thirty years through the badlands of Western history. When at last he dropped over the final rise that separated him from the fluttering Rebel flag, he was setting the pattern of his tangled, violent life.

Actually, this was his second desertion, for he had gone over the hill three months before, and had returned voluntarily.

We have no way of knowing why he deserted either time. Trouble with his officers—a bad situation at home—boredom —any number of factors could have been at work. Whatever the reason, he was on his way, and as he dug his heels in deep, the mount lunged forward in long strides which quickly ate up the hard Oklahoma soil. Night and day he traveled, over *arroyos,* across rivers, through hostile Indian country. Skirting established settlements and military areas, alert for danger, he headed home.

Home was the borough of Sherman, in Grayson County, Texas, a small frontier community still living within the shadow of Indian raids. Here the Selman family, with John as its sole support, had migrated just a few years before. Now the clan decided to move again, perhaps to remove the deserter from fear of pursuit, or perhaps just to satisfy John's desire for new experience, a trait which was to become more pronounced in the years to come. This time the family headed for the outermost edge of the Texas frontier.

Behind him John left a history so vague that it is difficult to follow precisely. He was born John Henry Selman in Madison County, Arkansas, on November 16, 1839.[3] At his birth he was the youngest of six children; others were born later.[4]

His father Jeremiah Selman, known as "Honest Jeremiah" [5] among his neighbors, was an Englishman who had been a Kentucky schoolteacher.[6] He married a Miss Underwood from one of the Carolinas and they moved to Arkansas. For a while at least, the family must have enjoyed some degree of prosperity; the census records for 1840 show that they owned five or six slaves.

In Arkansas Jeremiah Selman became a farmer and schoolmaster, although indications are that he made little progress financially. His neighbors were poor and so was he. A granddaughter has reported that not one of his students ever owned a book. Jeremiah's usual method of teaching was to write out some sentences which the students would copy and take home, returning in a few days to turn in their papers and get a new list of words and phrases.

John must have had an average amount of schooling for the time and place. If it was not superior, the reason might be that his father was bordering on old age when John was born. The 1840 census showed a sister over twenty and a brother over thirty.

Although large, the family was close knit and affectionate. Jeremiah regularly read aloud from a large family Bible and John once tanned a lamb's skin, softening the leather and forming it into a cover to protect the book.[7]

Around 1858 the Selmans moved to Grayson County, Texas, and here Jeremiah again taught school while his children tilled the soil. It was not long before they were known and respected members of the community. Suddenly, shortly before the outbreak of the Civil War, John's mother is referred to as the "Widow Selman." We know nothing more than this about the death of Jeremiah Selman.

The position of leadership now fell to John, his older brothers and sisters having undoubtedly established homes elsewhere. He was charged with providing for six persons, including himself. The 1860 census reports for Grayson County show his age as twenty; the others listed are his brother Tom, age eleven; Lucinda, a sister, age fourteen, and Mary Ann, another sister, age fifteen. His mother, age unknown, is not listed, nor is another sister, Elizabeth—age also unknown.

On December 15, 1861, John Selman enlisted as a private soldier in the Twenty-second Regiment of Texas Cavalry. The fact that he saw fit to join up right at the beginning of the Christmas holidays may indicate that John was in trouble at home. Whatever the reason, one day he said a hurried farewell to his family and friends and put on the Confederate uniform.

His first duty station was Fort Washita, C. N. (Choctaw Nation), where he reported for duty on December 28, 1861.[8] Some history was made at Fort Washita, but most of it had been scribbled at the cannon's mouth before Selman arrived. General Zachary Taylor had selected the site in 1842—an

21

advance of the frontier from the Forts Gibson and Towson line. Founded specifically to protect the immigrant Choctaws and Chickasaws from the Plains Indians, it became a way station on the heavily traveled Texas Road and Marcy Trail, favored by gold seekers on their way to California after the Mexican War.[9]

It was at Fort Washita that the first and only completely reliable description of John Selman was set down. This was probably his first experience with discipline, standing there in the darkened room as the sergeant glanced up occasionally and asked in a laconic grunt for the information he must have. The muster-roll card describes John as "twenty-two years old; five feet, ten inches in height; dark hair; dark complexion and blue eyes." He gave his place of birth as Arkansas and listed his occupation as farmer. A man who was always proud of good horseflesh, he furnished his own mount and riggings, the value of which the army put at $150.[10]

From comments and bits of description which were recorded later on, we can add a little bit to the official list of his characteristics. His eyes were a pale blue, so light it was hard to tell where the pupil left off and the white began. He habitually walked with them cast down and did not often look at people he was talking to. That habitual downcast gaze was no indication of abstraction of mind or inattention, however. He was as sharp and shrewd as they came; a sheriff who knew of his later misdeeds once wrote to a Ranger commander that Selman was "such a great thief and scoundrel, and withal so sharp that he can not be caught at his rascality." [11]

A good and skillful talker at need, unusually persuasive and logical, John had a way with men when he wanted something done. He was also a superb gambler, one whose poker-playing ability carried over into other aspects of his life, allowing him to put up a good bluff away from the card table.

22

For a while in the service things seemed to go smoothly. Selman evidently caught the eye of some of his superiors, and before six months were out he was promoted to the rank of Second Corporal in Company B of what was then called Stevens' Regiment of the Texas Dismounted Cavalry.[12] To make rank so quickly would indicate intelligence, an ability to learn and leadership qualities. No doubt his commanding officers thought of John as having the qualifications of a first-rate soldier. Had they been able to tame his wild, rebellious nature, they might have had an unusual fighter for the Con-federacy.

It is not difficult to imagine some of the characteristics and achievements which enabled Selman to become a corporal. Certainly he was a crack shot and an excellent horseman, but since his unit was composed primarily of Texans, he was definitely not alone in these capabilities. A safe bet, based on his activities in later life, is that he attracted others to him and showed ability to command. If the occasion demanded, he could be counted upon to swing men in line with his point of view, and this, combined with his other skills and abilities, was just what the army needed to keep his rough, hard-drinking and quick-shooting fellow soldiers under control.

However, John Selman was neither happy in the service nor impressed by his promotion. He had no sooner made corporal than he went AWOL. Where he went and why he took leave of the army so suddenly is difficult to understand, particularly since he returned, evidently of his own accord, in the early part of 1863. As his service file does not indicate any stockade time, apparently he was not imprisoned for the offense, but he was busted to private, and probably reprimanded.

John must have been bitter about his punishment; he went AWOL again on April 25, 1863, and this time he was determined not to return. The army, now out of patience, decided to throw the book at him. On the muster roll for the following May and June, the AWOL was changed to Desertion. He was never brought to trial for the offense.

There is no evidence that Selman ever saw any action against Union forces. He was in the armed services only a short time—hardly long enough to get used to his rifle—and since he was stationed so far from the main lines of battle it is unlikely that he ever smelled the smoke of conflict. The only recorded action at Fort Washita occurred around May 1, 1861, several months before Selman's arrival. Arriving too late to participate in any action, although the news of the fighting may have been the reason he joined, Selman saw only dreary months of post duty ahead of him. The barracks erected in 1850 were at that time the pride of the United States Army, but John was not impressed. He didn't mind sleeping on the ground as long as there was fighting, but with the US forces now gone and no action in prospect life was just too dull for him.

2

DEATH BECOMES NO STRANGER

AFTER HIS ABRUPT departure from the military and his return to Sherman, Texas, John Selman took his widowed mother, his sisters Mary Ann, Lucinda and Elizabeth, and his brother Tom and headed farther west.

There were few vestiges of civilization beyond Fort Davis, Texas.[1] Located on the Clear Fork of the Brazos River in Stephens County, the Fort was just a few miles east of the eventually to be established Shackelford County line[2] and about twenty miles northeast of present-day Albany. The community protruded deep into Indian country, like the muzzle of a gun, and was the settlers' first line of defense. Today only one silent blockhouse casts its shadow across a lonely countryside, but day before yesterday a small group of people lived a precarious life within its confines.

Named in honor of Jefferson Davis, President of the Confederacy, Fort Davis was never a fort in the true sense of the word. It was simply a compact settlement on the edge of the frontier where citizens banded together for mutual protection. No regular army soldiers were ever stationed there.[3]

There were many other tiny settlements scattered up and down through the Indian country—some even farther west—any one of which John might have chosen. His decision was undoubtedly influenced by the fact that John's future wife, a young lady from Sherman, had a brother, Jasper N. deGraffenreid,[4] living at the Stockton Ranch near Davis. The Selman family was not exactly moving in with strangers.

Of course there were other reasons for moving to the Clear Fork country. The area was amply endowed with tree-covered hills, crisp, cool-running streams and deep valleys. The luxuriant grama grasses grew high, and wild game, especially buffalo and deer, was abundant. In addition, this paradise was located in an obscure, out-of-the-way part of Texas where anyone hiding on the dark side of the law could find a refuge.

Until the outbreak of the Civil War, a community like Fort Davis had rarely been necessary. The Indians not already exterminated had been corralled on reservations, thanks partly to the troops at Camp Cooper, a few miles northwest of Fort Davis in Throckmorton County. Established in 1856, it stood between the Clear Fork Comanche Indian Reservation and the settlers scattered up and down the Brazos tributaries. A roster of its officers reads like a "Who's Who" of Union and Confederate greats.[5] Its most noted commander was Lieutenant Colonel Robert E. Lee, who at that time considered himself to be in the Siberia of America and looked forward to a quick and permanent transfer.

It was Lee's job to keep a tight security blanket around the Comanches, bottling up the reservation Indians and preventing the wild ones from gaining sanctuary and using the government land as a base for raiding and pillaging. In this job he was only moderately successful, once chasing a marauding band for 1100 miles and bringing back to the post only one captive, a woman.[6]

The last Union commander at Camp Cooper was Captain T. S. Carpenter, who, with a force of 250 men, was in charge in 1861. Many of Carpenter's soldiers undoubtedly had Southern sympathies and conflicting loyalties. Then, with the dark specter of war hovering over the nation and with both sides jockeying for position, Carpenter found himself surrounded on all fronts by Texas State troops under the command of Colonel W. C. Dalrymple. The Union captain, knowing that even if he might smash these state forces he would still be deep in enemy territory, and fearing the consequences to the whole nation if he did not surrender, reluctantly handed over his sword. Camp Cooper lowered its flag on February 21, 1861, thus avoiding a blood bath which might have stolen the historical headlines from Fort Sumter, which did not fall until two months later.[7]

After the outbreak of Civil War, with the Union troops driven out and Confederates pulled away for duty in other parts of the country, the Indians, with all restraints removed, reverted to their old raiding ways and soon the whole countryside crackled with flames and gunfire.

It was about this time that John Selman rode into the area. Camp Cooper was reduced to a sprinkling of Confederate soldiers, and the settlers were in a quandary because they had ventured into the country in the first place only because of the protection of the camp. Many widely scattered ranches had been completely dependent for their safety upon the horse soldiers. Texas could not supply the necessary protection for its citizens. As a result, the people panicked, rallied, held a mass meeting and decided to "fort up." The result was Fort Davis.[8]

Although it is at Fort Davis that John Selman first comes into historical focus, he and his family actually lived for several months at a small community a few miles below Davis known as the "lower fort." [9] Since Fort Davis was much the larger of the two places, however, they spent considerable time there. This we learn from the excellent record of life in that little township preserved in the diaries of Samuel P. Newcomb,[10] a semi-literate schoolteacher who was a friend of John Selman. Newcomb reveals the hard and precarious life led by the people on this remote frontier. On the first day of the New Year in 1865 he sat down to write in his diary. His meditations were gloomy, since only that day he had helped bury a child whose death, he thought, was caused by exposure. "As time rolls on," he wrote, "it is continually mowing us down, one by one; and how impossible it is for us to tell who of us will pass away with the present year." [11]

Lucinda, John Selman's sister, was in danger before the year was out. On May 8, 1865, Newcomb reports her near death with erysipelas as a doctor was sent for from Fort Belknap. John must have felt some of Newcomb's concern as Sam wrote, "Doctor Lindsley is not a doctor by profession, but he has some practice in giving medicine." Lucinda's survival was generally credited to a miracle brought about in spite of the doctor.

Death came in other and more violent forms since Indians were a perennial problem. Direct attacks upon the different forts were daily expected, but the closest Fort Davis ever came to being assaulted was in the early part of 1865. A large body of Comanches thundered almost into the community confines in pursuit of a settler named McCarty. Instantly all was in confusion, even though the Indians veered off at the last minute and disappeared. Some women began dashing about gathering up their children; while others were in tearful distress about husbands and sons who were out rounding up cattle. Newcomb remarked that "some were so badly frightened that they ran from place to place like they had lost all reason."

28

Several men who managed to hold their wits together saddled horses and after bellowing orders for their wives and children to seek safety inside the houses they rode off in pursuit of the Comanches. After tracking them all day, the men returned that night with nothing to show for their efforts but fresh saddlesores.

At other times, the settlers were not quite so fortunate. When John Selman rode in one day in June, 1865, he heard the story of the two Hitson boys and Press McCarty, all of whom had just barely escaped from the Indians. In company with a Negro boy, they were attacked out on the prairie by about twenty-five Comanches. McCarty made his escape but for the other three, a wild chase took place across the plains. Through mesquite and across gullies they rode. Eyes wide, faces flushed, hands gripping the reins of badly lathered horses, they wheeled, reversed, snapped off an occasional quick shot and searched for a place of safety. The Negro boy, lagging behind, had his hat blow off and made a fatal mistake when he stopped to retrieve it. The Comanches barely paused as they cut him down with rifle and arrow fire.

John and William Hitson made it to the river bank where they found a bluff with an overhanging top. Grabbing their rifles and spinning off their horses, they headed for the precipitous wall. Ducking under it, they made a stand—one which saved their lives.

Fording the river, some of the Indians tried to circle the boys for a good shot, while others splashed out in the middle of the stream to shoot at the youngsters. The accuracy of the redskins did not prove outstanding, so they tried rolling rocks down on the victims. This attempt was equally unsuccessful since the projection of the bluff made the boulders go over the boys' heads and drop harmlessly into the river. Finally, the Indians rounded up the horses, took a long angry look at the two elusive scalps and rode off.[12]

Selman and the other settlers had their hands full with all these Indian difficulties, although it is impossible to pinpoint any fighting that John participated in. Trouble occurred so frequently that Newcomb rarely pointed out any particular person involved, leaving the impression that everyone handled his rightful share.

Newcomb once remarked that it was strange they did not suffer more from thieves and outlaws. Although he reports some heavy drinking and a few violations of the moral code, only one serious case of thievery is mentioned in the diaries. Susan Newcomb describes a man named Andrew Jackson Marshal, commonly called "Jocko," a young fellow who stole a horse, a blanket and some other items. Jocko tried to escape by making a dash across the plains as a posse equipped with dogs followed close behind. Susan mentions only her brothers by name as members of this posse, so there is no way of knowing if John Selman was along or not. He may well have been.

After a chase which stretched almost to Weatherford, Texas, the outraged frontiersmen finally cornered their prey. Jocko, however, was a mentally retarded youth who, upon being captured, fell on his knees and began loudly to pray. This bothered some of the settlers so much they refused to help hang the boy, and soon hot words were flying through the crisp air. After a short argument, the posse agreed to whip the lad and let him go.

On February 18, 1865, candidates for public office rode into Fort Davis to do a little electioneering. Tod Willet was running for county clerk, W. R. St. John for tax assessor and collector, John Selman for sheriff.[13]

Sam Newcomb makes numerous references to Selman as being home from the army on "furlough." No one ever seems to have mentioned the fact that he had been on leave for a considerable time. Neither did his peculiar situation deter him from running for public office. He was just a young fellow now, apparently well liked by his fellow citizens—on who, up to now, had found no opportunity to display any of the virtues he may have had, or to commit any great sins. The fact that he wanted to be a peace officer is probably significant. It was an ambition which stayed with him for the rest of his life.

Although Stephens County had been organized for some time, county officials evidently did not wander very often into the Fort Davis area. The Newcomb Diaries, which cover a period of six years, do not once mention any state, county or federal officials other than Confederate Army troopers. Some of these county positions must have been filled simply because the law required it, but duties were so skimpy and pay so negligible that an officer usually had to seek other means to make a living.

Still, Selman must have taken to the campaign trail with a great deal of gusto, although Newcomb never revealed whether this gusto got him elected to office, or what happened to the other campaigners. But John showed up at Fort Davis with increasing frequency in the weeks that followed, and he appeared to have a faculty for making himself moderately conspicuous. His movements always aroused some comment from Sam and Susan Newcomb: "John Selman, Tod Willet, and S. Huff, left this morning for Weatherford," "John Selman and three others left for the Llano Estacado [Staked Plain] to go hunting," and so forth. John's importance and place in the community may be indicated by the position of his name.

By this time the Selmans had made up their minds to join the Fort Davis colony. The lower fort, situated about twelve miles down the Clear Fork from Fort Davis, was not as well located and could not offer its residents quite as much protection. So, on March 8, 1865, John had some pickets hauled for a home in Davis. Newcomb refers to it as "his mother's house," indicating that Mrs. Selman was considered the head of the family still. The schoolmaster goes on to say on March 14, "There was a home raised in this place today for Mrs. Selman by her son John, who is at home from the army on furlough." [14]

When the Selmans moved into Fort Davis, about 120 persons were living there, with others preparing to move in. The community was approximately 300 feet by 325 and held sixteen lots that were about seventy-five feet square. Two blockhouses on opposite corners were started but never completed. The Selman home was built next to the schoolhouse on the east side. [15]

The houses were erected with stakes, commonly called pickets, which were small trees cut in the vicinity. John and his neighbors built his in precisely the same manner that everyone else built theirs, each building varying only in the size and skill of construction. After the pickets were lined up for the walls, more pickets were laid across the top to form a roof. The top was then covered with dirt. Holes and cracks in the side were chinked with mud. Although dark, ugly and uncomfortable, the structure was warm in the winter and cool in the summer.

Mr. Newcomb himself built the finest home in Fort Davis, and by the 20th of January, 1865, he had it enclosed and a floor laid in one room. A floor was not only a rarity, but also a real luxury. An invitation went out to the young people of the community—starved for a little fun—to have a dance. They had a big one with many participants and a large crowd of spectators, to Mr. Newcomb's no small gratification. Two of the young ladies dancing to the lively tunes were Mary Ann Selman, age twenty, and Elizabeth Selman, probably about nineteen.

On March 15, 1865, Sam Newcomb finally saw the realization of a lifelong dream. He opened a schoolhouse in Fort Davis. The pedagogue recorded in his diary: "I have nineteen schollars at present, most of them are very rude and wild unacquainted with school disciplin." Obviously no great shakes as a speller himself, Newcomb held frequent spelling bees, the words coming from Webster's *Blue Black Speller*.[16]

In addition to worrying about the education of the settlers, Newcomb also fretted over their religious life. He once remarked, "the Sabbath is not much respected in this country," and it was largely through his efforts that the area circuit rider, the Reverend Mr. Slaughter, often stopped by. Mr. Slaughter would storm through Fort Davis in close pursuit of the devil, saving souls, praying over the dead, chastising the wicked, counseling the uncertain, baptizing the willing and giving Satan hell every night of the week in one of his fire-breathing, Bible-thumping sermons. People would sooner stay in bed during a Comanche massacre than miss one of the good man's performances and they would travel for miles to hear him preach the gospel. Nothing ever stopped the preacher but high water and Indian attacks,[17] and while no one ever denied the fact that many people were more interested in hearing another voice than in being saved, Mr. Slaughter had a persuasive way about him and was able to reap a harvest of converts.

The Selman family seems to have blended into the religious life of the community very well, and was apparently well thought of. This was due in part to the character of John's mother, who while she lived held the family together in a tight-knit unit. It was probably because of his mother that John Selman stayed on the straight and narrow path for the first few years of his life in Texas.

The widow Selman commanded respect for herself and her family not only because of her religious beliefs, but because she lived by them. Susan Newcomb wrote on February 21, 1866: "My mother is very sick. We couldn't have made it without old lady Selman. She is a faithful hand to wait on the sick, it seems like she never tires, she is always there ready."

Tom Selman, John's younger brother, is mentioned occasionally throughout the diary by Susan Newcomb, never by

33

Samuel. Judging from the meager information, Tom was a normal young man growing up on the frontier, mentioned when anything interesting happened to him. She once wrote: "Tom Selman and old lady Dotson's negro Bill, came up this evening afoot and said that the Indians had stole all their horses last night." [18]

Sam Newcomb's silence concerning Tom is rather ominious. One wonders if Tom was already showing some of the malevolence that characterized him a few years later. The younger Selman was then only about sixteen years old, his career not yet in full swing. No description of this younger brother is available, except for the fact that he is said to have been small-boned and in shaky health.[19] Whatever his health problem was, it did not deter him from cutting a wide, ugly path through Texas and New Mexico in later years.

On February10, 1866, the diaries record that the widow Selman was baptized by the Reverend Mr. Slaughter. He also married Lucinda Selman to Tod Willet. (Elizabeth later married Jasper deGraffenreid; Mary Ann Selman married a man named Clarke.[20])

The parson probably undertook a task which must have taxed all his power and used up all his patience, that of luring John and Tom Selman into making spiritual commitments. The diaries frequently record the fact that both of them attended church service, so they must have shown a spark of interest. March 3, 1866: "The old lady Dotson, John Selman and Tom Selman, came up to preaching this evening." [21] Perhaps the diary entry was made simply because it was so unusual to see either of the Selman boys at church service, so unusual that the Newcombs thought each attendance should be noted. At any rate, there is no evidence that either ever took the plunge into the icy waters of the Clear Fork in an effort to atone for past sins.

3

THE RE-ENLISTMENT

WHILE LIVING at the lower fort John Selman enlisted in the State Militia—the organization responsible for frontier defense.

The question arises: Why did he even consider enlisting again? Was it a matter of conscience? A lust for action? Did he think that no one would notice him in the state troops? Or did he just figure that the authorities would go easy on him if his straying from the Confederate cause was atoned for by a hitch in another outfit? Whatever the reason, he enlisted on February 8, 1864, as a private in the Stephens County Company of the Texas State Troops. His commanding officer was Captain J. W. Curtis.

The state troops were considered a home guard in Texas, and were never an integral division of the Confederate Army. The South having introduced conscription in April of 1862, all able-bodied men between the ages of seventeen and fifty had been hustled into the service and marched off to fight the Yankee invader.[1]

On the frontier, however, the situation was different and the drafting of eligible men did not apply. One not acquainted with the circumstances would be surprised at the great number of young men living in west Texas. Newcomb put his finger on the reasons for this when he commented after the war that a great many men were selling their stock and leaving the West now that the danger was past of being forced into the army if they left the frontier. He noted that "they are going back to older settled communities." [2]

Several states, including Texas, compensated for the lack of a regular army on their borders by equipping a home guard for service on the frontier where it was considered dangerous to leave women and children without some form of protection. Those exempted from the regular army draft because of their close proximity to Indian country were pressed into the state troops.

These units elected their own officers, scouted and fought the Indians and renegade whites, and prepared to defend themselves against armies from the North. The law in Texas which regulated this form of military conscription required the citizen to scout one-fourth of his time, and for the remainder, he was allowed to stay at home and attend to his own affairs unless he was in contact with an Indian enemy. Then he had to consider himself as being on duty until the skirmish was finished. [3]

John Selman acted as a liaison officer between Samuel Newcomb, Captain Curtis and General Throckmorton, suggesting that the captain and even the general were aware of his informal leavetaking from the regular army. At least, Newcomb knew he had been in the Confederate Army, and there is no reason to think Selman regarded it as a secret.

To some extent Selman represented the strength of the Stephens County Company. He was young and healthy, had a sixth sense for danger, and did not mind the work as he rode all over the country, checking defenses and notifying men of scouting duty. "John Selman came up from the lower fort this evening," Newcomb writes on February 28, 1865, "and brings news that we are released from scouting duty until further orders. He also brought me a note which was from General Throckmorton's headquarters, acknowledging the receipt of my map of Fort Davis." Though only a private, Selman was obviously a sparkplug of the frontier-defense organization.

Sam Newcomb describes a mission he, John Selman and one other man made. The purpose he never mentions, but evidently there was quite a bit of importance attached to the enterprise, because the men sat around fretting, waiting for John to secure a horse. Selman's being without a horse must have been a rare occurrence for him.

Finally a mount was obtained and they started for Fort Hubbard. Traveling light, they circled through Indian country but had gone only a few short miles when John's horse gave out. They camped that night in a dry, rocky *arroyo* and gave the animal as much nursing as possible. Their primary medical resource was a good bleeding, which they felt sure would cure all the animal's woes. Early the next day, however, after traveling only a short distance, the horse gave out again. This time in a short conference it was decided that Selman would take Newcomb's horse and go on to the destination. Again, there is significance in the fact that John was the one chosen to go on. Sam took Selman's animal and returned to Fort Davis. Everyone arrived safely.[4]

In the early part of 1865 Captain Curtis rode in with the news that it was time to go on scout again. No one liked the idea, feeling it was more important to get Fort Davis fortified as soon as possible. The two blockhouses on opposite corners were then being constructed and plans were being laid for at least two more. ". . . it is not the opinion of a few, but of everyone in this whole country, that the Indians and Jayhawkers will come down on us in the spring in numbers here-to-fore-unknown, and make an attempt to brake up this frontier." [5]

By the time the reconnoitering started, everyone had the hunting, rather than the scouting, fever. So they decided to combine the two enterprises into one. Eleven troopers under Lieutenant T. F. Maulding were accompanied by several men and boys with wagons who hoped to be able to bring back some buffalo meat. They traveled about twenty miles, found buffalo and all went on the hunt, the lieutenant included. In fact, the lieutenant charged in awkwardly on the windward side, stampeded the buffalo, and kept most of the others from getting a shot. Disgusted, they picked up their rifles and drifted back home with nothing more to show for their efforts than a few pecks of pecans.

A few weeks later Lieutenant Maulding was discharged from the state troops and an election was held to fill the vacancy. John Selman was nominated to fill the position.

Newcomb writes on April 15, 1865: "John Selman of the Confederate States of America was elected a Lieutenant. He thinks that by being elected to a commissioned office in the frontier militia, he will get a transfer. The people do not have much faith in it getting him out of the army, but voted for him to show their willingness to do all they could for him."

The transfer that Selman sought never came through. Newcomb said the election results did not reach headquarters. John's hour of reckoning had finally come.

On April 29, 1865, four Confederate soldiers from Fort Belknap came to Fort Davis and put John Selman in irons, charging him with desertion. Belknap was only about forty miles away, right on the doorstep of Fort Davis, yet up to this time no effort had been made to take him into custody.

Selman may have been surprised by the arrest. The indications are, however, that he had been expecting it for some

38

time, which was one reason why he volunteered for the lieutenant's job.

He surrendered quietly and was preparing to leave with his captors when Lieutenant Willet, his brother-in-law, stepped forward and guaranteed Selman's appearance in the morning if the soldiers would wait through the night. This would give John time to fix up his clothes, get his horse and settle his business before he left. The soldiers agreed and after supper they rode their horses out to grass.

The next morning the soldiers came in after their prisoner. He was on hand, and after brief farewells, all five of them rode away.

He never made it to Fort Belknap, nor was he ever courtmartialed for desertion. Newcomb wrote on June 5, 1865: "John Selman got back home alive and well today. He met his old company below Waco, disbanded and on their way home, so he turned around and came home also."

Waco lies at a distance of roughly 200 miles from Fort Davis. It would appear that Selman either had escaped from his captors or had been allowed to go free, and was riding around in south Texas when he ran into his old company.

In August of 1865, John Selman journeyed back to Grayson County, Texas, his jumping-off place for the wild frontier almost two years before. There, he married Miss Edna deGraffenreid on August 17, and took his bride back to Fort Davis with him the following month. Although not much is known of her, she came from a well known and respected family.[6] She was born in Arkansas in 1847,[7] making her about eight years younger than her husband. Judging by the diary entries of Sam and Susan Newcomb, she was well liked and blended into the community with little effort.

With the closing of the Civil War, Fort Davis began to break up. First one family, then another drifted off to better locations. Early in 1866 the entire Selman family moved to the Stockton Ranch, a few miles away, where Jasper deGraffenreid lived. It was here that John learned the butcher's trade.[8]

On May 8, 1867, the widow Selman died, an event which saddened the whole countryside. Sallie Reynolds Matthews says in *Interwoven* that her mother, who was past fifty, rode twenty miles by horseback to be with Mrs. Selman when she passed away.[9] She was buried in a small cemetery near the Clear Fork on what was then the Shaw Ranch.[10]

In 1869, a son, Henry, was born to the John Selmans at the Stockton Ranch.

For some reason, the Selmans and deGraffenreids now decided to move to Colfax County in eastern New Mexico. At that time Colfax was one of the wilder districts in the territory, virtually in a condition of anarchy. But this didn't discourage the two families. Taking a covered wagon, they crossed the Staked Plains in the Texas Panhandle and moved on into New Mexico. Here the Indians raided their outfit and drove off all their horses and cattle, leaving the families nearly destitute. Help came from Lucien Maxwell, owner of the Maxwell Land Grant, who gave them a quarter section of land.[11]

The 1870 census shows John Selman as a laborer in Colfax County with real assets worth $200. His personal property was valued at $1000. Although a great many stories have been told about John Selman's exploits in New Mexico at this time, it was not until nearly eight years later, when he returned, that his significant experiences there really began. Almost nothing is known of his life in New Mexico in 1870.

In May or June of that year a second son, William, was born in Colfax County. The family moved back to Texas shortly after that, or at least within the next year or two, and John Selman's career in bloodletting began.

4

THE ARMY POST AT FORT GRIFFIN

THE EXACT DATE when John Selman brought his family back to the Clear Fork country cannot be established, but since Texas military records show that his brother Tom enlisted on April 20, 1872, in Company C of the Montague County Minute Men, it can be assumed that all the Selmans were back in Texas by this time.

John's first act after his return was to build a small, one-room picket house on the banks of Tecumseh Creek in what is now Throckmorton County,[1] land which once had been part of the Clear Fork Comanche Indian Reservation, covering six square miles. After the transfer of the Indians to the Oklahoma territory in 1859, the region reverted to the state and was opened for pre-emption in 160-acre tracts. The requirements were only that a man be married and live on the land for a certain length of time.[2]

Although Selman originally had farming in mind, he soon gave that up because of the dryness of the soil, and turned to cattle raising. He had brought a small herd of steers back with him from Lincoln County on his way out of New Mexico.[3]

Some of the West's biggest herds were in the vicinity, the range was unfenced, as open as the blue sky, and as free as the immense herds of buffalo and antelope that fed on the tough grass. Barbed wire was unknown.

Near the river bottoms where John lived, among the pecan trees, briars, wild-plum thickets, elm and scrub oak, ran small wild game—rabbits, raccoons, opossum and red squirrel. If life was not easy, it was at least endurable, and no one went hungry.

About eight miles from John's place was the army post of Fort Griffin, first established as Camp Wilson in 1867 and renamed a few months later. For some years this frontier military establishment and the town which grew up nearby were important to John Selman. In fact, had Fort Griffin been less wicked and violent, the Selman story might have been different. It is here that his career as a gunman began and he made his first experiments in outlawry.

Actually the fort itself was badly needed in that uncertain and dangerous time to protect the settlements from Comanche and Kiowa Indians and white desperados more dangerous than either. It was ironic that a post with such a mission should attract a floating population of dangerous and degenerate characters who built a shack town of dives and brothels on the flat below the military establishment—a town in which John Selman found himself perfectly at home.

The garrison was composed mainly of Negro soldiers with white officers. Selman watched as the original buildings went up—a nightmare of green lumber, unbelievably shoddy workmanship and cramped, dingy quarters. The enlisted men lived in small, one-room log huts, six men to a building. Each hut was fourteen and a half feet long, eight feet wide and five feet ten inches at the peak. The only air allowed to circulate came from a small window in the rear and a door in front.[4] No wonder that drunkenness was rampant, and brawls became nearly a way of life. Perhaps the Army figured that men who could survive under these conditions would make rugged foes for the Comanches and Kowas.

Morale was almost nonexistent at the fort, especially among the enlisted men. They were not allowed to attend social functions at the outlying ranches and the dreariness of their lives was broken only by still drearier duties—drill, guard duty and latrine detail.

It took some time for the troops to bring the Indians under control, and defeats and reverses had to be endured first. There was, for instance, the Salt Creek Prairie massacre in May of 1871 when nearly a hundred Indians overran a wagon train bringing supplies to the fort. Two Kiowa chiefs, Satanta and Big Tree, went to Huntsville prison for that bloody deed.[5] After Colonel Mackenzie smashed the Comanche, Kiowa and Cheyenne encampment in Palo Duro Canyon in 1874, the day of big Indian raids was over.

John Selman was friendly with the Indian fighters, especially the Tonkawa scouts, who proved to be hardy antagonists, especially when going up against the Comanches, whom they hated fiercely. John was no Indian lover, and the Tonks were about the most unlovable of Indians; they were incredibly dirty and often drunk and quarrelsome in their camps. Nevertheless, he respected them as honest men and good fighters and allowed them to camp near his home.

The arrangement proved to be fortunate on at least one occasion. In 1872 (date and month unknown) Margaretta Selman was born to John and Edna. To celebrate, John killed two steers and invited the Tonks to join in the feast. The affair was hardly under way when a rider came pounding in, shouting that the Comanches had attacked the ranch of "old man Mathis" [Matthews?] and had carried off a boy and a girl.

43

The story handed down in the Selman family says that John vaulted into the saddle and with his band of Tonkawas pursued the raiders all the way to the Davis Mountains. In the battle that followed all the Comanches were killed and the children were recovered.[6]

John Selman, Jr., reports that at the time of his own birth in 1875 the family was holding the usual celebration when the Indians struck again. They broke into John's corral and took a stallion worth $1600. This time it took John and his Tonk friends only two days to overhaul the savages and to kill fifteen of them in a pitched battle. Four of the Tonks lost their lives, and one white cowboy was wounded in the leg.[7]

Indians were not the only dangerous creatures in the Selman neighborhood. One evening, as John sat in his home cleaning his rifle and talking to a neighbor named Webb, they were disturbed by the furious barking of the dog outside. John put up his gun and opened the door to see what was going on. At that moment the hound shot between his legs and took cover behind Mrs. Selman, who was boiling coffee. John barely got out of the way of a big mountain lion, which was right on the dog's heels.

Snarling and spitting, the beast jumped up on the bed where little William was lying, seized the boy and headed for the door. As it passed him, John struck it across the back with a piece of firewood. Turning on its assailant, the animal dropped the baby and Edna Selman rushed to pick it up. She paid a heavy price for this bit of bravery, for the lion struck her a crushing blow across the neck and breast, sending her reeling and leaving deep gashes.

Webb now entered into the fray. He grabbed the panther by the tail, and spinning swiftly, threw it into the fireplace. The cat cut loose with a terrifying scream and, throwing live coals all over the house, sought refuge under the bed where it cowered in fright. Selman by this time had reached the gun hanging over the fireplace and he shot the terrified animal. Stretched dead on the floor, the lion measured almost seven feet from tip to tip.[8]

William, the baby, escaped with only a few scratches, although one eardrum was damaged, leaving him slightly deaf for the rest of his life.

Very shortly after this incident, John began work on what was known to him and his family as the "Rock Ranch." Years later, after the Selman family was gone, it was renamed the Tecumseh Ranch.[9] Located just across Tecumseh Creek from his old picket house, the new structure had three large unplastered rooms arranged in the customary "L" shape. It was solidly constructed and considered one of the better homes in the Clear Fork area. Later, the public road from Albany to Throckmorton went past it.

Although the setting seemed peaceful, the countryside suffered from a lack of law enforcement. Until now, the federal government had been the only power in the region, but the troops were forbidden to intervene in strictly civilian matters. This rule was sometimes stretched, of course. White outlaws were often considered to be *comancheros*,[10] and their connection with the Indians gave the military an excuse and an opportunity to move against them.

Nevertheless, the outlying ranchers felt the need of additional protection and a citizens' organization began to form. Actually very little is known about it. It had no formal leader and no special name. It was called the Old Law Mob, or simply OLM.

No direct evidence links John Selman to this group, but most of the settlers did belong. Since the OLM gradually merged into a more sophisticated organization known as the Vigilantes, and since Selman was not only a member but a leader of the Vigilantes, it can be assumed that he participated in the Old Law Mob activities too.

This group set up its own kangaroo tribunal. The absence of a jail or other means of holding a lawbreaker made quick justice necessary. The guilty were promptly and cheaply hanged. When their grisly work was finished, the boys came drifting home, big grins on their faces, making joking remarks about how the outlaws "got away." [11]

At one time the mob nearly hanged Brock, a neighbor of Selman's who was suspected of killing a relative called Frank Woosley (or Woolsey). Brock was from the East and had acquired a sizable ranch which he invited his cousins Frank and Ed Woolsley to manage for him. One day Frank disappeared and for some reason everyone thought Brock had murdered him. Brock, who had a personality problem anyway, aggravated by a speech impediment, was not one who got along well with people. Before he realized what was happening, his head was in a hangman's noose. Just as his feet were leaving the ground, some of the OLM who had been arguing about the situation convinced the others that the available facts in the case did not warrant his death, so he was released.

Brock, almost blue and gasping for breath, vowed that he would find Woosley, and thus began a search which would last for years, cost a fortune and ruin Brock's life. Finding his cousin became an obsession with him. He sold his possessions and traveled all over the country, even to Mexico and Canada. When his money was gone, he stopped to work, but only long enough to get another stake. Then he was gone again on his lonely, never-ending search.

Years later, acting on a tip that Frank had been seen in Arkansas, he took a train to Hot Springs only to find that the man pointed out to him was not his cousin. Discouraged and heartsick, he turned wearily back to the station to purchase his return ticket. As he shoved his money under the bars, he glanced up and found himself staring into the face of Frank Woosley, the ticket agent.

46

When the news of Brock's discovery got back to Fort Griffin, the opinion developed that Frank had deliberately dropped out of sight, expecting the OLM to think that Brock had murdered him. If Brock had been hanged, the other cousin would have come into possession of the ranch. It could then have been sold and the two brothers could have joined each other in another part of the country.[12]

The OLM did not always confine its attentions to criminals. On one occasion, the wife of a local rancher wanted a divorce—something almost unheard of in that part of the country. A husband might sometimes desert his family, but a woman never asked for her freedom. Her mate was violently opposed but she was determined, and hired a lawyer named Fisch to represent her. Before long Fisch received anonymous warnings to drop the case. Stubbornly, he ignored the threats. A few days later he was given twenty-four hours to leave the country, and again he refused. Presently he was found hanging from a tree limb near the river bottoms. After several days the body was cut down and thrown into a ravine, where the bones bleached for many years.[13]

5

SODOM OF THE PLAINS

SINCE THE EVIDENCE has shown that John Selman had a nodding acquaintance with the Bible, one wonders if he ever compared the town of Fort Griffin with Sodom and Gomorrah. Like Lot, John saw fit to pitch his tent in a city of evil—one as wicked as either of those two Biblical towns. If a divine plan controlled Griffin's destiny, it called for retribution just as deadly. It was to destroy itself. Just as no stone was left standing on the Old Testament sites, so the dry Texas wind today blows over a flat valley and ripples the tall grass in a Fort Griffin that was.

To differentiate between the army post and the town, both called Fort Griffin, the settlers and ranchers usually referred to the post high above them as "Government Hill" and the town in the valley as "Griffin" or the "Flats." Here in the 1870's grew the largest town west of Fort Worth, having a population of over a thousand—and according to C. L. Sonnichsen, the historian of the local feud, an equally large number of "floaters." [1]

48

The town began originally as a group of squatter houses whose main purposes seemed to be furnishing whisky and other forms of entertainment to the soldiers. This proved to be a very profitable business, but when riots, fistfights and drunken debauches grew to outrageous dimensions and began to fill the army hospitals, the military decided to do something about it. They expelled the "businessmen," moving them half a mile away to the other side of the Clear Fork of the Brazos.[2]

The county of Shackelford was organized in 1874, however, and control passed to civilian authorities. Almost immediately the Flats below the fort were repopulated with every type of individual, mostly undesirable. Ranshackle wooden buildings lined the main street, a narrow, rutted road which ran from the foot of Government Hill to the banks of the Clear Fork. Signs with words misspelled hung above the door of every saloon and inside buffalo hunters, muleskinners, soldiers, gunfighters, outlaws, ranchers, gamblers, cowmen and merchants bellied up to the bar. Prostitutes plied their trade in the rough and broken streets, luring men to the shanties which lined the banks of the river.[3]

Tonk Indians, men and women, staggered about in a state of bleary-eyed intoxication, threatening those who crossed their paths. White gunmen armed with knives, rifles and pistols wandered the streets, screaming, cursing and firing their weapons. "Life was cheap," writes Ben O. Grant. "It was a town where all lived in the fury of the present."[4]

Although the town was built to cater to the desires and whims of the military, the buffao hunters and cowboys combined to establish it as a stronghold of sin and debauchery. Griffin had a reputation of being the most advanced buffalo town in the West during the 1870s, the decade of slaughter. The hunters swaggered through, exchanging meat and flint hides[5] for guns, ammunition and other essentials. In August of 1877 about 200,000 hides were traded, and each day saw many hide wagons entering or leaving the city. Joe McComb, Fort Griffin's most noted buffalo hunter, left Griffin in September of 1877 carrying a thousand pounds of lead and five kegs of powder. That month he had his most successful hunt, killing 4900 buffalo.[6]

The merchants of Griffin, realizing that the future of Griffin depended upon more industries than buffalo, began casting flirtatious glances at stockmen plying the Western Cattle Trail, which ran northward from San Antonio toward Kansas. Previously, the Chisholm Trail had been the most popular route for driving cattle to market, but now too many settlements were springing up along its path and new markets were opening up which could be reached more easily by other routes. So agents were dispatched by the Griffin merchants to eastern and southern Texas, and soon many herds that would have gone up the Chisholm Trail turned west at Belton and reached the new crossings on the Red River via Fort Griffin. The effect that the trail drives had on Fort Griffin can be seen in perspective when one considers that the Western Trail was second only to the Chisholm as the greatest of all cattle highways.[7]

The chagrin of Fort Worth merchants can be imagined. Heretofore, they had enjoyed almost all the cattlemen's trade, and now Griffin was about to usurp Cowtown's place in the sun.

And for a while it looked as if this might happen. Griffin began to boom. But cold-eyed killers and scoundrels were still predominant and respectable citizens, although they began showing up in increasing numbers, rarely showed their face in the Flats. They preferred to spend their time at the ranches, or in the more quiet and peaceful town of Albany.

Albany was really Griffin's chief rival. Located about fifteen miles to the south, Albany whisked the position of county seat right out from under Griffin's nose, and from then on it was all downhill for the hell-raising Flats. Albany got the railroads; Griffin got the soldiers, the buffalo hunters and the trail-driving cowboys. By the early 1880s, the soldiers, hunters and cowboys were nearly all gone. Griffin was dead.

Griffin's influence upon John Selman's character cannot be underestimated. He gives no indication of being anything other than an average settler up until this time, yet the record shows quite plainly that somewhere in his early years he became calloused and cynical in his outlook. After the lapse of so much time and in the absence of any sort of inscription, we can only surmise that John's immersion in the tough and soulless little world of Fort Griffin somehow changed him. Perhaps his latent tendencies merely came to the fore; we do not know. But it is certain that his contemporaries began to think of him as "a reckless two-gun man well known on the frontier." [8]

The erosion of character which he seems to have undergone did not, of course, deprive him of all humanity. He kept his devotion to his friends—in fact; he never lost that quality as long as he lived. His first killing at Fort Griffin is said to have resulted from his loyalty to his Tonkawa Indian allies. The episode cannot be documented but it has general and widespread acceptance in the Fort Griffin neighborhood.

It concerns one Haulph, a sub-human type known around Griffin as a good man to leave alone. Returning from a long trip, Haulph rode his weary horse into town one morning, eased himself out of the saddle, tied his horse in front of a saloon, went inside and proceeded to get drunk, as was his custom. In his intoxicated condition, he cared or thought little of his horse, which had remained tied all day in the boiling sun. Night came and the animal was obviously suffering, but no one wanted to risk Haulph's anger by moving or caring for it. The next day the horse was still there, tied to the hitching rail. A passing Tonkawa Indian, not knowing the circumstance and seeing the poor condition of the horse, untied the animal and

51

started to lead him around to the side of the saloon where there was water.

He had only gone a few steps when the owner lurched through the door and staggered outside. Steadying himself against the front of the building, wiping whisky from his beard as he stared with bloodshot eyes at the Indian, he demanded to know what was being done with his horse. Before the Indian could reply Haulph snarled, "I'll tend to my own damn horse," drew his pistol and shot the Tonk dead in the street. A few minutes later the authorities arrested Haulph, charged him with being drunk and put him in jail until he sobered up.

While Haulph was resting in jail, the news got back to John Selman. The dead Tonk had once befriended him and John wasn't about to forget. A few weeks later Haulph was found lying out on the prairie, staring with sightless eyes at the copper sun. He had at least one big bullet hole in him. An inquest was hastily called and the official ruling was suicide. Most folks winked at the verdict. They knew John Selman had avenged his friend.[9]

The man who called forth all of Selman's friendship and loyalty now stepped upon the stage. This was John Larn.[10] Selman's companion, employer and model, John Larn was perhaps the man who changed John Selman from the more-or-less-standard Western ranchman to John Selman the gunman. They lived only two miles apart, Larn's ranch being two miles down the Clear Fork from the Rock Ranch and right across the fence from old Camp Cooper, and their association was extremely close and confidential. An account of Larn's career, however brief, indicates that during these years Selman was subjected to powerful suggestions of evil from this man who may have been one of the most plausible, unscrupulous and deadly characters who ever appeared on the Southwestern frontier. We cannot be absolutely sure of this, Larn being an even bigger enigma than Selman himself. But Larn may well have been Selman's evil genius.

Relatively unknown today, Larn cut as wide a swath through Western history as any gunman of his time. His life was short, and he had little time or opportunity to make a deep impression on the history of his region, but his violent career and death are still matters for argument and speculation.

He was reportedly born in Mobile, Alabama, but drifted out to Colorado while still in his early teens. There he killed a ranch owner in an argument over a horse.[11] A month or so later he killed a sheriff in New Mexico.[12] By the summer of 1871, when he was twenty-two years old, he became a trail foreman for Bill Hays, a well known stockman around Griffin. Hays, not concerned with Larn's killings or with his background, hired him on the basis of his experiences with men and horses. W. P. Webb wrote that "some outfits preferred men who were on the dodge, because they stuck closer to business, avoided the towns, and were always ready to fight their way out of a difficulty."[13]

In the fall of that year, Larn drove a herd of 1700 cattle to the Colorado markets, an event punctuated by killings, cattle rustling and a near-shootout with some elements of the United States Cavalry.[14] Two men hired for that trip were Henry and James Comstock. Henry wrote a journal about his experiences. He had heard that "life in the saddle would be just like life in the rocking chair." His disillusionment came swiftly.

In Colorado, Hays had trouble selling his stock, and since branding time was approaching in Texas, he sent Larn, armed with a power of attorney, back to Fort Griffin to watch over his employer's cattle interests there.

In the summer of 1873, Hays returned to Texas. His creditors in Colorado had finally taken over his stock. Now, back at Fort Griffin, he found that Larn had accumulated a

53

small herd, and a dispute developed between the two men over brands. Trouble developed quickly.

When Bill Hays and his brother John left Griffin with a small herd of cattle bound for Fort Sill, Oklahoma, Larn swore out a warrant against him and his men, charging them with cattle theft. Larn, Riley Carter (acting sheriff), Lieutenant Turner, from the post at Fort Griffin, and thirteen Negro cavalrymen raced out of Griffin in pursuit of the alleged rustlers.

They swooped down on the Hays outfit as the cowboys were camped for their noon meal about forty miles from the Flats. Larn led the way as the posse stormed through the camp, shooting, yelling and killing. In the carnage which followed, Bill Bush, a tough young gunman and a former friend of Larn's, went down first because he was the most dangerous. The Hays brothers were then shot where they stood. Two others were killed and four captured. On the way back to Griffin the captives were killed while "trying to escape." Details differ over whether they were shot or hanged.[15,16]

Larn, fearing vengeance from friends of the Hays outfit, went heavily armed and continued to do so for the rest of his short life. Despite his bloodstained record, he became foreman for Joseph Matthews, whose descendants are still respected ranching people in that part of the country. Joe Matthews had one son and several daughters, most of whom married into the Reynolds family.[17] One of his daughters, however, was more headstrong than the others. In spite of her parents' objections, Mary was attracted to the handsome, dark-haired Larn, and the feeling was reciprocated.

Larn was said to be the kind of man whose enemies admired his virtues and whose friends admitted and confirmed his faults. He was certainly not a Paladin, yet this is the way many people around old Fort Griffin think of him today. He was a most unusual man. In spite of his murderous past, he made friends easily and nearly everyone liked him. His marriage to Mary Matthews was a happy one. He was never known to utter a harsh word to her, and she, on her part, even when his world came to an end in a burst of gunfire, never wavered in her belief in him.

His first home, now usually referred to as the "Honeymoon House," was built beside Camp Cooper. Larn knocked down some of the old buildings at the camp and used the rock to construct his house. The ruins still exist today, even to the heart and clover-shaped flower gardens which he designed and built for his wife.

His second home, built right across the Clear Fork and known as the Camp Cooper Ranch, is still occupied. Planned and constructed by Larn, it was beautifully symmetrical, architecturally far ahead of its time. It was composed of six large rooms and had a glassed-in cupola on the roof. Many historians have felt that this cupola was a watch tower, but such was not the case. On account of the flatness of the land a stranger could be seen coming for miles unless he came up the riverbed, in which case he could not be seen even from a lookout post. A cupola was simply considered a luxury of the day. All of the better homes had them.[18]

Divergent characteristics did not prevent John Selman and John Larn from becoming amicable. Selman was in his early thirties; Larn was in his early twenties. Larn is reported as being a faithful husband; Selman was frequently seen in the company of a notorious Fort Griffin prostitute named Minnie Martin, alias Hurricane Minnie. Their trysts became so well known that a wanted notice for Selman in 1879 included the caption that "Wherever a whore by the name of Hurricane Minnie is around, there will John Selman be." [19]

Although a glib and easy talker, Selman's personal qualities never ripened in the same way as Larn's. Selman had the knowledge, the stamina and the toughness to lead and direct rough and unpolished backwoodsmen like himself, but he never had the smooth personality that allowed him to enter the halls of the socially prominent as Larn did. Still, Selman was without any doubt the tougher and smarter of the two. When the chips were down it was Selman who survived and escaped.

The Fort Griffin and Albany newspapers do not often mention the exploits of John Larn and John Selman. It was not that the papers had an aversion to bloodshed, since they are often full of it; nor was an editor above squirting venom at those who aroused his wrath, as one did several years later on August 20, 1880, when he wished all the relatives of Amos Quitter would drown.[20] Much information is missing from these newspapers, apparently scissored out for one reason or the other; perhaps to keep the full story from being known. However, enough has been scraped together from these and other sources to give a reasonably accurate picture of the violence and death that stalked Shackelford County.

6

HEMP AND BLUE WHISTLERS

THE OLD LAW MOB had more or less faded out of existence by the time Shackelford County was organized in 1874. In its place was a more discerning organization known simply as the Vigilantes or Tin-Hat Brigade. C. L. Sonnichsen in his book, *I'll Die Before I'll Run,* remarks: "Nobody was supposed to know who the members were, but lists of membership (possibly conjectural) are in existence and several important names are on the rolls."[1] Larn was named by one authority as a "long time chief in the vigilance committee,"[2] and Selman, in 1880, admitted that he was also a member.[3] The names of some of the others, believed to have been given by John Selman, include W. R. Cruger (former sheriff), James Draper (deputy sheriff in 1878), W. H. Ledbetter (county judge in 1878), G. R. Carter, C. K. Stribling (former county judge), John Jackson and George Matthews.[4] The last mentioned George Matthews is reportedly not a member of the prominent Matthews family in the area.[5]

Another authority, an old buffalo hunter named Skelton

Glenn, left memoirs in which he wrote that "Larn and Sillman [sic] were the organizers and principle [sic] leaders of the Vigilent [sic] committee to supress crime in and around Griffin." [6]

John Selman's son, in his unpublished account of his father, makes no mention of his father's membership in the vigilantes, but he does speak well of them, saying that "they were absolutely necessary in those days." Of course, when the Tin-Hat Brigade bore down heavily on Selman and Larn, the boy changed his attitude, claiming that "my father and Laren were victims of their cunning." [7]

The vigilantes were a strong force at a time when strength was needed to curb some of the more aggressive rustling activities. It is interesting that they never "publicly" hanged anyone accused of anything other than stealing. Murder and crimes of violence were generally ignored; a man was expected to handle his own affairs in such matters. Homicide, while not condoned, was thought so little of by the vigilantes and law officers that the officials often considered it a waste of time just to bring a man in on that charge. One sample of Fort Griffin justice occurred when a private and a captain got into a drunken row on the streets one day. The enlisted man had stepped on the captain's toes and, instead of apologizing, had walked on. Infuriated, the officer drew his side arm and killed the man. He was acquitted at the trial, the evidence showing that "it was the only dignified thing he could do under the circumstances." [8]

But law was needed. J. C. Jacobs, the first sheriff of Shackelford County, was getting old and ineffective and the ranchers wanted a little more muscle behind the badge. So Larn was prevailed on to run for the office and on February 15, 1876, he was elected, although he was not sworn in until April 18. [9] W. R. Cruger, previously district clerk and assessor, had acted as deputy under Jacobs since January 7, 1875. [10] He continued serving as first deputy under Larn.

Larn's number-one chore was to get rid of the McBride, English, Townsend gang (Rister calls it the Bill Henderson gang), a band of thugs and desperados who made Fort Griffin their headquarters and rendezvoused in a shanty down on the Clear Fork owned by Indian Kate and her daughter Mag, alias "Swayback Mag." Both Kate and her daughter were prostitutes, living with a renegade Negro named Cato.[11] The cases against Swayback Mag consume a great deal of space in early Shackelford County Court records.

On April 2, 1876, the gang, accompanied by Sally Watson, another prostitute, stole twenty-six head of horses from Ellison, Dewees and Bishop's cattle ranch.[12] The rustlers, driving the stock before them, were barely over the horizon when Selman, Larn and some vigilantes struck the trail. Shaking the kinks out of their ropes, the pursuers grimly closed in.

As the determined vigilantes slowly overhauled the outlaws, the gang split up. Henderson (who was probably the real leader of the gang), "Kansas Bill," Hank Floyd and another thief struck out toward Dodge City, Kansas. The others, including Joe Watson, his wife Sally, "Reddy," "Larapie Dan" and "Doc" McBride, were driving a wagon and overtaken on or about April 14. On seeing the vigilantes, the horse thieves quickly scattered.

Sally Watson was captured and released. A few hours later Joe Watson, Dan and Reddy were hurt during a running gun battle, captured and hanged. Justice was swift and absolute.

McBride almost got away, making it nearly to Judge Ledbetter's place on the Clear Fork, where he hid in the heavy brush near the river bottom. Knowing he would never show himself to the searchers, the vigilantes devised the idea of sending a Negro to find him under the pretense of looking for a yoke of oxen. A few minutes later McBride was located, flushed from his hiding place and wounded. From the point of capture, he was brought in a little closer to Griffin and there, under a pecan tree, his horse was led out from under him. A note pinned to his clothes read: "He said his name was McBride, but he was a liar as well as a thief." [13]

After being turned loose by the vigilantes, Sally Watson went home and waited for her husband to join her. When he did not show up after several hours, she pawned her baby with Doc Neal, a rancher, for a saddle and six-shooter. She then rode straight across country to look for Joe, but met the vigilantes near MacKenzie's Crossing and asked where her husband was. The leader, presumably Selman or Larn, mumbled something about Joe being in jail in Griffin. She screamed, "You are a lying son-of-a-bitch. You did not have time to go to Griffin." [14]

As time had run out for Joe Watson and the others, so time was running out for Bill Henderson and one of his men who had fled north. John Larn was given warrants for their arrest and he left immediately. On April 27 William Gilson, City Marshal of Fort Griffin, received a telegram from Larn at Dodge City saying that Henderson and Hank Floyd were under arrest and he was returning to Griffin with both men in tow.

Upon arrival the two outlaws were locked in the narrow, poorly ventilated jail, and Larn began devising plans for cleaning up the town. One of the first men he consulted was John Selman.

Many authorities have called Selman a deputy under John Larn. Edgar Rye[15] and Skelton Glenn both claim it, and Don Biggers makes reference to a deputy who is probably Selman, but he gives no name. Yet there is no official evidence to support the contention that Selman was ever a duly appointed officer of the law in Griffin. The Shackelford County records, while admittedly not complete, do give an excellent picture of the over-all law-enforcement situation. In regard to John Selman they are silent. The evidence indicates that William Cruger, and he alone, served under Larn.

Selman, being a close friend of Larn's, may have been appointed as a deputy in an unofficial capacity. The legal requirements for an appointment and bond may have applied only to the first deputy. Though he was unsalaried, a man like Selman could collect enough in fees to support himself. At that time a law officer, in addition to enforcing the peace, was a tax collector, a license distributor and a receiver of fines, the latter hinging upon the number of arrests made and disposition of the cases by the judge.

In line with his official duties, John Selman made the entire circuit of Shackelford, once going to Reynolds City on business. Skelton Glenn said that herds of cattle at that time were being rustled in Mexico and delivered to Reynolds City by Tom Merrill. But this was not the reason Selman was in town. He had other things on his mind, and one evening he and Merrill got into a poker game. It soon developed into a hard-fought, high-stake game—so high, in fact, that Selman and Merrill were the only two left.

John, not having heard of his tall, slim opponent, was not on his guard that night; but Merrill had heard some pretty bad things about Selman and had his pistol lying in his lap while Selman's was in his scabbard. Finally it came Merrill's turn to pass, which he did, and John said, "I win," reaching for the pot.

"Not so damn fast," Merrill snapped and he grabbed his gun and pointed it at John's head. Then with his left hand he spread his cards out on the table, showing to all that he was high man. Of course Selman could only acknowledge that he was beaten, but he didn't have to like it. When he left Reynolds City that night, he vowed vengeance, claiming that through his carelessness he had failed to size Merrill up properly or the incident would never happened. It was a mistake Selman never made again.[16]

As Selman had learned something from Merrill, he also had the opportunity to learn from others, although not as pointedly. Strutting through the streets of Griffin at one time or the other came such gunmen as Wyatt Earp, Jim Miller, Bat Masterson (whom Selman once reportedly threw into the Fort Griffin jail[17]), Doc Holliday and his mistress Big Nose Kate, Pat Garrett and John Wesley Hardin. The latter must have been a mere youth at the time, and if he and Selman ever met here, history has not recorded it. Another bandit, soon to spread terror and fear through Lincoln County, New Mexico, was Jesse Evans. He frequently stopped at the Selman Ranch and, according to a living grandson of Selman's, buried $50,000 somewhere on the property, most of which has never been found.[18]

With all the gunfighters floating through the saloons and other deadfalls, Selman and Larn were bound, sooner or later, to run afoul of somebody. They tangled first with a young gunman named Shorty Collins. Shorty, a killer by reputation, had been drinking, and this fact, combined with the presence of a host of cowpuncher friends, was all that was necessary to bolster his courage. The lawmen and the outlaw met on the street. The little gunman was told curtly to throw up his hands. Yelling a colorful, unprintable epithet, he reached for his gun, but before it left his holster Selman, reacting swiftly, drew and shot him through the heart. The outlaw fell dead at Larn's feet. Edgar Rye bogs his story down in a great deal of invented conversation between Larn and Shorty's friends, who were considerably upset over their comrade's sudden demise. But the yarn ends on a happy note; the cowboys are satisfied, everyone has a drink together, and Shorty is buried.[19]

Don Biggers tells a much more credible and less sensational story involving the attempted arrest—of a man named Hampton, not Collins. While he makes no direct mention of Selman and Larn, he makes it quite evident that they were the two peace officers involved. Hampton was spotted walking across the street and was ordered to throw up his hands, which he did not do because he was partially deaf (he may have used his deafness as an excuse not to hear the command). The man was also not wearing a gun, but the officers may not have known this as Selman did not give him much time to prove it one way or the other. John jerked his pistol and commenced firing, emptying the weapon. The victim toppled dead. The slayer was then heard to wager that all the bullet holes in the body would be so close together that they could be covered with a silver dollar.[20]

The brutality of the slaying shocked even Fort Griffin and many angry comments passed up and down the main street. However, no effort was ever made to call the officers to account.

The slaying of Hampton (or Collins) is one of the few times that Selman stole the stage from John Larn. At no time did he ever become the dominant one of the pair, possibly because of Selman's instinct for fading into the background, a practice which he developed into an art in the early days of his life. Yet there is evidence to show that he was the more dangerous of the two, and especially the more feared and hated.

On the first of June, 1877, John Meadows, who worked for Selman and Larn, was due $300, which Selman promised to pay just as soon as he sold some steers. The fear gnawing away at this pledge was the rumor that the two Johns had a cheap and positive way of paying off their help. They shot them. Meadows was afraid this same treatment was destined for him, and his suspicions were aroused even further when friends told him he should forget the money, that his best chance for survival was to ride, far and fast. Hostile, bitter at the way he felt he was being treated, and frightened, Meadows saw John Selman riding up the road toward Fort Griffin and made plans to ambush him upon his return. In fact, Meadows made plans to kill both Larn and Selman when they came back that evening from town, but it was Selman that Meadows wanted most to kill. ("He was the meanest man that ever lived," John Meadows said.)

The ambush was planned to take place at Lamb's Head Creek, and a double-barreled goose gun with sixteen shot in each side was expected to do the job thoroughly. The plan was interrupted by a friendly neighbor who pulled Meadows from his hiding place, telling him that nothing would be served, regardless of who won or lost the fight. Meadows then left and a few days later went to work for Millet, who owned a ranch up on the Pecos.[21]

In telling his story, Meadows frequently implied that Selman was an older-looking man, or one at least who was prematurely gray. His descriptions always had the word "old" attached, such as "Old John," and in one particular instance, "this old son of a bitch."

Selman and Larn, in addition to their ranches, also owned some property in Fort Griffin at one time. In November of 1875 Selman purchased two lots for $150 and a month later sold them to Larn for $100.[22] Some old-timers seem to remember that John Selman owned a saloon, which might have been erected on this site. Joe McComb's son Milus seemed to recall his father's comments that on the night of October 26, 1875, buffalo hunters by the score poured into Selman's saloon when some soldiers from the fort threatened to burn the town.[23] The burning never came about, but several rifle volleys were fired into the village, wounding a few persons, none seriously.

On the 19th of February, 1878, John Selman purchased from Hurricane Minnie Martin "one house situated in the Town of Griffin, and one sett of furniture containing four

64

chairs, one bed stead, one beaura, and one wash stand." [24] John paid $200 for this property; no one knows what use it was put to.

Selman's ownership of property in Fort Griffin might have gave him a sense of community responsibility. On May 15, 1876, he sat on a grand jury,[25] and on October 18, 1877, he was one of a petit jury which tried Chas Mussleman for theft of a gelding. The accused received five years in prison.[26]

Mussleman must have had an uncommon amount of luck. He had somehow slipped through the hands of the vigilance committee, a feat that few before him had accomplished. On April 20, 1876, Houston Faught was caught stealing horses, and in very short order the vigilantes had jerked him into eternity. A card pinned to his clothes read: "Horse thief No. 5 that killed and scalped that boy for Indian sign. Shall horse thieves rule the country? He will have company soon." [27]

The Frontier *Echo,* defending the vigilantes, remarked: "He [Faught] was a well known and desperate criminal and if one out of every hundred crimes he is credited with were really perpetrated by him, then he deserves his punishment." The newspaper then went on to say that "the stealing of horses has become so frequent that the losers cannot purchase fresh stock fast enough to satisfy the demands of the horse thief . . . no medicine will reach the case but blue whistlers or hemp." [28]

On June 2, the Tin-Hat Brigade took for a midnight ride the two men Larn had brought back from Dodge City. At eleven o'clock the jail guards, George Wilhelm and Burner, were surprised (so they said) to hear a strange noise outside. They looked out and saw a force of at least fifty men on foot and twenty on horseback. Of course the jailors were disarmed and Henderson and Floyd were taken. The next morning the prisoners were found hanging from a tree near Hubbard's Creek. There are no signs of any weeping over their departure.[29]

65

On the following morning Captain H. L. Arrington of the Texas Rangers, along with Roberts, another ranger, were crossing Hubbard's Creek with Shackelford County Judge Lynch when they saw the two bodies dangling there. Turning to the judge, Arrington said, "Judge Lynch, I do not know whether or not you know anything about this, but it has got to stop. I am here to see that law is enforced." The judge gave a vague, non-committal answer, neither admitting nor denying that he was associated with the vigilantes.[30]

Arrington had other work waiting for him in town. Three horse thieves had been captured out on the prairie, and when it looked as if their necks were going to be stretched by the furious cowboys, Doc Neal took the culprits to Fort Griffin.

The situation in town wasn't any more pleasant for the thieves. Skelton Glenn says that the men had no sooner heard the cell door bang shut than "Selman and Larn made the boast that the vigilante committee would have them out of there before morning and swinging on a limb." Neal hadn't brought the prisoners that far just to see them die on a rope, so he asked Captain Arrington for protection. A squad of ten rangers was sent to guard the jail.

At the hearing the three men pleaded innocent, exclaiming that they had drunk five gallons of white-mule whisky before the thefts were committed and did not know what they were doing. Then they showed their gratitude to Doc Neal for saving them from Selman and the vigilantes by saying that he (Neal) was worse than they were. They accused him of killing in cold blood a mentally retarded fellow named Big Infant. Neal did not deny the charge; he merely explained that he meant to shoot someone else and Big Infant had accidentally wandered into the way of the bullet. The horse thieves were held over for trial.[31]

If the rangers were upset over the recent hangings, the governor was more so. "It should be made a rule of evidence," he said, in what was a direct slap at Selman and Larn, as well as others, "that when a jail is forced and prisoners taken out and murdered . . . that the Sheriff and jailors are accessories to the crime. . . . No Sheriff should be permitted to hold office another day after his jail has been forced. . . . I have never heard of a Sheriff, or a jailor being hurt, nor one of them hurting any assailants; nor have I ever known a bonafide, resolute resistance made by a Sheriff or a jailor to the demands of a mob, fail to be successful. . . ." [32]

The McKinney *Inquirer* and the Frontier *Echo* both came out in May of 1876 sharply disagreeing with the governor. The *Inquirer* noted: "A petition is circulating here and numerously signed, asking the legislature to pass a law to punish horse thieves as follows: First offense, whipping post; second, whipping and branding; third, hanging." The *Echo* snorted and offered a swift rebuttal, suggesting "hanging first and cremation second."

Regardless of the uproar, the lynchings went right on. The difference now was that information about the hangings became a little more difficult to come by. Nevertheless, on December 28, 1876, the area was electrified by an article appearing in the Austin *Weekly Statesman:* "No wonder the highwaymen are seeking security east of the Colorado. Eleven men were hanged ten days ago at Fort Griffin and four more are enroute to that merciful village." [33]

7

THE BEGINNING OF THE END

BY THIS TIME a great many people would have been glad to see ropes around the necks of Selman and Larn, although such a thing seemed only remotely possible. However, a rope of evidence in the matter of cattle rustling was beginning to twist itself around them. Though still within a step of a life of decency, they seemed determined to separate themselves from law-abiding people. Larn was still popular, but the number of his enemies was on the increase. Selman, who had balanced for so long between honesty and dishonesty, had now swung definitely toward the latter.

Both men owned small herds of cattle. John Selman's son remarks that his father was partial to red cattle, his steers becoming known in Texas as the Selman Red Herd.[1] It was no great effort for him to accumulate these animals. The country was overrun with "slicks" (wild unbranded cattle), and though it took a lot of hard work, an enterprising cattleman handy with a rope and branding iron could increase his herd quickly, provided he wanted to see his clothes torn to shreds in

the thickets and run the risk of being gored by a furious anu-
mal or knocked off his horse by a protruding tree limb. Even
then, other troubles could develop: a cowboy might not see his
neighbor's brand until, bleeding and sore, he had dragged the
bawling animal out into a clearing where he could examine his
catch. Then, full of anger and frustration, he was apt to claim
the steer through right of possession and cinch the matter with
a hot running iron.

Selman and Larn frequently ran their herds together,[2]
and as they grazed up and down the Clear Fork, mingling with
other stock, the Selman-Larn herd began to show an increase.
Some ranchers grumbled that the gain was at the expense of
their own cattle.

The trouble began in earnest in 1874 with a man named
Bryant, who lived in Larn's home and ran a few head of cattle
with Larn's herd. One day Bryant was killed by one of Larn's
ranch hands and the suspicion arose that it was done to get his
stock. Since Bryant had no friends or relatives who cared
enough or had nerve enough to investigate the matter, Larn
simply added the animals to his own herd and considered the
matter closed.[3]

By now some of the other ranchers were becoming uneasy. The casual way men were dropping out of sight was
enough to frighten anyone, but to this was added a real concern over the cattle that were regularly disappearing. The
ranchers, suspecting that the steers were stolen, tried to force a
showdown. Larn's father-in-law, the highly respected Joseph
Beck Matthews, stepped into the picture before things had
gone too far and used his influence to bring about a settlement
—an uneasy abatement of differences which a short time later
finally exploded in violence.[4]

When Larn was elected sheriff in 1876, he was in the
unique position of having the blessings of both friends and
enemies. His friends were delighted because of his power and

authority. His enemies hoped he would get killed. Undoubtedly they wished the same for John Selman.

Most authorities credit the officers with doing a good job
of law enforcement in Griffin,[5] although no one spells out exactly how he arrives at this conclusion. A few outlaws were
shot or hanged, but these efforts were primarily the work of
the vigilantes—an organization in which, of course, the two
men played a significant part. Killings seemed to go on at a
constant rate.

It appears that Sheriff Larn and Deputy Selman spent
most of their time at the Stone Ranch, an old and imposing
structure owned by the Matthews family. Several friends con-
gregated there also, among them Tom Selman (now called
Tom Cat by nearly everyone), Billy Bland, Charlie Reed,
Billy Gray and Jack Lyons, all of them tough, hard-bitten gunmen. Nightly meetings were held, a lot of whisky was con-
sumed, and some cattle were supposedly rustled.[6]

John Selman's brother Tom now shows up for the first
time at Fort Griffin, although in fact he may have been there
for quite awhile. After being in the Montague County Minute
Men for four months, he was discharged on August 20, 1872.
Probably he had lived with his older brother since that time,
the activities and personalities of Selman, Larn and the others
being so engrossing that Tom Cat was accorded scant mention in the records.

The Larn-Selman gang might have continued to do pretty
much as it pleased for a long time if its membership had stayed
out of trouble. However, that was not to be. A big shoot-out
was the beginning of the end.

On the evening of January 17, 1877, Billy Bland and
Charlie Reed, thoroughly intoxicated, came galloping into
Griffin, swearing and yelling and firing six-shooters into the
air. Reining up in front of the Beehive, a combination dance

hall, saloon and gambling emporium, they jumped off their horses and swaggered through the doors.

Once inside, the boys decided to liven up the place and shoot the lights out. They were going merrily about their task when First Deputy W. R. Cruger and County Attorney William Jeffries stepped into the saloon with drawn guns. Reports differ as to whether or not Cruger asked the men to surrender and lay down their weapons. Bland, who was taking aim at a light while standing in the door between the saloon and the dance hall, turned and fired when he saw Cruger facing him with a pistol. The bullet inflicted a flesh wound on the deputy and at that moment the Beehive exploded with sound and fury. Shots were fired in every direction and when the smoke had cleared, a number of innocent bystanders lay dead. Dan Barron, a young lawyer recently married, lay sprawled on the floor, a hole in his forehead. Lieutenant Meyers, recently of the 10th Cavalry, was sitting in a chair, shot, dying and about to fall to the floor. Billy Bland was down, rolling in agony, his eyes already starting to glaze. William Jeffries, a gaping hole in his lungs, survived, as did Cruger, who was wounded only the one time.

Charlie Reed, credited with killing Barron with a wild shot, managed to escape unhurt. He slipped outside but found some angry saloon customers watching his horse and waiting for him to come after it. He reversed his direction, passed unnoticed out of town and walked twelve miles to the camp of Newton J. Jones, who was living out on the prairie. Jones gave him refuge for the night and the next day Reed found his horse, which had been turned loose. He left the country.[7]

Larn and Selman were quite bitter over Bland's death, feeling that the shooting had been unprovoked. On March 7, 1877, Larn resigned as sheriff and it was generally believed in Griffin that his resignation was a protest against Bland's killing. Deputy William Cruger was appointed to succeed him.[8]

Bill Cruger, a man with a fascinating career that can only be touched upon here, was widely considered a good citizen. Once again, however, we see a complex personality who was well thought of in spite of his faults. His name appears on the vigilante membership list and the story is told that once while he was feeding the prisoners, the vigilantes came in and took some of them. Cruger turned them over and then went right back to his meal.[9]

Larn, Selman and the others continued meeting at the Stone Ranch, still getting drunk, still rustling cattle and now planning to avenge Bland's death.[10]

There is no way of knowing when Selman and Larn pulled out of the vigilantes, although a good guess would be that they withdrew when the rustling charges could no longer be ignored. The fact that Cruger had violated a tacit taboo against harming a fellow member didn't help the cohesion of the gang, either. Whatever the reason for the difficulties, the men at the Stone Ranch felt that the vigilantes were out to get them, and they would leave the ranch at night and ride up into the hills to sleep. The feud was rapidly approaching a point of no return when the Vigilance Committee apparently tried for a reconciliation. Two representatives of the Tin-Hat Brigade, Alonzo Millet and a man known only as Young, contacted Larn and his men and offered a deal. Details are few, but the conditions seemed to be that if they "would quit getting drunk and doing as they were, the vigilantes wouldn't bother them." Larn, John Selman and his brother Tom, plus some other gang members, accepted the proposal. Jack Lyons and Billy Gray became suspicious and saddled up.[11]

The first fruit of the truce seems to have been an appointment to a position of public trust for Larn and Selman. On April 28, 1877, they were appointed Deputy Inspectors of Hides and Animals for Shackelford County. As part of the oath of office, both men solemnly swore that they had never fought a duel with deadly weapons or acted as a second. The bonds, $1000 each, were co-signed by J. B. Matthews and F. E. Conrad.[12]

The duties of this office were several, the chief one being to inspect cattle herds entering or leaving the county. Also, butchers had to make a quarterly report to Commissioners' Court listing the number of beeves butchered, and they were required to furnish hides as proof. This was a very strict requirement. Those who did not come voluntarily were brought in by force.[13] Selman, who appears to have learned the butcher's trade while living at the Stockton Ranch after leaving old Fort Davis, was certainly qualified for the job of supervising butchers.

The herds which passed through Griffin going up the Western Trail all came under the scrutinizing eye of Selman and Larn. John Meadows remarked that Selman did most of the inspecting, getting seventy-five to one hundred dollars from some of the trail drivers, most of which went into his own pocket.[14] If what Meadows alleges is true, the shakedown could have involved considerable amounts of hard cash.

While they were inspectors, the two men also received a contract to furnish beef to the army post of Fort Griffin. Meadows says that they had a contract from the government to feed the Tonkawa Indians at the fort, too. Reports differ, but the best available estimate is that they butchered between one and three beeves per day. Immediately trouble broke out with the ranchers again, they claiming that the slaughtered was stolen. The situation was certainly ideal for a successful rustling operation. Expenses were almost non-existent, profits were munificent and their position as inspectors gave the men a perfect opportunity to cover their tracks.

Even the most ideal situation sometimes turns sour, however, and that happened here. On October 10, 1877, the

73

money-making world of John Selman fell apart when the state of Texas filed suit against him, William A. Martin and L. H. Kelly for recovery of $1000 each in forfeited bond costs. This suit brings up all sorts of questions, none of which can be answered with any accuracy. In the first place, the suit seems to have been filed because Selman and the others were accused of taking part in some illegal action, no doubt connected with their position. But why was no legal prosecution made against Larn? And how did Martin and Kelly get mixed up in it? Selman and Larn may have secured minor appointments for them, but unfortunately no records exist beyond a bare mention of the affair. Only the trial verdict is available. The court decided that the reasons given were sufficient for forfeiture of the bond and the case was dismissed.[15]

Presumably Selman and Larn did not continue as inspectors, although court papers give no indication that they ever resigned or were dismissed.

8

THE CLEAR FORK HIDES

THE TEXAS RANGERS had been in Shackelford County at least as early as 1876, the year two of them found Henderson and Floyd hanging from a tree. Yet in spite of some mutterings about law being enforced, there is no indication that they ever took any direct action to end the lynchings. The slaughter went right on.

In June of 1877 Captain Arrington was transferred and Lieutenant G. W. Campbell took over.[1] With a force of nearly thirty rangers—some of them, like Newton J. Jones, recruited from the local residents—Campbell showed signs of being a tough third party intent on driving a hard wedge between the warring factions in the county.

As Campbell took command, the situation between the hostile parties was daily becoming more ominous and threatening. Selman and Larn, with plenty of hired guns in their camp, were beginning to step up their cattle operations and were accused, as usual, of doing it with other people's stock. Selman's son, who was an infant at the time all the troubles took place, says that his father and Larn were small ranchers fighting to hold their land against the encroachment of the rich cattle barons. Larn in fact was later killed, directly or indirectly, by his former friends and comrades, the large cattlemen, or at least with their tacit approval.

It appears at the beginning of the feud that the two men were in league with the big operators and were used as tools to drive the grangers (dirt farmers or nesters) off the range. At least, it was the farmers rather than the large ranchers who seemed to be complaining about the activities of the gunmen. Striving hard to make a living in a difficult, dry soil, the nesters could not afford to lose even one cow.

On the basis or rumors that Larn and Selman were throwing hides into a waterhole on the Clear Fork near Larn's slaughter pens, a search warrant was issued and Lieutenant Campbell led a party of thirteen men, mainly non-rangers, out to the Camp Cooper Ranch to drag the river.[2]

On arriving at Larn's home, Campbell instructed the others to wait outside while he went in to serve the papers and discuss the proceedings. John Larn met the lieutenant at the door, glanced out at the posse, and upon hearing Campbell's statement, offered to turn over his pistol. The ranger refused the weapon saying, "I just came here to see this place searched and if you won't refuse that, then I don't need to take your gun."[3]

Larn was not alone in the house. John and Tom Selman, plus a gunman named Tom Curtis, were also there. The group argued and talked with Campbell for about an hour and finally Larn reluctantly agreed to allow the search. Then everyone went outside. Larn flushed as he once again saw the other riders in the road. Stamping toward them, he began cursing and dared them to come through his yard.[4] Campbell tried to quiet him, but the situation was touchy, fraught with danger, and further arguing might lead to bloodshed. There was also the chance that John and Tom Selman had moved to advantageous positions near the house where they could bring a great deal of firepower to bear on the posse at a second's notice.

Trying to ignore the gunmen, Campbell led his deputies around the yard and down to the riverbank where grappling hooks were thrown in. Their efforts proved successful, Campbell saying that "six beef hides were found in the bed of the Clear Fork, not of their brands—Selman's and Larn's." [5] It is not clear whether these were the only hides found or the only ones with different brands.

The story is told that as the searchers were dragging the river, Larn and Selman, heavily armed, came down to the other side and asked the party to call out the names of the different brands they found. Since the area here was so brushy and the side leading up to Larn's house so steep, it was possible to call out questions from a short distance away and still be hidden from view. It is not hard to imagine the searchers glancing up occasionally, all the time wondering if unseen rifle barrels were pointed down at them. At any rate, when the question was repeated, it developed that the whole bunch had a pretty severe case of laryngitis and nobody could speak above a whisper. [6]

Larn and Selman maintained afterward that the hides were thrown into the river to frame them, and there may have been truth in this claim. Of course some whispers were heard that over 200 hides (all of them bearing different brands) were found in the creek bed, but this story seems to have been deliberately fabricated in an attempt to make a small alleged rustling operation look huge. It also conflicts with the testimony of Campbell and others who were at the scene.

One of the deputies, R. A. Hutchison, said only four or five hides were found in all and only one that could be definitely identified. Hutchison went on to say that the man who owned the hide was "offered $50 to keep quiet about it being his, as they could not afford to let too much get out." [7] Who offered the bribe was not revealed, but the implication is that either Larn or Selman attempted to pay the man off in order to keep him from pressing charges.

Lieutenant Campbell suggested that the accused rustlers surrender to him. Both men promised to come to Albany the next day and answer charges. True to their word, they showed up at the county seat the next morning. Walking into the magistrate's court, they dragged the main witness (who either owned the identified hide or hides, or claimed to have seen the rustling) out into the street and suggested he move to another part of the country. He did. Now only the hides remained in court as evidence, but the other witnesses were too frightened to testify. Apparently only the rangers would speak out, but not being injured parties they could not secure convictions. Finally, a compromise of some sort was reached and the two accused rustlers were released.[8]

Lieutenant Campbell, quite angry at what he considered a miscarriage of justice, wrote bitterly to his commanding officer, Major John B. Jones. The letter lashed out at how the court was conducted and expressed amazement that no bill was found against the parties who killed all those cattle. Campbell then went on to explain why privilege had been substituted for law in Albany. He swore that the majority of the county officers were members of the vigilantes and that there were at one time about eighty of them. The local officers, being members themselves, would take no action against any other member.[9]

This was not to be the last frustration Campbell was to experience in trying to bring law and order to Shackelford County. A brave, conscientious officer, he did not mind stepping on sensitive toes when he thought the occasion demanded it, and the jailing in Albany of the noted gunman William A.

"Hurricane Bill" Martin gave him just the opportunity he sought.

Martin had a criminal record longer than the Clear Fork of the Brazos. He and his band of gunmen, called the Texas Gang, had terrorized Wichita, Kansas, in the early 1870s until the vigilantes there had broken the gang's back and sent Hurricane Bill running for the Rio Grande.[10] Back in Texas, he drifted into Griffin, one of his old hangouts, and there became a member of the vigilance committee. He had been sued along with Selman for forfeiture of bond, as noted earlier.

But now Martin was in jail on a warrant from Sheriff Cruger for attempted murder, and his recent friends, the vigilantes, were making some very unkind remarks about him—so unkind, in fact, that Bill was in fear of his life. He sent for Lieutenant Campbell and offered to make a deal.

Bill told the lieutenant that the mob was persecuting him and he wished "each and every member of those bloodthirsty and cut-throat Tin-Hat committee to be checked in their murderous career." He said he could "show the skeletons of upwards to seven victims of this terrible mob foully murdered in the past years." Then he made the remark that he was not a member of the clan, but "had been with them when they done some of the killings." [11]

These are quite remarkable statements, considering that Skelton Glenn says that Bill Martin was not only a member in good standing along with Selman and Larn, but had the job of tying the ropes which held the victims—then cutting them down later. For this he received a fee, plus what he took off the bodies.[12]

Martin was also bitter at the committee for other actions against him. They had forced him to marry a prostitute named "Hurricane Minnie" Martin. After the ceremony they changed their minds and nearly hanged him for going through with it.

In view of John Selman's relations with Hurricane Minnie, one wonders just how much he was involved in this situation.

Campbell was elated over Martin's information, which he took at face value and immediately relayed to Major Jones, giving him all the information and saying that Hurricane Bill had offered to point out the guilty parties and furnish the names of eyewitnesses who would confess if they were promised protection. Requesting permission to move in and make arrests, Campbell awaited a reply.

If the letter itself was not a mistake, mailing it from Fort Griffin certainly was. The local badmen and rowdies considered nothing safe, not even the mail.[13] Campbell's letter was evidently opened, for a copy fell into the hands of people opposed to the arrest of their best Tin-Hat citizens.

Judge J. R. Fleming fired a letter off to Governor R. B. Hubbard. In it he played the role of an injured party whom Campbell was trying to embarrass. Fleming said that he understood such an organization as the vigilantes had once existed and might even still be around, but he had used every exertion to find out who the guilty members might be and had come up with no information. Highly shocked and grievously shaken that a Texas Ranger would believe such tales, Fleming said that if those named by Martin were arrested, all the best citizens would be in jail. The letter ended with a request that Campbell be transferred to some other county.[14]

The governor passed the word down through General Steele[15] that the lieutenant must go, and on May 18, 1878, Major Jones sent a brutal order to Campbell "directing him to discharge all the men in his company except six on the 31st of the present month, then turn over all public property and funds in his possession to Sergeant Van Riper and then consider himself relieved from duty." The excuse for this action was that he (Jones) "was reducing the forces of the command to bring the expenditures within the existing appropriation for frontier defense." [16]

The rumor soon swept the county that Campbell and his men had been dishonorably discharged.[17] Major Jones was then forced to make several public pronouncements that the discharges were honorable and the reason was economy.

Campbell's ordeal was not ignored by the better citizens of Shackelford County. Letters and telegrams poured into Ranger headquarters imploring Jones to change his mind. The good judgment of some of the settlers was not enough to get Campbell or any of his discharged men reinstated, but his dismissal was lifted and he was transferred to another county.[18]

9

THE DEATH OF JOHN LARN

WHEN JOHN SELMAN and John Larn walked away from the magistrate's court in Albany, they realized that the grangers would have to be driven out of the country. Dividing their gang, which was now composed of about sixteen men, they slashed across the countryside, discharging their firearms into houses, galloping into the very houses of the farmers at midnight and shooting through the flimsy walls. Cattle were shot dead on the prairie and run over cliffs.[1]

This was sufficient cause for scandal, but there was more to come. Two stone masons were hired by Larn for $500 to build a rock fence on his ranch. Selman had a stone wall around his ranch too[2] and quite possibly had recommended to Larn the same men who had built his.

Larn made a down payment of $100 when the work was started, and when the four-mile-long job was complete, the builders demanded the balance of their money. Then they disappeared. A few days later, two bodies were found floating in the Clear Fork and suspicion was immediately cast on Selman and Larn. Decomposition had already set in, however, and no one could swear for certain that the two bodies were those of the actual fence builders. The coroner said he was not convinced and refused to call it murder.[3]

Sergeant Van Riper filed a report on the inquest which not only disagreed with the coroner's, but practically accused him of being a confederate of the murders. The ranger sergeant remarked that Selman and Larn were members of a certain "clan" and the coroner was a member of this clan also, as were practically all the county officials. It was obvious that Van Riper was intent on calling a spade a spade.

The rangers had been given orders to guard themselves against any undue sympathy with or prejudice against any of the parties to the feud. Nevertheless, they had their private opinions as to the rights and wrongs in the dispute and their feelings often carried over into their correspondence. At this time they favored the grangers.

It was not only the grangers who feared the combination of Selman and Larn; the rangers did also. Van Riper remarked that Larn had sworn to have the lives of five men, that two were already dead, that he and Lieutenant Campbell occupied the top position among the remaining three. They were nightly expectant of a raid, and once Van Riper swore that a plan was laid to ambush him while returning to camp with a prisoner, but for some reason it was not carried out.[4]

John Selman was having his trouble with ambushes also. He and Larn were bushwhacked by an unknown rifleman who aimed a little high and only succeeded in knocking Larn's hat from his head. There was no other damage and the murderer got away. A few days later a rider came by the Selman ranch and asked Mrs. Selman if he could speak to John. When informed that he was not at home, the rider left.

That afternoon as John drove some steers down a brushy *arroyo,* a shotgun blast tore off his saddle horn. Weaving through the rocks and brush, Selman had presented a difficult target for the killer, in spite of his being so close to the gunman that the shot did not have an opportunity to spread. The slugs passed within inches of him but he was not injured.

The bushwhacker's luck was not holding as well. John swung his buffalo gun around and fired into the brush where the shot had come from. A few seconds later he was rewarded by finding a dead man sprawled among the dirt and stones of the hillside. Selman then went on home and got an old wood-hauling wagon, threw the body in and drove to the ranch, letting the legs hang over the tailgate. The next morning some riders came by and reported they were looking for a missing cowboy. John motioned toward the wagon where the buzzards were already feasting on the corpse. After some discussion among themselves, one of the men threw the body across his saddle and they all left. John watched silently and grimly, his buffalo gun cradled in the crook of his arm.[5]

Though both sides were doing their best to exterminate each other, it was the grangers who bore the brunt of the suffering. One of the farmers disappeared. He went out to check on some cattle and never came back. No one could be sure whether he had been run out of the country or was lying dead somewhere. Obviously the harassment—having their homes shot into, their stock killed and run off and armed riders calling on them at all hours of the day and night—was beginning to play havoc with the farmers' nerves. One newspaper article commented that the recent acts had "terrified the grangers so that they ceased to work their crops, kept close to their houses, and would not go out to their cowpens to milk; sending their wives out to transact all their business that was attended to." [6]

But though events looked bad for the nesters, matters suddenly took a worse turn for Selman and Larn. Something had happened; the truce between the vigilantes and the gunmen which was put into effect after the killing of Bill Bland had apparently fallen apart. Whatever the reason, something had occurred grave enough to put Larn and Selman in fear of their lives from their former comrades. They sent a note to the rangers, promising to meet them in Albany and turn state's evidence. Although all six of the rangers hurriedly went to Albany and waited several days, the two men never showed up.[7]

A granger named Lancaster did come in, however, and swore to the sheriff that Larn and Selman had chased him along the Clear Fork river bank for miles—had shot at him, wounded him, forced him to hide out in the brush and would have killed him if the opportunity had presented itself.[8]

A week or so later, in June of 1878, Larn ambushed a well known rancher named Treadwell. Fortunately for the rancher, Larn had to make a long rifle shot and Treadwell escaped unhurt, but his horse was shot out from under him and killed.[9]

For Larn and Selman it was a case now of open war against everybody, and the ranchers and farmers responded by going to Joe Matthews and demanding that he do something about Larn. Matthews talked to his son-in-law and got nowhere. Throwing up his hands, he told his neighbors there was nothing more he could do.[10]

The civil authorities, who had turned a deaf ear to the escapades to the two men while they were fellow vigilantes, now decided they were a threat to law and order and made plans to hunt them down relentlessly. Sheriff Cruger, plotting their arrest, picked his men carefully. This was no job for amateurs. A mistake or hesitation could be fatal. On the night of June 22, 1878, plans were laid to take the two men into custody.

Hurricane Minnie, the prostitute, seemed to have a way of knowing when things were happening or about to happen around Fort Griffin. Somehow, she learned about the planned arrests and lost no time in securing a horse and riding out to warn both men.[11] In the dark she missed Larn's ranch but rode on to warn John Selman. On hearing the news, he grabbed his rifle and cut across country to Larn's place, either to warn him or to join him. He arrived just in time to see, from a bluff overlooking the ranch on the other side of the Clear Fork, the sheriff and his deputies moving in.[12]

Selman could see that only a few men were in the posse, and none of them were Texas Rangers. John did not know it at the time, but the rangers were not even aware of what was taking place, and Cruger had planned it that way.

Included in the posse were Deputy Sheriff Dave Barker and two of Larn's in-laws, George and Ben Reynolds.[13] Two others have been identified as William Gilson, former city marshal of Fort Griffin, and Treadwell.[14]

Glenn Reynolds, also a relative of Larn's by marriage and the first sheriff of Throckmorton County, Bill Hawsley,[15] and some unidentified possemen had previously left the main party and circled around to Selman's Rock Ranch, hoping to catch John in the net too; but, already warned, he had escaped.

It now appears that most of Larn's relatives were bent on his destruction. Reasons can only be surmised. The most logical is that he had probably gone too far in his endeavors to drive out the grangers and was pulling the structure of lawlessness down upon the heads of everybody. When violence had been visited primarily upon the nesters, the authorities could afford to turn their heads and pretend they saw nothing. But when everyone and anyone became potential victims of the assassin's bullet or the lynch rope, then corrective measures had to be taken.

Cruger probably used Larn's relatives to make the capture easier. Although the gunman was not likely to be on smiling terms with the Matthews and Reynolds families, there is no

86

reason to suspect that the situation was so bad that he feared capture or death from them.

At the rear of Larn's house the land dropped off sharply toward the Clear Fork. Here the cow pens were located out of sight of his home, and as Larn sat down to do the morning milking, the sheriff and Ben Reynolds covered him and placed him under arrest.[16]

Edgar Rye says that Larn was not armed at the time of his capture, that he offered money to be allowed to get his gun and fight it out.[17] Other more reliable stories indicate that he was indeed armed, wearing a revolver which he unbuckled and handed over to Cruger with the remark that he had noticed some men near the house earlier but had thought they were rangers and was not expecting trouble.[18]

It appears that Larn surrendered readily because he thought he would be taken to Fort Griffin, thinking that in Griffin there were friends whom he could count on to free him. His complexion changed when he was informed that the warrant was for an Albany court. He knew then that the situation was deadly serious.

With worried thoughts churning in his mind, Larn began considering a means of escape. He asked permission to go inside the house, planning to get another gun. His request was refused. Angry now, and desperate, he demanded his pistol back and an opportunity to fight it out, but his captors, having fretted all night about the risks involved in taking him, were adament in their refusal. Dave Barker, a deputy, said elatedly, "We've got the nest egg." [19] Nobody wanted to risk losing it. Larn then snarled that if he ever got out of custody, they would all die. But for these threats he might not have been mobbed later.[20]

As John Larn accepted the fact of his arrest, his biggest fear was that he would be murdered on his way to Albany. The posse might either hang him to the first convenient tree, or simply bypass all that trouble and shoot him. In order to circumvent them, he asked that his wife and son Will be allowed to accompany him to town. The request was granted—the Reynolds men probably did not know how to refuse.

The procession rode through Fort Griffin and on into Albany, where Henry Herron, a deputy, took Larn to Charlie Rainbolt's blacksmith shop to have shackles riveted to his legs.[21] Then with the chains clanking and the populace staring, he was taken to a thin-walled shack which served as a jail. There, along with the other prisoners, he was chained to a spot over the fireplace.

Meanwhile, Mrs. Mary Larn had stopped off in Griffin and obtained the services of a young lawyer named John W. Wray. He went to Albany and demanded that his client be allowed to go free. The demand was flatly refused.

At ten o'clock that night John Poe,[22] former buffalo skinner for Joe McComb and now Deputy City Marshal for Fort Griffin, relieved R. A. Slack, who was guarding the prisoners. Slack stretched his arms, gave a long yawn, retired to a small side room and went to sleep. Two hours later he was awakened by a poke in the ribs with a six-shooter. Jumping swiftly to his feet, he found himself surrounded by masked men who seized his arms.[23] John Poe was there also, and he too had been overpowered. Poe's name, however, appears on the alleged vigilante membership list and he may not have been too reluctant about giving up.

Nine men (some reports say eleven, others say twenty or thirty) wearing slickers and bandannas, stamped into the jail and Larn rose to face them. "In recognition of some of your better qualities," one of the masked men is reported to have said, "we are not going to hang you." Then nine rifles cracked in the night air and John Larn fell dead. Slack later said, "He was the gamest man I ever saw and he smiled placidly as the mob shot him to pieces." The leader of the executioners was reputedly a relative.[24]

One of the odd things about the killing was that each of the prisoners thought the mob had come for him individually. Most of them turned their heads to the wall when they heard the hoarse shouts and the clumping of boots. No doubt some of them had seen this many times before. One prisoner (it was Hurricane Bill, who was still in jail) said, "It would be a pity to bloody such a nice pallet, so I'll just get up."

As the burst of gunfire echoed and re-echoed across the street, Mrs. Larn, who had taken up residence in a local hotel, emitted a piercing scream. She didn't have to go see what had happened. She knew.

The next day a verdict of death from gunshot wounds by parties unknown was rendered and Mrs. Larn sadly took her husband home. He was buried in the back yard of his Camp Cooper Ranch, where a tombstone marks the grave today.[25]

10

THE ESCAPE OF JOHN SELMAN

THERE ARE several stories about what happened to John Selman after he witnessed the sheriff's posse close in on John Larn and take him away. Edgar Rye says he immediately rode over the countryside rounding up friends, of whom the two men had no shortage. That night a spectacular prison break was planned and as darkness fell men from all over the county began to cluster on the outskirts of Albany. As they grouped, Selman began to explain the tactics. Then as he talked, a volley of rifle shots reached their ears and they knew it was all over. Jumping on their horses and riding fast, they scattered into the night.[1]

John Selman, Jr., picks up the story there and says his father stayed around Shackelford County all winter, killing several men and giving the county a great many constructive funerals. According to his story, John took to the hills and, with his buffalo gun doing the talking, avenged Larn's death many times over. There is no secondary evidence to back up this story. Newspaper accounts, ranger reports, court records and personal letters give no hints that Selman was even in the neighborhood during the weeks and months following Larn's death.

Phin W. Reynolds tells a much more credible tale. He says that when Selman saw Larn being arrested, he headed eastward, showed himself at Tom Lanier's ranch in Stephens County to give any possible pursuers a false lead, then doubled back to Larn's ranch where he took a $300 chestnut sorrel stallion and rode northwest. A posse later followed him to the "foot of the plains" where they lost the trail.[2]

The story of Selman's departure from the county is further substantiated by a letter written by Ranger Newton J. Jones to J. R. Webb in 1947. Jones noted that after Larn was captured, Sheriff Cruger sent word for the rangers to meet him and the others at Treadwell's place. "As soon as God will let you come," was the way the message read. So Sergeant Van Riper took all six of his men and rode out there. Upon arrival, they found the vigilantes "falling out among themselves," some being in favor of killing Larn and the others wanting to let the law take its course.[3]

The sheriff told the rangers that the Selman brothers, John and Tom, had escaped, and he wanted Van Riper's men to pursue them. The sergeant was suspicious, however, feeling that Cruger had hidden motives for suggesting the chase— such a motive, for instance, as getting the rangers out of the area and leaving it free for the activities of the vigilance committee. There is no indication to tell us why, if they had such suspicions, that they did not provide Larn with around-the-clock protection.

Van Riper's men did not comply with Cruger's request. Instead, four of the six returned to Albany and the other two, Jack Smith and Newton J. Jones, went to see Mrs. Selman at the Rock Ranch. She told them, and they seemed to find it difficult to believe her, that the vigilantes would kill Larn. She also substantiated the statement that John and Tom Selman, along with John Gross, had left the vicinity. As an afterthought, she told Jones that her husband would have surrendered to the Rangers.

Although the rangers made no attempt to find the Selmans and Gross, the posse did. Their efforts, however, proved futile. After pursuing the fugitives for over twenty-four hours, they rode weary and empty-handed back into Albany a day or so after Larn's death. There they found the rangers in the midst of an investigation of the slaying, an investigation which shook the foundations of Albany so hard that it appeared blood might again flow in the streets. The vigilantes were violently opposed to letting any details of the murder get out, and they threatened to kill the rangers. John Poe walked up to Jones in a hostile manner, evidently trying to scare him into deserting his friends. Jones said, "I am one of the six." Poe did not answer, but stood there glowering. Just at that moment the posse rode into town.

Seeing Glenn Reynolds among the possemen, Jones and another ranger walked past Poe and began talking to Reynolds. "We cannot understand the situation," Jones said. "We have been told that they [the vigilance committee] would kill us just the same as they [did] Larn."

Reynolds replied, "If you are going to get evidence, there is nothing they will not do to stop it."

How much of an inquiry the rangers were able to make in view of the hostility of the citizens is not known. It evidently was not much because no reports are available and no indictments were ever handed down.

The only charges to be filed were those made by county officials against John Selman. On October 19, 1878, a grand jury convened in Albany and indicted John H. Selman on nine different counts of cattle theft, ranging in date from March 15, 1876 to February 15, 1878.[4] Each indictment was for one cow or one bull each, making a total of nine beeves he was accused of stealing. His brother Tom was also named in three of the charges.[5] Warrants for John Selman's arrest were sent to all the surrounding counties. On May 20, 1879, an *alias capias* was sent out with the following footnote attached:

Dear Jack:

[Send] copies to Presidio and El Paso counties for Selman. He was in Fort Davis some time ago. Perhaps you had better send a description of him with it.

John Selman is about 45 years of age—5 ft 9 or 10 inches high—eyes hazel—hair and whiskers black sprinkled with gray—generally wears only mustache—downcast look—compactly built—weight about 155 or 160 pounds—good and plausible talker—If a whore by the name of Hurricane Minnie is around, there will John Selman be. Hear that he goes by the name of Smith.

[Signed] J. R. Fleming[6]

John Selman was already gone from Shackelford County, but the legacy of hate he left behind was soon visited upon his wife and children. The Selman family claims that the Rock Ranch was surrounded by vigilantes who thought John was inside. They fired on the house for several hours, keeping Mrs. Selman and the children pinned down under a bed. When finally the shooting stopped, Mrs. Selman who was expecting another child, was prostrated. While the complete accuracy of this story is doubtful, there is sufficient evidence to prove Mrs. Selman did suddenly become quite ill, the best guess being that the recent events had triggered a physical reaction that she was unable to cope with. A Fort Griffin doctor came and pronounced her condition as critical. Her brother, Jasper N. deGraffenreid, then took her and the four children to his ranch in Stephens County. Mrs. Selman's condition became worse, however, and a week later she died in premature childbirth. A deal was later made with J. C. McGrew, a rancher whose wife was a niece of Mrs. Selman's, to take care of the children until John could send for them.[7]

Several stories have been told to account for John Selman's activities after his hasty departure from Griffin. One, substantiated by Selman's son, says he rode sixty miles and struck the cow camp of Charlie Siringo. Both Siringo and John Selman, Jr., agree that Charlie welcomed him with opened arms and outfitted him with a supply of food and ammunition. Here the agreement ends. The Selman story is that John rode on and stayed out of trouble. Siringo accuses John of stealing 2000 sheep after leaving his camp, a theft which was punctuated by the killing of two Mexican boys who were guarding the animals. After shooting the youths, John supposedly drove the sheep to El Paso and sold them for a dollar a head.[8]

The odds are that John Selman was not guilty of the theft charge. For one thing, there is solid evidence placing him in New Mexico on a killing rampage less than two weeks after leaving Fort Griffin. A man could not possibly drive 2000 sheep over 300 miles of rough country and return that distance in less than fourteen days. Also, since neither authority mentions Tom Selman or John Gross in the narrative, neither may be correct in his statements.

Selman and the other two did stop at a camp out on the prairie, but it belonged to Fred Tucker, a Texas horse dealer. Tucker, at the time Selman came upon him, had twelve men and seven wagons, and was driving a herd of horses to market in Leadville, Colorado. Selman and his friends got permission to stay the night. The next morning, while most of Tucker's men were scattered out on the range, Selman seized all the guns in camp and put Tucker's cowboys in a tent. As the others straggled in throughout the day, they were taken prisoner also. The wagons were then plundered, the loot was

94

loaded on Tucker's horses, and the three men rode off toward southern New Mexico.[9] The next few months found them at the scene of a bloody factional dispute known as the Lincoln County War.

11

KING OF THE OUTLAWS

By summer of 1878, guided by his sure instinct for finding trouble spots, John Selman was a part of the activities known as the Lincoln County War. As usual he sought the fringes rather than the center, and the part he played in these marginal activities has never been—perhaps never can be—thoroughly explored. But we know enough about his depredations to be sure that he did his share of bloodletting and caused his share of trouble. To place him properly against this blazing background, we shall need a quick survey of the major developments in the Lincoln County troubles, remembering that no event in Western history has been more written about or more wildly distorted. Billy the Kid, for instance, has been so fictionalized that almost any point of view one wishes to adopt can be justified by reference to one "authority" or another.

Lincoln County in 1878 was larger than some states. It reached from the Pecos to the Rio Grande and beyond: Lincoln, the county seat and hub of the conflict, was surrounded by moutains—the Sacramentos, the White Mountains, the Jicarillas and the Capitans—where several hundred square miles of virgin timber flourished, but it included great expanses of desert waste. It was, in fact, a little world, where all sorts of terrain and all sorts of people could be found.

The town of Seven Rivers, located at the junction of the Pecos and a few small tributaries, was the headquarters for rustlers, especially those who raided the ranch of John Chisum, the cattle king whose vast holdings lay northward along the Pecos. Near Chisum's headquarters was the town of Roswell, with Bosque Grande still farther north and Fort Sumner farther still, probably the outermost limit within which the war was fought. To the west lay Lincoln and White Oaks (a mining town); the Mescalero Apache Indian Reservation sprawled over the western slopes of the Sacramentos; and tucked in the middle, convenient to all sections of the county, was Fort Stanton. Occasional ranches and small farms dotted the valleys, sometimes even forming into small settlements such as San Patricio, which lay near the junction of the Ruidoso and Hondo Rivers.

Although the conflict raged over politics, cattle and land, it was the life-insurance money of one Emil Fritz which brought the hostilities blazing into the open. When lawyer Alex McSween, for reasons still not fully understood, failed to turn over the money to the Fritz heirs (money which he had been engaged to obtain), he ignited passions ready to burn because McSween and John Tunstall had announced their intentions of going into the banking and mercantile business—an activity in direct competition with the enterprises of the Dolan-Riley faction. In February of 1878, John Tunstall was brutally murdered by a band of hired assassins. McSween, then backed by John Chisum, employed his own band of gunmen, among them a young killer called Henry McCarty, *alias* William H. Bonney, William McCarty, Henry Antrim, Kid Antrim, Bill Bonney, Bonnie, Bonny, Kid, and Billy the Kid. Tunstall had previously given the Kid a job and perhaps it was only out of gratitude that he, along with the others, took to the vengeance trail after the Englishman's death. Although the youthful gunslinger played no part in the instigation of the feud and was never much more than a hired gun, he is the legendary character that people remember today. Pat Garrett, his slayer, and the big names around which the war revolved are all but forgotten.

Supporting the Dolan-Riley faction was a young renegade named Jesse Evans. Boasting that he had on call nearly a hundred men, Evans, who was a close friend of Jimmy Dolan, the political boss of Lincoln County, organized his group of killers under the name Seven Rivers Warriors, their chief purpose in life being the obliteration of the McSween party and the rustling of John Chisum stock.

Opposing the Warriors was the other group of gunmen known as the Regulators, nominally headed by lawyer McSween, although as the war turned more and more against him, control slipped to Billy the Kid, who knew little about the niceties of politics, but was more adept at fighting for his life. While neither side had an overabundance of charity and good will toward each other, the facts seem to indicate that the Regulators were the aggrieved or injured party.

It was the Seven Rivers men who gradually gained the upper hand, finally gaining recognition as deputies under Sheriff "Dad" Peppin. In July of 1878, as the tide of war swept bloodily toward a showdown in the famous five-day battle in Lincoln, the Regulators were holed up in McSween's house. Outside, their enemies waited with cocked guns and warrants for their arrest. Since the Kid and his friends refused to come outside to certain death, and none of Peppin's deputies dared go inside, the building was finally set on fire. Alex McSween was killed and the Warriors emerged victorious, although the Kid managed to escape the fiery trap, as did most of his friends. This climax, however, signaled the end of organized fighting on both sides. The Kid became a wanted fugitive, his luck running out with the crack of Sheriff Pat Garrett's pistol in Fort Sumner in 1881. Evans could not survive the victory either. He himself rarely showed his face in his rustling hangout of Seven Rivers thereafter, and his Warriors broke up, wandering the area in small groups, raping, pillaging, looting. All thoughts of honor, glory, loyalty—if they ever existed— were thrust aside as they all fought for survival. It was about this time that John Selman rode into the area.

John Selman was not one who advertised his presence. He galloped into Lincoln County when the war was in full bloom, and thus his activities were largely eclipsed by the deeds of more familiar gunmen such as Billy the Kid and Pat Garrett. The countryside was full of warring bands, living off peaceful citizens and crossing each other's trails in a fashion calculated to frustrate and confuse the historians of a later generation. Only one historian, Robert N. Mullin, has succeeded in putting all the facts together in a pattern that makes sense.[1]

On the 8th of July, 1878, John Selman and his brother Tom, and probably John Gross and a few other men he had picked up during his travels across Texas and into New Mexico, raided the ranch of George Coe on the Hondo River. Coe, who was at John Chisum's ranch helping to defend it against the threatened onslaught of some of Peppin's deputies, complained that the rustlers under Selman burned his house to the ground after looting it of everything of value, including some treasured pictures and an old violin.[2]

As the flames billowed and crackled, the outlaws spotted a farmhand working in the fields and attempted to take his horses. The farmer wasn't easily buffaloed by the gunmen, although he did allow them to take the teams belonging to Coe. He threatened to fight if his own animals were molested, so he was left in peace.[3]

It is at Coe's place that John Selman is definitely identi- fied by name. According to Mullin, he now begins to use the *alias* of John Gunter or Gunther, an *alias* also occasionally used by John Gross. In fact, it is often difficult to tell who was who among the gang as the members were known to use each other's names interchangeably, as well as fictitious ones.

Meanwhile, some of the Warriors, still using the name of the old band, reorganized at Seven Rivers. Most of them were fugitivies from Texas and the toughest and meanest of Peppin's possemen. The two Selmans and Gross joined the organization and the group's firepower soared.

The captain in charge of these deperados was William Harrison Johnson.[4] He was destined only to last for a few short days because his father-in-law, Hugh Beckwith, had a passionate dislike for the man on personal grounds which had nothing to do with the Warriors. On the 17th of August, 1878, Mr. Beckwith became enraged over the way his son and John- son were handling property belonging to the Beckwith family. He attempted to shoot both men and did manage to kill John- son, although he himself was badly wounded and had to be taken to Fort Stanton to recover.[5]

Now another fast gun, Caleb Hall, *alias* Sam Collins, *alias* the Prowler, took charge. Hall's tenure of office was nearly as short as Johnson's. Near San Patricio, on a sweep up the Ruidoso Valley, the Warriors stopped at the home of John Newcomb, and demanded that Mrs. Newcomb serve them a meal. Mrs. Newcomb who judged rightly that the group was bent on plunder, served them a meal that none of them ever forgot. Caleb Hall felt flattered over what he thought was spe- cial attention, but it turned out to be more than just that. She put some poison in his drink and it was not long before the Prowler was thrashing about on the floor, deathly ill. Realizing what was happening, the other outlaws drew their guns and upon pain of death forced the lady to produce an antidote.

100

Fortunately, one was available and Hall survived. Nevertheless, his health was broken by the experience and he soon dropped out of the gang, going to Silver City to live.[6]

Near the first part of September, John Selman tried to seize control, but he ran swiftly into trouble with some of the older members who resented his attempts at power grabbing. Hart, a resentful gunman and a close friend and lieutenant of Hall's, felt he rightly should be in charge and his belligerent attitude indicated that he had no scruples whatever over his manner of getting it. John quietly held back and did not press the point at this time. He simply announced his generalship and waited to settle the issue permanently on another day.

Besides John Selman and Hart, some of the other members known to be with the gang were Tom Selman, *alias* Tom Cat, John Gross, William Dwyer (or Dyer), Bob Speakes (believed to have been a former Texas Ranger), V. S. Whitaker, Charlie Snow, *alias* Johnson, Reese Gobles (or Gobly), John Nelson, Rustling Bob Irwin (sometimes know as Jim Irvin or Irving), Jake Owens, Marion Turner and a weird character known only as the Pilgrim.[7] A two-page incomplete letter in handwriting which has been identified as belonging to John B. Wilson (justice of the peace in Lincoln) identifies some of the gang as Bill Jones, Jim Jones, John Jones, George Davis, John Smith or Sillman and Tom Cat Sillman. Wilson said he knew nothing more about the members, except that "they are killers and desperate men." [8]

The gang now rode weary horses over the eastern slopes of the White Mountains and started down the Rio Feliz, heading in the general direction of the Pecos River and Seven Rivers. During the trip some Tunstall cattle were rustled and a man named Martin was taken prisoner. Here they killed one of their own men and this may be where the question of leadership was settled.

No one knows precisely what happened, but Hart was sitting at a table waiting for a meal to be fixed and Selman killed him. The accepted story, according to Mullin, is that John, sitting on the other side of the table, slowly pulled his gun and without warning fired a shot up through the boards. The heavy slug ripped through the table, smashed Hart alongside the nose, ranged up through his head and tore off the top of his skull.[9]

Now the gunmen, with John Selman firmly in control, turned north past the ranch of John Chisum and rode up the Hondo in the general direction of Lincoln and Fort Stanton. Toward the middle of September they stopped at the home of Cleto Chavez, a small farmer, and called for watermelon—then shot Cleto and his son Desiderio when they complied with the request. Then, flexing their muscles on almost defenseless victims, they robbed a neighbor of Chavez and left the farmer wandering naked in the brush. Of course all the horses to be found in the vicinity went up the river with the outlaws.[10]

Arriving now in the general area where the Bonito and Ruidoso rivers flow into the Hondo, the Warriors decided to spend some time on what looked like easy pickings. Small fruit farms dotted the landscape and offered ample opportunities for men with nothing to do but kill and destroy. Within a few days the Seven Rivers men attacked a party of laborers cutting hay near the home of Jose Chavez on the Bonito River. Chavez was not there, but two of his sons were, along with a mentally retarded youth named Lorenzo Lucero. According to most reports, the outlaws were in the process of running off the horses when the Chavez boys objected. This objection was handled in the customary manner: both lads, besides the "crazy boy," were shot and killed. Their bodies were discovered the next day and the father, badly shaken, went to Fort Stanton to procure coffins.[11]

Striking south now, the band slashed fifteen miles to the home of Martin Sanchez, later a lieutenant in the New Mexico

Mounted Rifles.[12] There, Martin's fourteen-year-old son, Gregorio, was shot three times and killed. A farmhand was wounded, but managed to escape.[13]

Selman's men now drifted down to the junction of the Hondo and Ruidoso and there on September 17, 1878, they practically demolished Avery Clenny's store after looting it. Clenny escaped, but decided to retire to a fruit ranch, figuring his chances for a long life would be better.[14]

The gang had now attracted the attention of the military authorities at Fort Stanton, several letters being written concerning them by Colonel Dudley, the commanding officer. He was beginning to give minute attention to the group's movements. For some reason, Dudley referred to the desperados not as warriors but as Wrestlers, or Rustlers. This new name could have been an attempt to show a thin line of difference between the old gang of Jesse Evans and the new members under John Selman. Or it could have been merely a misspelling or mispronunciation which Dudley failed to correct.

On September 28 and 29, 1878, Dudley took the testimony of a Mr. Klein (or Kline), a mail contractor. Klein stated that the Wrestlers (no specific names mentioned) had visited the Bartlett Ranch on the Bonito River, eleven miles from Fort Stanton. Bartlett had a grist mill and two married employees living just a short distance from his house. "The Wrestlers took the wives of these two men," Dudley wrote, "forced them into the brush, stripped them naked and used them at their pleasure. One of the women in this nude condition went to the house at 2 A.M. and told her sad tale to Mr. Bartlett." Klein refused to give the names of these women as their husbands wanted the incident kept quiet.[15]

The Wrestlers had now fired their guns at so many people that they were running low on powder; and in order to replenish their supply, they agreed to rob the house of Isaac Ellis, a dealer in ammunition who lived on the outskirts of Lincoln.

The outlaws were overconfident—so sure of themselves on account of the success of their depredations thus far, that they assaulted the house without first reconnoitering the area and came dangerously close to having their ranks decimated. Several men besides Ellis were in the house and they were experienced fighters, some having fought with the Kid. In the ensuing battle the Wrestlers began to retreat, but the retreat soon developed into a rout as the outlaws were forced to abandon horses and merchandise they had stolen.[16]

When the pursuers finally gave up and turned back, Selman regrouped his men near Fort Stanton. There they began to break up for the first time under his leadership. Jake Owens deserted, as did a few others. Their places were filled, however, by some new men who came into the organization, among them Gus Gildea, who immediately became Selman's lieutenant and coined the term "Selman's Scouts." [17] Perhaps Gildea felt John's endeavors needed more prestige and dignity. If he did, he was disappointed. The new name fooled no one in New Mexico.

Only nine men were left now, the rest having either turned off to better and greener pastures or been slain by some of their own companions. Among those left were John and Tom Selman, Gus Gildea, Bob Speakes, Bill Dwyer, V. S. Whitaker, Charles Snow, John Nelson, Bob Irwin and Reese Gobles. Some reports say Gobles was wounded, but Dudley remarked that it was Gunter (John Selman) who was suffering from a rifle-shot wound.[18] He did not comment on the circumstances surrounding the shooting.

Spreading the word that they were the advance unit of a gang sixty to eighty strong,[19] the Scouts set up their headquarters at Lincoln in the Hudgens Saloon, which at one time housed the brewery of G. L. Murphy. They next tried to force Hudgens to go to the post trader's store at Fort Stanton and buy a large quantity of ammunition but he refused to do so.

After a short conference, the Scouts sent four of their own men to purchase the needed supplies.

The plan might have worked had not Hudgens slipped from his saloon and run breathlessly to the fort, where he informed Colonel Dudley of what was afoot. Furious, the colonel wasted no time. The four men were ordered arrested, the supplies were taken from them and their money was refunded. Then they were escorted to the post boundary and shoved across after being warned never to return, under threat of being put in the stockade.[20]

When the men got back to the saloon and told their story, tempers became so inflamed that the Scouts wrecked the building in anger and the wife and sister of Hudgens were "abused and insulted." A bystander named Shepherd tried to protect the women and received a battered head for his pains when the gunmen savagely pistol-whipped him. As for Hudgens, he could not be found and so missed his share of the ill treatment, though the boys left word with his wife that he would be killed on sight.[21]

A week later, the army received a call for help from farmer George Nesmith at Three Rivers, nearly forty miles away. The fact that the military this time sent soldiers to assist in a purely civil matter calls attention to the reality that only armed and naked force could control the situation. By the time the soldiers arrived, however, the outlaws were gone.[22]

Some people disputed the statement that the soldiers were really after the Scouts. Billy the Kid (who might have been a little prejudiced) claimed that the gang burned Lola Wise's house and "moved in sight of the soldiers, taking horses, insulting women." [23]

In October of 1878, anticipating a raid, a group of citizens set up a roadblock in the Hondo River, not too far from its junction with the Pecos. Startled by this display of determination, the Seven Rivers men turned northward. Another posse under the leadership of Juan Patron, a prominent resident of Lincoln, made a wide-swinging trip up the Pecos in search of them. The two groups made violent contact, the Scouts at first attempting to fight their way through and then recoiling, to flee north once again along the Pecos. In a long pursuit, two of Selman's men were killed between Lloyd's Crossing and Fort Sumner. Still Patron closed in relentlessly. Three more Scouts, unidentified as were the others, were reported killed near Puerto de Luna in what is now San Miguel County and almost on the outskirts of Fort Sumner.[24]

By now the whole countryside was up in anger and actively searching for the desperados. The gunmen were tracked, hounded, shot at and forced to take refuge during the last part of 1878 in the *Bosque Grande* on the Pecos. Five were reported caught and jailed when they tried rustling some cattle from the ranch of Pat Coghlan at Three Rivers.[25]

Dissension among the outlaws followed. Men began dropping out, looking for new and safer worlds to plunder. John and Tom Selman, Bob Speakes and a few others rode over to John Slaughter's ranch. Slaughter was reputed to have the toughest group of gunmen in Lincoln County at that time.[26]

But nowhere was there peace, even with each other. With nothing but time on their hands, they began to fight among themselves. Tempers flared and quarrels flowered. There are two stories about the gunfight at Dead Man's Crossing on Rocky Arroyo, a small watercourse which empties into the Pecos. One is that John Selman and several of his Scouts were playing poker on the banks of the stream and an argument erupted which terminated in the sudden death by gunfire of one of the participants. The slaying is generally charged to Selman. The other anecdote says that Selman and two others were playing cards and following a heated dispute, Selman killed both men. Regardless of which story is correct, a day or so

106

after the incident, some of the Jones boys found the body or bodies lying twisted among some scattered cards. They were buried where they lay. Mrs. Eve Ball, a leading Lincoln County historian who relates the last version, adds the comment that the Jones brothers recognized Selman's handiwork because of a peculiar hoof print left by his horse.[27] Who the victims were can only be guessed at; however, Billy the Kid said that Irvin, Reese Gobles and Rustling Bob Irwin had been killed by members of their own party. Perhaps one or two of these were the Selman victims.[28]

The event which actually doomed Selman's Seven Rivers men to banishment from New Mexico occurred on September 30, 1878. That was the date that Lew Wallace was appointed governor. Samuel Beach Axtell, who had served since July 30, 1875, had been suspended from office following a complete breakdown of law and order in the state, and Wallace accepted reluctantly the vacated post. A former Indiana favorite son for the Republican presidential ticket, Wallace had won glory in the Mexican and Civil Wars. Now all he sought was a political position where he could practice his literary skills. He hardly regarded New Mexico of being worthy of his talents, but he had accepted the position with as much dignity as he could muster. His mission was simple: Restore peace and harmony to the state and create an atmosphere conducive to the attraction of more settlers.[29]

Wallace's primary concern was to get rid of the outlaws who had invaded the region. In November of 1878 he issued his now famous Amnesty Proclamation in which as governor he promised a general pardon to all the fighters on both sides of the factional dispute known as the Lincoln County War.[30] This did not apply to gunmen, such as John Selman's fellows, who had drifted in from outside the state. For these people there was no choice except to stay and be killed or to flee. Selman and most of his men chose the latter alternative.

107

On March 11-12, 1879, Governor Wallace furnished a letter to Captain Henry Carroll of Fort Stanton, in which he listed most of the wanted outlaws in New Mexico, particularly those who had infested the eastern part. Several versions of the letter exist, all of them in Lew Wallace's handwriting. Well over thirty names are written there, among them John Selman (who is number 3), and Tom Selman, *alias* Tom Cat (number 4). The names of his Scouts, some of whom were in all likelihood already dead, are also given. All of the wanted men were charged with murder or grand larceny. John Selman and his brother Tom, along with Gus Gildea, Bob Irvin, Reese Gobles, Rustling Bob, Robert Speakes, and the Pilgrim, were charged with the murder of Gregorio Sanchez, the two Chavez (Chaves) boys, and the "crazy boy." [31]

The list is a hodgepodge of names, giving the appearance that Wallace wrote in everyone he could recall who was not either in jail or dead. His wanted notice proved to be very controversial, depending upon which side of the dispute you happened to favor. The Mesilla *News* printed an editorial claiming that the wanted men were peaceful citizens being arrested without benefit of indictments or warrants.[32]

The Mesilla *Independent,* choking with anger, printed a counter editorial criticizing the stand taken by its competitor and saying, "The *News* submits a list of names of the 'peaceful' citizens. . . . Prominent among the list of names is that of Andrew Boyle, a friend and correspondent of the *News.* A quiet citizen you say. Not everyone in Dona Ana County will agree with you. Then there is Tom Cat, whose very name suggests suspicious habits. Gus Gildy, Rustling Bob, who was rightly named for his occupation, Bob Speakes, the Pilgrim, Jesse Evans, Jim French, the Kid. Are these the quiet and peaceful citizens?" [33]

Neither the Lew Wallace list of wanted outlaws nor the quarrels of newpaper editors were of any consequence to John

Selman. By March of 1879, he, his brother Tom and John Gross were out of New Mexico and blazing a path of terror and fear up and down the western part of Texas, their operations ranging from the Panhandle to Presidio on the Rio Grande.

Here John Selman organized a new gang, much of it built around the nucleus of the old Wrestlers or Scouts. Fortunately for the good of society he never succeeded in welding his new band into an effective fighting force. The Southwest was too large, communications were too poor, his men were too scattered. But had John's ambitions succeeded in just a little greater degree, "the force would have swelled to such a number that only an army could subdue them.[34]

On the 15th of June, 1879, James McIntire, a highly regarded former Texas Ranger, was camped near Tascosa on the Canadian River in Texas. That day a party of horsemen, eight or ten in number, rode into his camp and mistook McIntire for a man on the dodge. "They told me if I wanted to come to them," McIntire said, "to come from Fort Griffin to Devils River and there inquire for Buck Smith or Long John and I would be all right. Long John told me that Buck Smith is the alias now worn by John Silliman [Selman]. [He] showed me alias names of Silliman's gang on a paper, they have adopted names of women, such as Annie, Sue, etc. Said Silliaman was up above at the 'other plaza' but did not explain where this place was. . . . Silliaman's brother Tom is with them and known as Tom Cat. John Gross is with them under an alias I do not remember." [35]

The leader of this small group was a new Selman lieutenant calling himself John Long, or conversely Long John. He was a man whom McIntire recognized as being under indictment in Shackelford County for killing Vergil Hewey and a colored soldier of the 10th Cavalry at Fort Griffin. Long had enjoyed an adventurous life during the Lincoln County War,

109

having been named a deputy under Sheriff Peppin. On July 13, 1878, armed with a warrant, he was looking for Billy the Kid near San Patricio. He met the Kid along with John Copeland, Alex McSween and eight other men along the Ruidoso Road. The meeting was quite unexpected for Long; he barely had time to rein his horse up short before the animal was shot out from under him and he was running for his life. He returned to Lincoln with the warrant unserved.[36]

Less than a week later, on July 19, Long, Marion Turner and Sheriff Peppin were trying to serve warrants on the Kid, McSween and the others who were holed up in McSween's house in Lincoln. The efforts to arrest the barricaded men proved fruitless, so Peppin and Long decided to burn them out. That afternoon, John Long, helped by a man known only as "Dummy," slipped into the McSween home and poured coal oil on the kitchen floor. It burst into flame, smoldered and went out. That evening, Long went back alone. This time he used shavings and pieces of kindling previously saturated in oil, and the house was quickly enveloped in flames.[37]

McIntire noticed that, though poorly mounted, Long's men were well armed and sporting new Winchesters and six-shooters. After mentioning that they had robbed a bank in New Mexico of $1500, Long made several inquiries about local conditions, especially the number of troops stationed at Fort Elliot. He implied that the gang intended to attack and wipe out the army post.[38] Long remarked that Selman had about 175 men under his command, although scattered from the Canadian to the Devil's River. Right then, only about seventy-five were with Selman, and John was uncertain whether to put their guns to work against Fort Griffin people (against whom he was making many angry threats) or to bring them down for use against Fort Elliot.

After Long and his men had left, McIntire hastily went to Moses Wiley, the county attorney for Wheeler County, and

110

told his startling story. Shaken, Wiley fired off a letter to Major John B. Jones, Commander of the Frontier Battalion of the Texas Rangers, and a man to whom the name of John Selman was doubtless familiar. Wiley told Jones that the army was forbidden to cooperate with the state civil officers, and could defend nothing but government property. He then went on to say that no one seriously thought Selman would attack the military, but if an attack were attempted and skill used, the chances were that the assault would be successful:

> Would the Governor's or President's proclamation, if it could be obtained against these outlaws, serve to authorize the military and civil authorities against these outlaws? It is impossible to say where or at what point they will strike, but when as many desperados as they have now are banded together for the express purpose of outlawry and depredations it is probable that they will accomplish something startling. And occupying as they do the interior lines of communications, they can readily concentrate upon any given point of the frontier which makes a circle about them.[39]

No more than this is now known about John Selman's supposed ambitions to create a six-gun empire of his own in the Southwest. Only occasionally—for instance, in a brief mention by Charles Goodnight that Selman's gang was stealing cattle that passed along the Canadian River—are the band's predatory activities mentioned.[40]

12

CAPTURED

AFTER A BRIEF period of success, John Selman's gang disintegrated. It may have been that internal strife and dissension ripped the loosely knit organization asunder. Men like John Long, Selman's ablest and toughest lieutenant, suddenly dropped from sight, leaving the impression that much of the band's strength was filling shallow graves across the prairie.

Another possible factor in the gang's decline was the fact that Selman fell victim to the Mexican black smallpox. The available evidence suggests that he was out on the open range when it happened. His comrades probably brought him to Fort Davis for medical treatment. An indication that John was not a Davis resident at this time lies in the treatment afforded him. He was put in a tent about a mile outside the village limits and a "bar fly" was assigned to tend to his wants. Isolation in the case of a rare disease was not a new or unusual treatment on the frontier, but the cold, amost indifferent way Selman was handled by the townspeople suggests that he was little known.

This did not mean that Selman was necessarily unpopular; it would indicate more that he was a stranger in a harsh and unfeeling land, a man who expected the treatment he got and would have been surprised had it been any different. Following recovery, he went on living in Fort Davis and even opened a business.

His male nurse did not last long. After being with Selman only a day or so, he went to town for a drink of whisky and never came back. How long Selman lay alone after that is not known, but he must have been near the brink of death when attention was brought to his plight by a line of buzzards perched on the ridgepole of the tent. A traveling Mexican tailor, Guadalupe Zarate, investigated the scene and found the gunman, starving, raving and almost mad with thirst. Covering Selman's body was a mass of blow flies; John had scratched his bleeding shins where maggots had entered.

The tailor, who was accompanied by his daughter Niconora, took his wagon into town and brought back a large brass kettle and a barrel of water. Soon the water was being heated over a roaring fire and Selman's clothes were tenderly stripped from his body. When the water had reached the proper temperature, he was lowered into the brass pot and with the aid of carbolic soap and a stiff brush, he received his first bath in several weeks and the maggots were dug out. After a few days John began to mend. His son later commented that he offered to pay his benefactor from a large, gold-laden money belt which was strapped around his waist. The offer was refused with thanks, and from then on John Selman always had a warm spot in his heart for Mexicans.[1]

Although Selman rapidly recovered, his face was badly scarred and pockmarked, a circumstance which completely altered his appearance. Now, thinking he was so pitted that no one would recognize him, he shaved off his beard, opened a butcher shop in Fort Davis and operated it under the *alias* of

113

Captain John Tyson.[2] He also contacted elements of his old gang, including Jesse Evans, who was still in the vicinity, and became, according to ranger reports, not only the leader of the group, but its agent in Fort Davis.[3] This group, as headed by John Selman, was not large, numbering perhaps twenty men in all. Small in size, it was lethal in its operations.

Fort Davis and its neighbor Fort Stockton had suffered a series of outlaw raids for over a year now, with John Selman's older and larger group no doubt involved in some of them. With Fort Davis as their base, the thieves traveled all the way from their haunts on the Pecos to the Rio Grande, ranging over an area encompassing several hundred square miles. As was the case in Selman's old domain, his forces swept back and forth across this region at diffrent times during the year, harrying ranchers and merchants.

The two towns were wilderness sin spots, used to hard-eyed individuals passing through. However, the indications given by the rangers are that the outlaws did not live openly in either place, which accounts for Selman's ability to live and work in Davis without recognition or at least without being suspected of criminal activities. Heretofore, in order to gain information about events taking place in town, one of the gang would stroll in and combine a little business with pleasure— watch preparations for trail drives, observe merchants who seemed to be growing prosperous (always with the idea of ending that prosperity) and visit that oldest of amusement places, the sporting house.[4] John Selman's men visited the towns for pleasure as usual, but his own continued presence in Fort Davis gave the gang a better over-all idea of transactions taking place.

If John Selman was actually funneling information to the outlaws as the Rangers reported, he finally overstepped himself. On May 21, 1880, the Fort Davis citizens fired off a letter to Governor Roberts bemoaning the fact that "lawless men congregate around the cattle camps in New Mexico and from there come in large parties to depredate upon the peaceful and law abiding citizens of this state." The correspondence describes holdup methods and lists a twelve-month series of robberies, capping it with an account of the offenses committed within the last week.[5]

The letter mentions that aid had not been requested before "in the hope that these lawless men could be driven from the country without such assistance . . . longer delay is useless as these depredations are becoming of alarming frequency. The presence of a few Rangers would undoubtedly have a good effect."

Two weeks later, a company of Texas Rangers, under the command of Sergeant Caruthers, rode into Fort Davis. A squad of ten men under Sergeant Sieker went to Fort Stockton.[6] By this time the situation had deteriorated so much that many of the petitioners to Governor Roberts were afraid to step outside their doors and welcome the Rangers. Caruthers wrote his commanding officer: ". . . upon my arrival . . . all was quiet, but I find it to be the supressed calm of absolute fear, all the merchants here expect to be attacked daily." [7]

Caruthers made no mention at this time of peaceful citizen John Selman. But he had plenty to say about the Selman gang. Jesse Evans, Bud Graham (*alias* Ace Carr) and Charles Graham (*alias* Charlie Graves) had robbed Sender and Siebenborn's store in Fort Davis and escaped with "400 pieces of silver of the denomination and value of one dollar each and the current coin of the Republic of Mexico $200 and $200 United States greenbacks." [8] Selman's old companion, John Gross, using the *alias* of John Gunter, waited in town while the robbery was being committed. He was, most likely, a lookout for the bandits.[9]

A few days after picking up the money in Fort Davis, the gunmen, Evans, Ace Carr and Graves, planned to spend it in

Fort Stockton. The boys were soon whooping it up and on the verge of treeing the town when a fight broke out between them and the local residents. Ace Carr was captured, but the other two made it back to Horsehead Crossing on the Pecos, where they made plans to free their luckless comrade.[10]

The townspeople evidently blundered into taking Carr captive. Ranger Caruthers wrote Lieutenant Nevill on June 8, angrily complaining that in the fight only Carr had been caught, the citizens handling the affair in such an awkward manner that the other two had escaped. The gun battle seemed to have been a sham; the taking of Carr a prisoner, an accident. The people, frightened over their blunder, huddled in fear and waited for an assault on the town. Fortunately at this time Sergeant Sieker and his band of Rangers arrived and took charge of the criminal. This put the Rangers in a quandary: it took so many of them to guard Carr around the clock that they actually became prisoners of the prisoner, and enough men could not be spared to go out on patrol and look for the others.[11]

The circumstances were literally the same in Fort Davis. Already in fear of the outlaws, the citizens hoped desperately that Carr would not be transferred to their town. This made the problem difficult for Caruthers, and while he was not getting much cooperation from the townspeople about where to start looking for the desperados, he at least found some unnamed person who unearthed the role of John Selman in the current troubles. The Ranger wrote Major Jones on June 14: ". . . their agent here is Capt Tyson, his real name is John Selman, who I find is [indicted] in Shackelford County. I think from what I can learn that he is chief of the gang."

Caruthers then described some of his difficulties in coping with the changing situation. "They [the outlaws] have threatened the life of the Sheriff here and he is afraid to do his duty simply because he cannot get the proper support. The outlaws

116

are lying out in the mountains, in groups of five to seven, watching this point and Stockton. I think their main object now is the release of Carr. The Sheriff was afraid to bring Carr to this point . . . so I left him in Stockton in charge of Sergeant Sieker. In fact, if he were brought here, they could not hold him 48 hours without Rangers." [12]

It was then that matters took a turn which gave Caruthers a plan. The jailor at the Fort Davis jail, hearing that Carr would be brought there, resigned in a funk. When this happened, the sergeant, who had been reluctant to arrest Selman because "I know I could not hold him here," hit upon an idea of what to do with John, who was evidently getting suspicious of the Rangers interest in him. ". . . as he [Selman] was getting very scary I had him appointed Dept. Sheriff and jailor," Caruthers wrote.[13] Clearly the sergeant hoped this would calm Selman down and keep him in town without the need of actually imprisoning him.

While plotting to hold Selman by trickery, the sergeant at the same time was planning to apprehend the rest of his men. Caruthers wired Sieker at Fort Stockton to bring Ace Carr to Fort Davis and hold him there. Shortly afterward, Carr was brought in under heavy guard and lodged in jail. Then information was "leaked" to the outlaws that Caruthers would be away for a few days, thus affording them an opportunity to raid the jail and release Carr with the connivance of their leader and associate, Selman. The idea was to plant deputies in the buildings along the street and shotgun the raiders when they arrived.[14]

The plan was nearly ready for operation when Sheriff Wilson learned of it, got drunk and spread the story all over town. With his hand thus forced, Caruthers promptly went to the jail and arrested John Selman before he could escape. John now shared the same cell with Ace Carr, and this time he didn't have a key.[15] Snapping with fury, Caruthers wrote out a report to Jones: "I think he [Sheriff Wilson] is totally unfit for the office, the Hon. County Judge O. M. Keesey is no better, I had to arrest him for Asst. to murder . . . the justice of the peace, Frank Duke is under the thumb of the county judge . . . the citizens will not cooperate with us openly. . . ." [16]

His unexpected confinement must have been extra irritating to Selman for he had just got married—to none other than Niconora Zarate, the daughter of the Mexican tailor who had nursed him through the smallpox. The wedding took place in the offices of Justice of the Peace Francis Duke on June 26, 1880, just two days before John's arrest. [17]

With Selman and Carr firmly behind bars, Evans and Company decided that the hot breath of the Rangers was getting too close. So Jesse, John Gross and two others struck out for Presidio, trying to give the impression that they were fleeing to Mexico. In order to let the pursuers know where they were, Evans openly purchased a pair of boots in Presidio. [18] Then the gang turned north toward their hide-out in the Chinati Mountains, hoping they might have fooled any followers.

Their hopes were in vain. The Rangers learned of the outlaws' plans from a Negro, and Sieker, Caruthers, Ranger Privates Tom Carson, Dick Russel, Sam Henry and "Red" Bingham rode all night for seventy miles, surprising the gunmen around noon on July 13. [19]

After a running gun battle which covered a mile and a half, the desperados were finally cornered on a mountaintop where everyone dismounted and took cover behind rocks. One of the fugitive Graham boys zeroed in on Ranger Carson and shot his hat off. The next bullet knocked the Ranger's horse out from under him. Carson's luck held, however, and in another exchange of shots he managed to wound Graham in return; and Sieker, catching Graham when he raised up to look around, shot the outlaw through the head.

118

With one fugitive now dead, the Rangers stormed the barricade and the others quickly surrendered, throwing away their guns and begging for mercy. The reason for their pleas soon became apparent. Ranger Bingham was dead and the Evans gang knew it, although the Rangers had not yet missed him. In the frenzied hostilities no one had seen him fall and his loss was not even discovered until later when Caruthers, searching for his knife, stumbled across the body. Sieker raged when he found out Bingham was dead—"I should have killed them all." [20]

That evening a heavy rain began to fall. "It was a sad sight," Sieker wrote, "to see the two bodies covered with blankets, prisoners tied with ropes, lying by a brush fire." Bingham's body was buried just a little way down the mountain, a feat which took hours to accomplish as the ground was hard and rocky, their only tools being hands and knives. " . . . our little squad showed him all the respect we could. We formed and fired three volleys over his grave, and with saddened hearts we wound our way through the mountain passes to Davis." [21]

John Selman and Ace Carr never had an opportunity to watch as the last of the Selman gang was brought into town. In their dim, cramped quarters called the "bat cave" because it was constructed underground beneath the courthouse, the two prisoners learned of the capture of Jesse Evans only when the trapdoor above them was opened and the others dropped through. It was not long before John Gross began pleading for fresh air, crying that he was paralyzed in the leg and arm from the cramped and stuffy quarters. He was then lifted up, taken outside, laid down and closely watched. The Rangers figured he was bluffing when they saw him cross his "paralyzed" leg several times, but they really got indignant when a fiddler who was playing a waltz switched to a jig and Gross "went to patting his feet pretty lively." He was promptly jerked off the ground and dropped back into the bat cave where he got "well very fast." [22]

Trying not to let any opportunity for freedom slip by, Evans sent a note to Billy the Kid saying he "was in a damned tight place" and suggested the Kid raid the camp and get him out. The Kid and Evans had been bitter enemies during the Lincoln County conflict, so if Billy ever did receive this message he must have got a great deal of enjoyment out of reading it. At the moment he could scarcely care less about Jesse's woes; besides, he had plenty of troubles of his own.

Lieutenant Nevill of the Texas Rangers had arrived in Fort Davis on August 5, and it was he who intercepted Evans' note to Billy Bonney, or Billy Antrim, as the message referred to him. That Nevill knew little of the Kid or his reputation is evidenced when he wrote Jones, "I understand this man Antrim is a fugitive from somewhere and noted desperado." [23]

On October 15 Jesse Evans went on trial for the robbery of Sender and Seibenborn and the murder of Ranger Bingham.[24] John Gross, standing trial under his and Selman's old *alias* of John Gunter, was charged only with murder.[25] Evans received ten years on each count and Judge Blacker set the sentences to run concurrently. Gross was also convicted and sentenced (the file does not say for how many years), and journeyed with Evans to the penitentiary at Huntsville. His trail ends there. No more is known of his life. Jesse Evans escaped shortly after his confinement and vanished. His trail ends also the moment he drops over the wall.

The only one who did not go on trial at Fort Davis was John Selman. The Rangers seemed more interested in turning the old gunman over to the Shackelford County officials than indicting him at Fort Davis. The Ranger records were also vague as to the amount of evidence proving Selman to be associated with the outlaws. Apparently they were more interested in subjecting him to intensive questioning about the Fort Griffin troubles in 1878, although all we know here is that they obtained the names of the principal members of the Shackelford County "mob"—information which was probably not news to anyone except the Rangers at Fort Davis. Before Selman revealed this much, he asked for protection, claiming that if he were "turned over to the officers of that county, that he would be killed as his business partner John N. Larn had been in 1878." [26]

The odd thing about all this was that the Shackelford authorities expressed no desire for his presence. So the Rangers were in the awkward position of having on hand an indicted offendor that nobody wanted.

After several letters and telegrams were passed back and forth between Sheriff Cruger and the Rangers, Cruger bluntly wrote Major John B. Jones and told him he saw no reason whatever why Selman should be returned. The letter is quoted in full.

Day before yesterday I telegraphed you to the effect that I could not answer for John Selman's life if I brought him here, and also that the charges against him cannot be sustained in law. It is true that I could bring him here without his getting killed, but it would take a larger force than I have the means to defray their expenses with.

I have examined the indictments against Selman and find that a portion of the witnesses have left the country and the majority of those here are only to prove ownership of marks and brands.

I have talked to several witnesses and they say that the charges cannot be sustained. I have also talked to several of our leading citizens and they agree with me in saying that charges against Selman will not be sustained and will amount to nothing except to involve Shackelford

121

County in great expense, which she is ill able to bear; and that the indictments were probably found in order to keep him out of the country, as he is such a great thief and scoundrel and withal so sharp that he cannot be caught in his rascality.

What I have written and telegraphed you about Selman's being hung I wish you to keep secret as it might cause me trouble; but in regard to the other matters in this letter I beg to refer you to C. K. Stribling, J. B. Matthews, or any other good citizen of the county.

If the charges against Selman cannot be sustained & there is the strongest probabilities that his life will be lost, what good will it do to have him brought here?

Our county is free of mobs and there is nothing here to incite one to action, but I fear that the arrival of Selman will be a renewal of the times we have passed through, without the least show of doing any good, but on the contrary a good deal of harm.

I have written this letter, so you may have all the lights thrown on the subject, and that whatever you do in the premises, you may act accordingly.[27]

The puzzling part of this letter is the fourth paragraph where mention is made of references to "Selman's being hung." The telegram and letters Cruger refers to are missing from the Ranger files, but obviously Cruger is not referring to John Selman. The only other Selman he could have meant was Tom, and since his name is not mentioned in any of the Ranger reports, a conclusion can be drawn that he was not with his brother at Fort Davis, an unlikely situation unless something drastic had happened. He had not been known, up until this moment at least, to stray far from John's side.

The hint that Tom had been lynched is substantiated by

an item which appeared in the Galveston *News* on August 21, 1880. The story has a Comanche, Texas, August 20 dateline.

John Selman, who stands indicted in Shackelford County for theft of cattle and arrested recently in Fort Davis, was brought here yesterday by a squad of Rangers and lodged in jail. He will be held here until Court commences in Shackelford County. It is considered not safe to carry him to Shackelford without a guard, as Dorn Selman, brother to the defendant, was murdered by a mob after he was arrested and in jail.

The name "Dorn" is undoubtedly a printer's misreading of a scribbled-longhand "Tom," and it seems certain that Tom Cat came to an unhappy end, probably by strangulation. It may be noted that when Tom was placed in West Texas in 1879 by the testimony of McIntire, this is his last recorded appearance. Never again does his name crop up in the Selman chronicle.

Cruger's final appeal was to no avail. On the 6th of August, 1880, Sergeant Sieker and his detachment put John Selman in heavy irons and delivered him to Comanche County to await transfer to Shackelford.[28]

Shortly afterward, court was set in Albany and Selman was transferred there, but not to stay. His guards—Bill Jeffries, Bill Hawsley, and George Shields (or Shailes)—took him behind a store, gave him a flea-bitten horse belonging to John Sauers, shook hands with him and told him to ride. As Selman dug his spurs in deep, the guard pulled their guns and commenced firing in the air. Jeffries later admitted that they were only pretending to try to stop him. Sauers, who donated his horse to the escapee, received another mount from his employer, George Reynolds.[29]

123

John Selman was allowed to escape because of a desire for self-protection on the part of Shackelford County officials and citizens. The county had everything to lose and nothing to gain by sending the gunfighter to jail. Records indicate that he would not have been convicted anyway because of a paucity of evidence and witnesses.[30] And if Selman had decided to speak out bluntly from the witness stand, his testimony might have been embarrassing to many people. His escape created no uproar throughout the county, nor is there any evidence that wanted circulars were mailed out. That part of the country just seemed glad and relieved to be rid of him.

No one knows which way John rode when he shook the dust of Shackelford County from his feet for the last time. A good guess is that he met his wife Niconora somewhere around Fort Davis and from there journeyed to San Pablo in southern Chihuahua, Mexico, where Selman opened a saloon. Next he sent for his children.

For the story of what happened to the Selman children it is necessary to go back a year and a half to April 22, 1879. On that date, somewhere in Presidio County (probably at Fort Davis, which was then a part of Presidio County), John Selman signed a power of attorney enabling John C. McGrew, his brother-in-law, to sell the Selman ranch and conduct other business. On the 22nd day of the following month John McGrew, attorney-in-fact for John Selman, received five dollars and a promissory note for $800 from J. A. Matthews for the Selman holdings. The money was supposed to be paid to Mrs. Selman, but according to the deed records she was already deceased. They do not indicate details of her death. McGrew made application to be the guardian of the minor Selman children.[31]

On September 15, 1879, guardianship of the person and estate of Henry Selman, William "Billy" Selman, Margaretta Selman and John Marion Selman, minors, was granted to Mc-

Grew and the property was then sold for the eight hundred dollars, which was to go for the support and education of the children. J. A. Matthews paid the money.[32]

That the money actually benefited the children is questionable. John Marion later described some of the alleged ill treatment he and the others received from McGrew, remarking that the children were farmed out to neighbors and forced to do hard labor almost from the time they were old enough to walk.[33]

Although John Selman later sent for all four of his children, only William and John Marion were allowed to go since they were too young to be of much assistance around the Mc-Grew Ranch. Margaretta was told that her father did not want her, causing the girl to be quite bitter about his memory in later years. However, the real reason she was required to stay behind seems to have been that Mrs. McGrew did not want the girl growing up in a strange land and marrying someone not of her race.[34] Margaretta and Henry never saw their father again.

William and John said a tearful farewell to their brother and sister and left by train for El Paso. Then, crossing the border, they took another train south for 285 miles to San Pablo. The journey must have been made in 1881, as John Marion wrote that he was baptized in the village Catholic Church in 1882, several months after his arrival. Earlier, his father, due to his wife's influence, had accepted the Catholic faith and, reportedly, repeated his wedding vows in a church ceremony.[35]

The boys' new mother was a schoolteacher, a devout Catholic and, from all accounts, a very charming and gracious lady. Under her tutelage, the youngsters obtained a good education although much of John Marion's higher learning was gained outside of class. He says that within a few months he spoke fluent Spanish as well as any native and "could outcuss any kid on the block."

Soon after the children's arrival in San Pablo, Ike Blum

and John Breen, two of John Selman's friends who had been living in El Paso, came to Mexico and together the three men formed a partnership and opened a gambling house and saloon at the site of every big fiesta in the republic. The festivities usually lasted only a week. When the last couple quit dancing, the Yankee enterprise would shut its doors and wait for the guitars to twang in another town. The partners were very successful at their trade; however, the younger Selman once related that a "circus woman" bucked his father in a monte game and won 4000 pesos in silver.[36]

After a year or two had passed, John Selman decided to drop out of the saloon and gambling business and spend more time with his family. An outbreak of smallpox had struck the village of San Pablo and both his boys were seriously ill. While the youngsters did manage to survive, William, like his father, was left with a badly pitted face. Even with that, the Selman family escaped almost unscathed compared to tragedies occuring all around them. All day long for weeks a stream of funeral processions passed by their house, and the deceased was usually a child being carried to the cemetery in a small casket resting on top of the father's head.

As the disease ran its course, John turned his attention to a rich silver claim some forty miles from San Pablo. His mining methods were primitive, but he still managed, with the help of several employees, to extract considerable ore from the shaft before the bottom fell out of silver prices.[37]

As the mining business had now failed, Selman turned again to a saloon venture, opening another bar in San Pablo. This venture did not last long, however; he came down with the yellow jaundice, becoming so ill that a physician was brought from Chihuahua City to tend him. After several weeks he wasn't getting any better, but the thought of seeking medical treatment elsewhere had not occurred to him until he discovered that his medicine was only common baking soda. Angered, John sold his saloon to the first buyer and loaded his family on a train. They did not stop until reaching Paso Del Norte,[38] probably in 1883 or 1884. There John commuted back and forth across the Rio Grande, getting medical treatment in El Paso[39] and slowly regaining his health.

When Selman was again able to travel, they journeyed to Fort Bayard, New Mexico, where they spent a winter. In the spring he sent his wife and son John Marion back to San Pablo and he and William began a prospecting trip around Kelly. Here John met a friend from Texas and so William was left working in a hotel in Magdalena while his father and the friend prospected and hunted in the Mogollon Mountains. When they returned three or four months later, John was absolutely broke but in good health. He borrowed twenty-five dollars from his son's hotel earnings, entered a poker game and twenty-four hours later owned $800 in cash, a saloon and its fixtures.[40]

Selman opened the saloon under new management, but mining still claimed his interests and what money he made in one enterprise, he lost in another.

One day on the streets he chanced to meet an old enemy from Fort Griffin. Gotch was the man's name—a carpetbagger, according to John, one whose hand had been turned against Selman since the early 1870s. They exchanged a few strong words, and in a fast exchange of gunfire it was John who proved to be the quicker. As Gotch rolled in the street, Selman grabbed his son, sold his saloon for cash in one of the fastest transactions on record, and with the boy headed for San Pablo. It was not until years later that Selman learned much to his disgust that Gotch did not die—he had only been shot in the arm.[41] Back in Mexico, John successfully sold farm equipment for the John Deere Company.

In May of 1885, a sensational murder took place near Sierra Blanca, Texas. Ranchman Tom Merill—whom Selman long before had the dispute with over the cards in Reynolds City and who, according to Phin W. Reynolds, may have been one of the men who helped kill John Larn[42]—and his wife were brutally stabbed and hacked to death with a knife and ax. Tom was disemboweled with a slashing blade and his wife, coming to her husband's assistance, was savagely and literally chopped into pieces. The murderer or murderers were never caught. One theory regarding the crime was that the killers were smugglers from Mexico who had been caught stealing and had slaughtered the couple to cover up their act. Skelton Glenn, however, says flatly that John Selman hired two Mexicans to murder the ranch owner and his wife, out of a desire for vengeance.[43] Glenn offers absolutely no evidence to back up his allegation, and the buffalo hunter, who admittedly was no friend of John Selman, may have been trying to even some old score with Selman by accusing him of a crime that a great many people may have had reason to commit.

In the meantime John's wife had apparently died. At least, after Selman's return to San Pablo from Magdalena, no further mention is made of Niconora, the memoirs becoming resoundingly silent concerning her. This is particularly puzzling in view of John Marion Selman's loquacious writing in which nothing, no matter how remotely related to his father, seems to have escaped his eye. Perhaps Niconora succumbed to one of the ailments which had plagued her husband and her children.

In April of 1888, the 34th District Court in Albany, Texas, dismissed the cattle-rustling charges against John Selman for lack of evidence.[44] Hearing the news, he and his two boys moved to El Paso.

John Larn, Shackelford County sheriff and gunman-rustler, in photograph taken shortly before he was locked in his own jail and shot to death.

John Selman at Fort Griffin, Texas, about 1875. *Courtesy Edna Selman Haines*

Home of John Larn, rancher, father, husband, sheriff, rustler, manslayer, in Shackelford County, Texas.

Newton J. Jones, in retirement. Jones was a Texas Ranger at the time of the Shackelford County troubles. *Courtesy Texas State Archives*

Sitting, left to right: Bob Speakes and John Jones; *standing, left to right:* Jim Jones and Billy the Kid. Speakes and the two Jones boys were reputed to be members of Selman's Scouts. Bob Speakes was supposedly killed by John Selman during one of the Scouts' disputes. Billy the Kid was identified by Bill and Sam Jones, brother of the Jones boys shown here. Reprinted, by permission of the authors, from C. L. Sonnichsen and William V. Morrison, *Alias Billy the Kid* (New Mexico, 1955).

Above, left: John W. Poe a few years after the Shackelford County troubles when, as a guard, he allowed vigilantes to subdue him and kill his prisoner, John Larn. *Courtesy James Shinkle*

Above, right: Governor Lew Wallace during the time he rid New Mexico of Selman's Scouts and other outlaws (about 1870). *Courtesy William Henry Smith Memorial Library, Philadelphia*

A. M. Gildea, as he appeared with Selman's Scouts, in New Mexico, 1878. *Western History Collections, University of Oklahoma Library*

A. M. Gildea, as he appeared
with Sellman's Scouts, in
New Mexico, in 1878.

Bass Outlaw, the little gunman and Texas Ranger, slain by John Selman during a shootout at Tillie Howard's brothel in El Paso, Texas, 1894. *Western History Collections, University of Oklahoma Library*

John Selman in Fort Davis, Texas, shortly before his arrest by Texas Rangers. *Courtesy Robert N. Mullin*

Tillie Howard, El Paso's most famous madam. She blew the whistle for good on Bass Outlaw. *Courtesy Colonel Walter Stevenson*

Joseph G. Hardin, father of John Wesley, in Civil War uniform. *Courtesy Joe Hardin Clements*

John Wesley Hardin as a young cowboy in Abilene, Kansas, 1871. *Courtesy Bob McNellis*

Joe G. Hardin, the lawyer-brother of John Wesley Hardin, who was hanged by a mob in 1874. *Courtesy Joe Hardin Clements*

John Jr. and Molly Hardin, children of John Wesley Hardin. *Courtesy Joe Hardin Clements*

Martin Morose and Tom Finnessey in Juarez, Mexico, shortly before Morose's death. *Courtesy Robert N. Mullin*

El Paso Chief of Police Jeff Milton and United States Deputy Marshal
George Scarborough in El Paso about 1895. *Courtesy J. Evetts Haley*

Helen Beulah Morose and child, probably the son
of Martin Morose, in a photograph taken in Juarez,
Mexico, 1895. *Courtesy Joe Hardin Clements*

Romula Granadine in her wedding gown on August 23, 1893, when she married John Selman in El Paso. She was sixteen; he was fifty-seven. It was not a happy marriage. *Courtesy Rosabelle W. Moore*

"Uncle John" Selman about the time he killed John Wesley Hardin. Selman used the cane because of a leg wound he received during a gunfight with Bass Outlaw. *Courtesy Robert N. Mullin*

Bud Selman in a photograph taken during the 1890s, probably in El Paso. *Courtesy Bob McNellis*

John Selman, Jr., El Paso police officer in the 1890s when he arrested Hardin's mistress, Beulah Morose, and caused her to be fined fifty dollars. *Courtesy Edna Selman Haines*

John Selman and son (John Jr. or Bud) in a photograph taken in El Paso during the 1880s and found in the scrapbook of Big Alice Abbot, the madam of the most notorious brothel in El Paso. Selman was the only male to appear in Big Alice's scrapbook. In the original photograph a large X is scratched across Selman's genitals.)

Funeral card commemorating Jane Bowen Hardin (Mrs. John Wesley Hardin). *Courtesy Bob McNellis*

Callie Lewis, John Wesley Hardin's teen-aged second wife, in a photograph allegedly taken on their marriage day in Junction, Texas, 1895.

John Wesley Hardin, Jr. during the
time he came to El Paso for the
settlement of his father's estate.
*Courtesy Southwest Texas State
University*

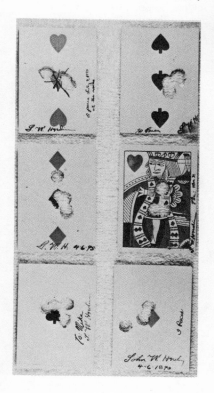

John Wesley regularly practiced
shooting holes in playing cards,
signing them, and giving them to
his admirers. These were shot in
El Paso's Washington Park on July
4, 1895, for the benefit of a crowd
from the Wigwam Saloon. *Courtesy
Joe Hardin Clements*

The Gem Saloon on South El Paso
Street, scene of two holdups by
John Wesley Hardin. In the
foreground, obscured by the
telephone pole, was the second-
story office of John Wesley Hardin.
Courtesy Bob McNellis

The first-floor bar of the Gem Saloon in El Paso. Hardin robbed the upstairs
gambling den. *Courtesy Bob McNellis*

John Wesley Hardin
*Western History
Collections, University of
Oklahoma Library*

An early magazine artist's rendition of gambling in El Paso. Drawing by W. A. Rogers, magazine unknown. *Courtesy Bob McNellis*

Top: the Smith & Wesson .44 caliber revolver, #352, that John Wesley Hardin was carrying in his waistband when he was killed; *bottom:* the Colt .45, #141805, used by John Selman to kill John Wesley Hardin. *Courtesy Jim Earle*

Top: John Selman's Colt .45, #36693, taken from Selman by Cole Belmont as Selman lay in an El Paso alley after being shot by George Scarborough; *bottom:* the Colt .45, #141805, used by John Selman to kill John Wesley Hardin. *Courtesy Jim Earle and John Bianchi*

The Colt .45 #154940, carried by El Paso Sheriff Frank Simmons when he arrested John Wesley Hardin for the robbery of the Gem Saloon. Also shown are Simmons's badge and Hardin's arrest warrant. *Courtesy Bob McNellis*

The Colt .38, #84304, dime, and Elgin watch, #4069110, presented to John Wesley Hardin by James B. Miller in El Paso in April, 1895, for assisting Miller in the prosecution of Bud Frazer. *Courtesy Bob McNellis*

This Colt .41, #73728, was used by John Wesley Hardin to rob the Gem Saloon in El Paso on May 1, 1895. Note Hardin's professional card. *Courtesy Richard Marohn*

The Colt .45, #130272, used by United States Deputy Marshal George Scarborough to kill John Selman. The gun was given to Frank McMahon, Scarborough's brother-in-law, who sold it to Joe Kopf, the owner of the Gem Saloon, in 1908. *Courtesy Herbert Kopf Collection*

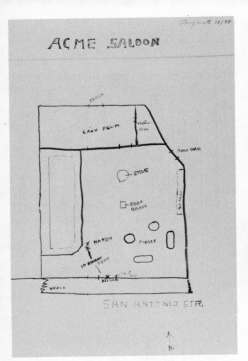

Albert B. Fall, defender of John Selman for the slaying of John Wesley Hardin. Fall is wearing a Spanish-American War uniform in this photograph taken about four years after the Selman trial. *Courtesy Mrs. C. C. Chase*

Left: The sketch by Sheriff Frank Simmons on the night of Hardin's death showing the positions of Selman and Hardin at the Acme Saloon. *Courtesy Bob McNellis*

An artist's conception of the shooting of John Wesley Hardin in the Acme Saloon. *Courtesy Jim Earle*

San Antonio Street in El Paso (looking east) at about the time Hardin was killed. On the right, behind the carriages, is the Wigwam Saloon where John Selman was slain. Across the street, and perhaps a half-block farther east, is the Acme Saloon. *Courtesy Bob McNellis*

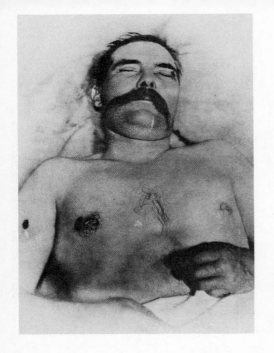

John Wesley Hardin after his death on August 19, 1895. Both shots are entry wounds. *Western History Collections, University of Oklahoma Library*

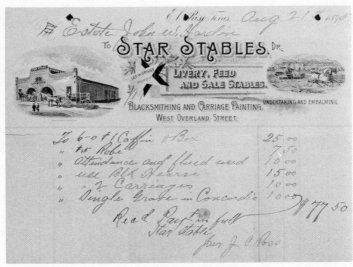

Funeral statement for the estate of John Wesley Hardin. *Courtesy Bob McNellis*

13

EL PASO

EL PASO in the 1880s and 1890s was the kind of community that would attract a hard case character like John Selman. It was still a frontier settlement, isolated from civilization and free from most of the restraining influences which were beginning to shackle other towns throughout the Southwest. Although it lacked the buffalo hunters and the trail-driving cowboys who had given Fort Griffin such splash and color, it was still a wide-open, gun-toting, hell-raising, sin-soaked town sprawled at the gates of Mexico. The little adobe crossroads had shown few signs of progress since that day in 1827 when José Mariá Ponce de Leon took up land across the *Rio Bravo* in what is now the center of El Paso. Then in 1881 the first railroad engine chugged into the sleepy little village of 500 persons and the community awoke with a jolt. By 1890 there were nearly 10,000 residents.[1]

The town grew up below a narrow pass, the Pass of the North, through which flowed the wide and turbulent, yet sometimes gentle, Rio Grande. And right across the river was the tumultuous and untamed region known as Mexico. Six-gun law frequently appealed to either side. El Paso's best known marshal, Dallas Stoudenmire, had set a precedent for copious bloodletting. Receiving his appointment in 1881, he racked up a total of four dead men in almost as many months before he himself met death, via a bullet from behind.

It was an Anglo town, although Mexicans accounted for seventy-five percent of its population. The Americans accounted for the city's growth. It was they who were able to attract business, industry and railroads. It was they who created a municipal government. It was they who had the power and influence in the faraway state capital at Austin. It was they who rode roughshod over their neighbors and each other, and were primarily responsible for the town's bloody past and its even bloodier future. If they built the churches and other respectable civic enterprises, they also built the unrestricted gambling casinos and saloons and the accompanying whorehouses.

To a stranger the town must have appeared squat and ugly, its dirty brown adobe buildings baking under a simmering sun. Rain was rare, yet it was a land of contrast. A shower in the Franklin Mountains would send a wall of water rolling down the gullies and canyons, inundating the town, ripping ragged holes in the streets. Then as quickly as it came, the flood would disappear, leaving only sand from the desert and rocks from the mountains in its wake. A few hours later nature might revisit the town in the form of a howling dust storm during which the looser sections of New Mexico and Arizona passed in review.

Although John Selman may have been somewhat of a stranger to the town, he was not necessarily a stranger to its residents. He had survived by the gun for too long to be considered just another gunman striding through the dusty streets. Many of those who did not know him personally were familiar with his reputation. John was getting along in years now, old for a gunfighter, and no matter how inconspicuous he tried to be, the mere fact that he was still around was enough to cause whispers and stares wherever he went. Many of the hardcases he brushed against were, like himself, drawn to El Paso—attracted by something they may not have understood themselves.

In such a place Selman's notability overawed very few. The city was always full of rough, hard, quick-shooting men who were working for and running from the law. Any distinction between the two, judging by the way they killed and their utter callousness, was usually impossible to make.

Oddly enough, although John Selman later became one of the more familiar sights around El Paso, almost no reliable description of him has filtered down. One man, thirty-eight years after Selman's death, wrote: "I saw John Selman frequently, but knew very little about him. I doubt if anyone else knew much more. He was rather a large man, big-boned, rough-hewn and shaggy. He moved slowly, did not talk much, and drank plenty of whisky. Fearless, he was deadly with a pistol." [2]

An almost completely opposite view was set down sixty years after Old John's death: "John Selman looked as little like a killer as is possible to imagine. He habitually wore a boiled shirt, a well tailored suit, and highly polished shoes. He was soft spoken and polite to one and all. This led some to believe they were dealing with a meek, harmless, little old man. That one was about as harmless as a gila monster." [3]

Selman's son wrote that his father was appointed city marshal in 1885, immediately after the resignation of Marshal James Gillett. [4] The son's statement has misled many people, and some writers have commented at length on Selman's alleged activities in this respect. [5]

El Paso police records go back only to 1912, but the

records of the city council are in existence and the names of all the city marshals are filed there. John Selman's name is not among them and there are no blank spots which would indicate that a name has been omitted. The local newspapers, the El Paso *Times* and the El Paso *Herald,* likewise make no mention of Selman during the time he is supposed to have been a marshal.

What probably occurred was that Selman applied for the position and was turned down. Sometimes the turnover in that office was rapid because of death,[6] corruption,[7] or a change in city government. The office was, in effect, a part of the political spoils system.

The rumor persists among old-timers that during one of these fast change-overs John Selman offered his name for consideration. The members of the city council, not quite sure that they wanted a man of Selman's notoriety, engaged in a heated argument over the appointment, finally deciding against it. While there is no record in the council minutes of any incident such as this, newspaper articles do indicate that often a great deal more went on within the council chambers than was officially noted.

It would appear that when Selman first came to El Paso to live, he tried to be inconspicuous and blend into the community. The records of the American Smelting and Refining Company show that on June 3, 1888, he was working as a weigher and pot puller, hardly the trade that one would expect a feared and noted gunfighter to engage in. At any rate, even though he was soon promoted to dump boss at $3.25 per day, John must have felt the price of anonymity was too great, and he quit a year later, on June 5, 1889.[8]

William "Bud" Selman worked for A. S. & R., also as a weigher, and John Marion (now calling himself John Selman, Jr.) was an office boy. Both of them started and quit within a month or so of their father.

132

In September of 1891 a party of men including E. C. Roberts of El Paso, who may or may not have been the leader, stopped at Hueco Tanks,[9] dragged John Gilan, commonly called "French John," out of his bed, and for some unknown reason beat him unmercifully. The old fellow was a recluse who lived in a cave. The gang sauntered off after the beating, but a few weeks later a ruffian named Rhodes went back to the cave to give French John a second installment. Gilan met him with a rifle and warned him not to dismount. Rhodes laughed and jumped off his horse anyway. A rifle ball hit him in the arm and another knocked his legs out from under him. The wounded man now struggled back on his horse as fast as possible and hurried to town where he swore out a warrant for Gilan's arrest.[10]

On October 22, Gilan was fished out of the Rio Grande just a short distance from El Paso. Marks on the body indicated that he had been knocked senseless by several blows on the head and his throat had been cut. One ear was missing. A feeling among investigating officers was that the assassins had taken the ear to show their employer that the gruesome task had been accomplished.[11]

This brutal act shocked even the hardest of citizens and strenuous efforts were made to bring the murderers to justice. Although Roberts and Rhodes were arrested, however, they were never convicted.

Around six o'clock on the evening of November 3, 1891, John Selman was in the Mint Saloon rolling dice for drinks with some friends. A few hours later, after he had absorbed all the liquor he could hold, he and Frank Clark stepped outside and began discussing the mystery surrounding the Gilan murder. Two men in gray suits walked by them several times and seemed interested in the conversation, but for some reason Selman and Clark paid no attention.

At last Selman started for his home, which was on Santa

Fe Street in the lower end of El Paso. On the way he noticed the same two men following him but concluded that they were railroad workers. Then as he approached Second Street, a terrific blow smashed him under the right eye and across the nose. Knocked unconscious, he fell toward the sidewalk as a knife flashed toward his throat. The blade went between his lips, slashed across the right side of his jaw bone, and buried itself in the back of his mouth. Blood gushed forth so rapidly that the murderers, thinking they had slashed the jugular vein, pushed the victim from the sidewalk to a vacant lot, some three feet below. No attempt was made to rob him.[12]

A passerby reported to Officer Kline that he had found a dead man. Together they returned and picked up John Selman, dazed and unable to say what had happened. The two men took him home.

For some mysterious reason the incident was kept very quiet. An El Paso *Times* reporter learned of it two days later, but the article he wrote raised more questions than it answered. He quoted Selman as saying he was struck from behind; yet the approach had obviously been from the front, since that was where the blows and knife wound came from. An impression is left that Selman knew his assailants, but for reasons of his own did not care to name them.

Old John did make some astonishing statements to the press, but unfortunately he did not fill in the details. "I had received numerous warnings that my days were numbered, but did not dream the scoundrels would attack me in the city," Selman is quoted as saying. "I believe my assailants knew all about the killing of Gilan and I want to say right here that I would not be surprised at any time to hear that J. C. Jones and Dick Blacker have all been murdered. We have all been threatened." [13]

Selman went on to say that the men who had attacked him were horse thieves. Jones and Blacker, when contacted, agreed that the two men who had assaulted Selman and killed Gilan were all members of the same rustling gang.[14]

The only explanation for these charges (and this one leaves much to be desired), comes from the memoirs of John Selman, Jr. He notes that a band of horses had been stolen in old Mexico and a party of *vaqueros* had engaged Old John to aid in the search for the bandits. With a group of cowboy friends whom he managed to round up on short notice John struck the trail at Hueco Tanks and finally overhauled the rustlers on the banks of the Pecos River. In a pitched battle four of the thieves were killed and three or four captured. All of the horses were recovered and turned over to the Mexican authorities in El Paso. The prisoners were locked up, but since the offense had been committed on Mexican territory, they were released. It was shortly after this that the stabbing occured and the younger Selman blamed it on members of the outlaw band.[15]

For almost a year after the attempted murder John Selman is not heard from. Frank Collinson describes him at this time as working for the Mexican Central Railroad and later as a bouncer in the Wigwam Saloon.[16] E. L. Shackelford, a broker, testified that Selman worked for him at one time, but no date has ever been established.[17] His son says that when he had recovered from his wounds and felt strong enough to ride, he and his two boys accepted a commission to drive a large herd of cattle from Abilene, Texas, to the Sacramento Mountains in southern New Mexico. It was about the first month or so in 1892 when the herd got under way and a few weeks later, upon the completion of the drive, John undertook another contract to drive 10,000 cattle from a spot somewhere near El Paso to the foothills of the Sacramentos. He and Bob Gooley represented the firm of Moore and W. A. Irvin, the latter being an El Paso druggist. While little is known of Moore, Irvin was an agent for the power faction trying to unseat Albert Bacon

Fall and Oliver Lee,[18] two men who completely dominated the political and cattle interests in the Tularosa Basin of New Mexico.

The memoirs suggest that John Selman broke away from his employers and he and his cowboys went to work for Fall and Lee. How this was done is not explained; the scene merely shifts from one working aspect of his career to another as Fall, whose rise to fame and subsequent disgrace were yet far in the future, made occasional visits to the range. Most of the horses for Selman and his men were purchased from Lee, the Alamogordo and Dog Canyon ranch owner. He was later indicted by Albert J. Fountain for branding cattle not his own, the evidence showing that this operation went on for several years,[19] some episodes occurring in the same area where we have placed John Selman and his cowboys. No mention, however, has been found of Selman's direct involvement.

As the nights grew cold, tempers grew short. John showed that he was ready for action once again when he became so angry he nearly killed a man. A puncher from one of the adjoining outfits asked for breakfast one morning and when he bit into a loaf of sourdough he found it raw in the middle. Wiping batter from his chin, he began swearing and applied some unkind epithets to Old John. Selman drew his gun and rammed it twice with hard, jolting punches into the fellow's ribs and snarled, "Eat every damn crumb of it or I'll blow a hole in you."

Young John laughingly concludes that "the loud mouthed gentleman lapped up every crumb . . . and from the way he licked his chops, I guess he thought it was pretty good." [20]

Selman returned from New Mexico just in time to make the election race for Constable of Precinct 1 in El Paso.

The election of November 8, 1892, was the quietest one

136

ever held in the city up until that time. Anticipating trouble, the town fathers had banned the sale of whisky until the polls were closed, and as a result the proceedings were so dull that the newspapers found little to write about. A big item of the day concerned a voter in the first ward who could not remember his name. He was finally sent out to look for a responsible party who could identify him.[21]

John Selman had many friends in El Paso and one of the best was Jim Burns, a shrewd Scot who owned the Red Light Saloon. John Selman, Jr., tells a tongue-in-cheek story about the way in which he and Burns corralled some votes for his father. It seems Burns threw a big dance on the evening before the election, bringing several girls over from Juarez, Mexico, to do the entertaining. Selman's boy was guarding the door and Burns instructed him to admit every male over twenty-one, but not to let anyone leave before he was properly instructed on how to vote in the next day's election. He then handed the boy a big stick.

"What's this for?" John asked.

Jim said, "If any of them try to leave, hit him over the head and make a damn good Democrat out of him."

Burns also left a bundle of sample ballots, those of the Democratic party having the image of a rooster at the top. When the Mexicans left the dance, the boy collared each man individually, showed him the ballot and impressed upon his mind the rooster, also making the intoxicated man repeat, *"el gallo, el gallo"* (the rooster, the rooster).

When the polls opened the next morning, hacks began picking up Mexicans to take to the polling places. Naturally they all voted the right way.[22]

All the citizens, of course, took their politics seriously. As the voting places closed, the saloons began to show brisk signs of life. The Wigwam, the Bacchus, the Gem and the Café were jammed with pushing, smoking, drinking, swearing crowds of men waiting to hear the results. The next day the *Times* happily headlined the story:

DEMOCRATIC PARTY MAKES
CLEAN SWEEP. THE COUNTRY IS SAFE.[23]

John Selman, who ran as a Democrat against C. E. Jones, was not expected to get more than a few token votes. The El Paso *Herald*, which supported Jones in the race, claimed two weeks before the election that he (Jones) was a "walk over who does not have to work much." They went on to insist that "Jones has for an opponent a first class man but he got out too late to make a winning race." [24] Nevertheless, Old John had managed to buttonhole a lot of voters. When the tabulation for Constable was complete, he had an eighty-eight-vote majority out of 1486 ballots cast.[25] On November 15 he made bond for $1500 and started his new job.[26]

14

THE DEATH OF BASS OUTLAW

THE EL PASO jail was not built especially to please its inmates.[1] Jim Thompson, a gunman well known around town, had spent what he felt was more than his share of time on the inside of one of the cages, and when a Selman deputy arrested him again on the basis of an old *capias* his rage boiled over. He was even more indignant when it was discovered, after he had already spent twenty-four hours in jail, that his time had previously been served for this offense and everything was all a mistake. When the door opened, Jim Thompson stormed out, blaming John Selman for his false imprisonment and snarling threats. Grabbing his gun, he went out to look for the Constable.

He ran first to the Red Light Saloon, where Selman could ordinarily be found, but on this particular morning John was not there. Thompson shoved his pistol under bartender Matt Lyter's nose and snapped that he would kill him first and dispose of Selman later. Lyter, badly frightened, slapped the gun aside, took two or three long leaps, burst through the door and

139

ran for his life. He found Selman somewhere down the street and gasped out an account of what had taken place.

John hitched up his trousers and started to look for Thompson. They worked different ends of the street, each man elbowing his way through the saloons, saying nothing, gazing coldly about, then strolling out and entering the next place of business. They almost collided head-on at the door of the Café Saloon as Thompson was coming out. John was the first to go into action. He pulled his gun and rammed it savagely into his adversary's stomach, while telling him he was under arrest. Thompson gasped, backed into the Café and drew his own pistol. For some inexplicable reason neither man fired. They stood glowering at each other, weapons drawn, each seemingly waiting for the other to back down or start shooting. Selman finally outstared his man. Thompson's nerve cracked and he pitched his six-shooter behind the counter. Meekly he was led off to jail, although on the way he got over his fright, recovered his bravado and began threatening Selman again.[2]

Why Selman did not not kill Thompson will have to be attributed to a quirk of character. This omission was certainly out of line with John's past conduct. Even the newspapers were surprised at the way he handled the affair and lavished all sorts of praise on the Constable, complimenting him on his patience and skill. Obviously it was Selman's instinct which told him that the gunman was a bully and a braggart who lacked sufficient nerve to risk a shootout. Although his judgment proved correct, it was a dangerous gamble—the kind of bet he almost never made when the stake was his life.[3]

Although none of the El Paso saloons suffered from any lack of notoriety, John's favorite hangout, the Red Light, enjoyed as nefarious a reputation as any in the Southwest. In addition to dancing and hard whisky, Jim Burns furnished girls and a dozen or so small cribs where his customers could enjoy all the delights available.[4]

140

Such activities finally aroused the wrath of the El Paso *Times,* which fired some scathing editorials at the Red Light and undertook a campaign to close its doors. As a friend of Jim Burns, John Selman was dragged in and took a thrashing, as did nearly every city official in El Paso.

The trouble really came to a head when seven of Burns' female attractions at the Red Light were arrested and lodged in jail by Officer Johnson, whose business was to collect fines from lewd and vagrant women. Burns became so indignant about these arrests that he threatened to have the officer removed from his position. Carried away by a sense of his own importance, he boasted that he controlled the police department, the city council and one of the newspapers. Had he quietly paid the fines instead of becoming loquacious, his troubles might have ended there. Now, however, the *Times* had a red-hot issue, and interest among El Paso residents began to rise. Everyone was wondering just where Burns was getting all his power.[5]

The *Times* was then in need of a flaming issue. Burns was about to go on trial for attempted murder and the *Times* was demanding a conviction. The jurors would hear about Burns' boasts and act accordingly. Few of them were beyond the reach of the newspapers' editorials in those days.

The trouble had started when a group of hilarious soldiers in the Red Light insisted that a mulatto cavalryman be allowed to dance. Burns objected to this: the house would furnish the needed entertainment. The troopers grew insistent, but Burns was firm. He finally ran everyone out of the building, closed the doors and turned out the lights.

Gradually the noise outside subsided as the soldiers disappeared up the street. Then Burns unlatched his doors again, turned on the lights and reopened for business.

A few minutes later John Selman, accompanied by a group of cattlemen, walked into the saloon. The cowboys de-

141

posited their six-shooters with the bartender and soon all were enjoying themselves. Presently the white soldiers came back and it was not long before a feud began shaping up between the two crowds of men.

As tension quickly mounted in the saloon, five Negro soldiers drove up in an army ambulance and came in with their rifles. The Negroes were not looking for trouble, but their white comrades were, and the weapons gave them an idea. They took the rifles, began a manual-of-arms drill on the Red Light floor, and several times managed purposely to run into the cowboys, whom they were trying to antagonize. Tempers flared and the cattlemen demanded their guns back so they could fight.

Selman at this point stepped into the altercation and told the white soldiers to settle down or he would arrest them. The cavalrymen then turned away from the cowboys and began to abuse Burns for letting Selman take charge. They spoke very unflatteringly of his lineage, referring to him as a "gray headed son-of-a-bitch," and saying they would get paid later and settle accounts with him then. In the meantime Burns could wait for his money.[6]

Burns, now working himself up into a rage, said he was going to close again. He turned off the lights while everyone was still in the building, squatted down behind the bar and fired a shot into the ceiling. Pandemonium resulted. His patrons stampeded toward the door, trampling each other in their rush to get to the street. Burns helped them all through the doorway by firing a few shots just a foot or two over their heads. Now in a frenzy over all the excitement he was causing, he dashed to the splintered door and blasted a couple more rounds at the fleeing figures. One of the bullets smashed the shoulder of a Mexican youth who had been in the building but was not involved in the dispute.[7]

Jim Burns was jailed on a charge of attempted murder,

but when he was brought before the jury the offense was described as aggravated assault.

The trial was given considerable space in the April 27 and 28, 1893, edition of the El Paso *Times,* but the newspaper account differs greatly from the court records. The latter are unusually full since this is one of the few cases where the testimony of witnesses is preserved.

The defense was a comedy. Burns introduced Constable John Selman and Deputy W. H. Wheat in a blundering and obvious attempt to influence or intimidate the jury. Burns himself waved his arms and flew into wild ravings during the trial, interrupting witnesses and screaming, "Lies, lies!" at each bit of damaging testimony. After being repeatedly called down by the judge, he was finally threatened with expulsion from the courtroom.

The conduct of his defense attorney, Charlie Patterson, was on a par with that of his client. He closed with the statement that "all citizens and taxpayers derive a certain amount of benefit from the Red Light in the way of licenses, taxes, etc." Then he appealed to the jury not to convict Burns because of "general principles."

The Red Light proprietor was found guilty, however, and fined $25 and costs. The *Times,* elated at the conviction, screamed in black headlines: THE HIGH AND MIGHTY JIM BURNS CONVICTED. A sub-headline read: HIS PULL LIMITED TO A FEW POLICE OFFICIALS AND DOES NOT REACH OVER JURORS.[8] The editor did not comment on the relatively light sentence.

The newspaper, now sensing that the prey was on the run, took up the cudgel with renewed vigor, slashing at Burns for saying that he controlled the police chief and the mayor. They wondered why the bosom friend of Burns, Chief of Police Caples, allowed the Red Light still to operate. "This dive on Utah Street is nightly filled with the worst class of prosti-

143

tutes and the most irresponsible of criminal classes," they howled. "These lowest and most dangerous of criminal women have been to a certain extent free from the fines and penalties inflicted upon other vagrant women." The newspaper was now hinting at bribery.

On May 4, 1893, Jim Burns went on trial for conducting a disorderly house (the Red Light). On this, the first of five charges, he was fined $100 and costs. The doors of his saloon were now shut tight.[9]

John Selman had sat quietly through all the difficulties his friend was having. Now he could contain himself no longer. He told Burns he would be a fool to pay the fine until he had spent his last dollar in fighting the case. He even offered to throw into the defense half the value of a house and his share of 240 acres of land lying alongside the Rio Grande, owned jointly by himself and Burns.[10]

It must be said in defense of John Selman that his association with Burns was based on friendship and not money. There is no evidence that Selman ever took a dime in bribery from the Red Light owner. One of his few virtues was sticking by his friends no matter how odious they were, and Old John never backed away or ignored Burns when trouble came. The others, including Chief Caples, whom Burns said he paid two dollars a night for a license, stammered a red-faced farewell to a former friend who was now only a political liability.

As the troubles over the Red Light began to die down, John turned his attention to romance. On August 23, 1893, in the office of J. R. Harper, a Justice of the Peace in El Paso, John married Miss Romula Granadino. She was the ward of W. H. Wheat, Selman's first deputy, who was appointed on November 24, 1892. The deputy signed a statement before the ceremony took place, swearing that "John Selman is over the age of 21 [he was almost fifty-four] and Miss Granadino is of the age of 16 years and that there is no legal objection to the marriage of said contracting parties and I [W. H. Wheat] forthwith swear that I am the guardian of Romula Granadino, do give my consent to her marriage with John Selman." [11]

Considering Wheat's marital record it is difficult to understand how he ever became guardian of anyone. He was continuously caught lifting the wrong skirts and the papers are full of his escapades in and out of the divorce courts. He was charged with the rape of one maiden; they married but the charge, instead of being dropped, was reduced to seduction and he was jailed. [12] Immediately upon his release he charged his wife with desertion and adultery.

The newspapers the day after Selman's wedding gave good coverage to the event, remarking that he had been younger, but had never looked handsomer or happier. John, dressed in a black suit, answered the judge's questions with a conscious smile. Who wouldn't be nervous? City hall was packed with well wishers impatiently waiting for the ceremony to be over and the music to begin. When John finally developed enough courage to kiss the bride, [13] it was time for the handshakes to start and the presents to be given. The dance lasted until 12:15 in the morning—and the hall was filled until the end. [14]

The marriage proved to be a stormy one. Dishes sailed through the air quite regularly, and John, Jr., was frequently called upon to act as peacemaker between the two. Old John's children, who now had a stepmother younger than they, were not pleased with the marriage. [15] Ashamed of their father's actions, John, Jr., and Bud Selman moved uptown. [16]

Old John was not one to let his marriage interfere with his constabular activities. While the docket books do not give many details of the arrests he participated in, they still reveal an active officer who was taking his work seriously. The pages are literally covered with the names of people arrested by him and charged with such offenses as disturbing the peace, drunkenness, burglary, swearing at an officer of the law, theft and so forth. There is even one charge of adultery. Most of the fines were for five dollars.[17]

Although Selman's time now seemed to be spent in handling more or less petty offenses, his days of crossing trails with dangerous gunmen were far from over. One fellow, a man whose reputation never rivaled Selman's but who was feared because of his speed and accuracy with a gun, was ex-Ranger Bass Outlaw (this seems to have been his real name). About five feet four, lithe and very strong, with pale gray eyes, weak mouth and receding chin, Outlaw was a terror when drinking.[18]

Supposedly born in Georgia of a good family, he had more than the average share of social graces and education. He reportedly killed a man in Georgia and ran away to Texas where, in 1885, he enlisted in Company E of the Rangers. In 1887, he was transferred to Company D.

His life was a tragic one. He was never able to maintain any kind of position—either in law and order, in business or in friendship. Mrs. Alonzo Oden, wife of Ranger Oden, felt that the man was brilliant, misunderstood, and incapable of being anything more than what he was—his own worst enemy.[19]

Alonzo Oden himself, one of the few who were able to maintain a friendship to the last with Bass, wrote upon his death: "Bass Outlaw is dead. Maybe all of us knew something like this would come to Bass—Bass, who was so kind; who could laugh louder, ride longer, and cuss harder than the rest of us; and who could be more sympathetic, more tender, more patient than all of us when necessary. Bass had one weakness, that—at last—proved to be stronger than all his virtues. Bass couldn't leave liquor alone, and when Bass was drunk, Bass was a maniac. . . ."[20]

146

Although Outlaw was rapidly promoted to Sergeant, his alcoholism worked even faster. He was finally forced to resign from the Rangers by Captain Frank Jones for being drunk on duty in Alpine.

Sometime later, Bass managed to secure an appointment as a Deputy United States Marshal with headquarters in Alpine. In spite of his habits, he was extremely popular there and the residents in large numbers petitioned Marshal Dick Ware to retain Outlaw in that district. Out of deference to public wishes this was done. Ware foresaw trouble with the quick-tempered little man, however, and warned him repeatedly about his drinking, threatening either to discharge him or force his resignation.[21]

No matter where Outlaw went in the Southwest, his reputation proceeded him. He was so well known in El Paso and such a terror to the town at one time that a policeman was assigned to keep him quiet.[22] On June 21, 1892, he wound up in bed with the white mistress of a Negro dive keeper named Watts. Watts became very indignant over this, but was afraid to object for fear Outlaw would shoot him. Finally he got up nerve enough to file a complaint in court. When Outlaw sobered up, however, he cheerfully gave the woman back and the charges were dropped.[23]

On April 5, 1894, Bass was in El Paso once again, this time as a court witness. Drunk as usual, he was making numerous threats against Marshal Dick Ware, who, Outlaw claimed, had sent another deputy marshal into his territory to serve papers. This rested uncomfortably in the pit of Outlaw's stomach because there had been some fees connected with the paper-serving task which Bass felt should have gone to him.[24]

The little marshal went first to Tillie Howard's sporting house—probably the finest establishment of its kind in the Southwest—where he sought to drown his sorrows in a woman's charms. Ruby, one of the girls, took Bass by the hand and when he left a few hours later, he appeared to have lost his anger.

Next he stopped at Barnum's Saloon and then wandered on up Utah Street, where he met John Selman and Frank Collinson. As the three joined in conversation, Bass's old bitter feelings began to return and he started making threats against Ware once again. Selman and Collinson tried to get him to go to his room and sober up, but Bass waved these suggestions aside. He wanted an encore with Ruby.[25]

Selman and Collinson, trying to humor the man, strolled with him back to Tillie's. Once inside, Selman and Collinson sat down in the parlor and began chatting. Bass wandered off into a back room. He had been gone only a few minutes when a shot rang out in the bathroom and Selman smiled, glanced over at Collinson and said, "Bass has dropped his gun." [26]

Getting up, John was just starting toward the rear of the house when Tillie burst out of her apartment, ran to the back and began blowing a police whistle. This was a normal occurrence when trouble developed. She was pursued by Bass Outlaw, who chased her out into the yard and attempted to take the whistle from her.

Others recognized the tweet of the whistle also. Joe McKidrict, a Texas Ranger who was in town testifying before a federal grand jury, was talking to a friend in front of a printing house down the street when he heard the shot fired and the whistle blow.[27]

Selman stepped out on Tillie's back porch just as McKidrict came into the back yard. "It was an accident, Joe," Selman said. "He's all right."

"Bass, why did you shoot?" McKidrict demanded.

Outlaw, still holding his pistol in his hand, snarled, "You want some too?" With that he stuck his pistol up against McKidrict's head and jerked the trigger. The bullet struck the

Ranger directly over the left ear, and as he toppled to the ground, Bass shot him once more in the back.

John Selman jumped off the back porch, reaching for his gun. Outlaw had the drop, however, and he fired almost directly into Old John's face. The ball whipped past the constable's ear, the powder searing his eyes and almost blinding him. Reeling backward, John pulled and fired by instinct at the dim, blurred figure of Outlaw. His shot hit Bass above the heart, the slug ripping its way through the left lung and emerging beneath the right shoulder. John stood there blindly, holding his gun with one hand and his eyes with the other. He felt he had hit the gunman and thought he was staggering, but he could not be sure.

Bass, though mortally wounded, had a perfect opportunity to kill the constable; but he was so weak he could not lift his pistol high enough to do the job. Retreating, he fired two more shots, one hitting Selman just above the right knee, the other cutting through the thigh and severing an artery.

Still in retreat, Outlaw fell over the fence and staggered around the house onto Utah Street, where he met Ranger Private Frank M. McMahon of Company D. He surrendered to McMahon, giving up his revolver and begging the Ranger to protect him from the mob which he felt, incorrectly, would be pursuing him. McMahon and a passing Mexican helped Outlaw into the Barnum Show Saloon, where he staggered into a corner and slid, sick and terror-stricken, to the floor.

He was lifted up and laid on top of the bar, where Dr. T. S. Turner examined him. Concluding that nothing could be done to help the dying man, he had Outlaw transferred to a prostitute's bed in the back room, where he died about four hours later at 9:15 P.M. Bass knew he was going and he kept crying over and over, "Oh God, help!" Then he asked, "Where are my friends?" [28] Nobody answered.

Joe McKidrict, who died within a few minutes after he

was shot, was taken back to his home in Austin for burial. His real name was Joe Cooly. It had been changed to keep his mother from knowing where he was. He was about thirty years old and a former member of the San Antonio police force.[29]

After the shooting John Selman struggled into a carriage and went to see Dr. White. While his wounds were not diagnosed as serious, he was confined immediately to bed and it was two weeks before he was even able to walk around the room. After that he spent the rest of his life with a cane. He did not recover the full use of his eyes, John Selman, Jr., reporting that he was nearly blind at night.[30]

Old John was charged with murder and on October 30, 1894, he went on trial in 34th District Court in El Paso. Judge C. N. Buckler told the jury in his closing statement: "There being no evidence before you that the defendant John Selman is guilty of the crime of which he is charged in the indictment in this case—you are therefore instructed to find the defendant not guilty." [31]

15

ENTER JEFF MILTON

PROSTITUTION, a trade practiced for centuries before El Paso was anything more than a desert of scraggly tumbleweeds and mesquite, was as much a part of the town as hard liquor and the six-gun. Its popularity was attested to by the fact that it was legal and thriving when other forms of entertainment, such as gambling, had been banned. On May 1, 1890, the city council established a trade territory for the girls which became popularly known as the Tenderloin.[1] Here the harlots were licensed to operate and for this privilege they paid ten dollars a month into the city's coffers.[2]

In a town as wide open as El Paso, it would have been easier to stamp out the West Texas dust storms than the bawdyhouses, even if their elimination had been desired—which it was not. Confining the females to one section of town, however, did bring together the rougher class of citizens and in essence limited them to an area where they could be more easily controlled. This allowed trade and business in other parts of the city to expand normally, while also protecting the

151

eyes of the virtuous from gazing upon the ranker aspects of the town's life.

Along with prostitution, gambling had long been a thorn in the side of El Paso. The city finally decided that there would have to be a choice made between the two and for some reason the officials determined that prostitution was there to stay, but gambling was condemned as evil and banned.[3]

This was the decison of a reform group of politicians elected in 1894, and at once Mayor Johnson began looking around for someone to clean up the town according to the edicts of the city council. They needed someone who could be just as mean and ornery as anyone El Paso could produce. Tough Jeff Milton, who was currently punching tickets for the Pullman Company, responded to the call. On August 10 he was sworn in as City Marshal of El Paso.[4]

There has been much talk of difficulty between John Selman and Jeff Milton. The suspicion is that Selman felt he deserved the city marshal's job and made a few unkind comments about Milton's intrusion. One story has it that Selman remarked to friends about how he would take Milton's guns, jam them into the seat of Jeff's britches and kick the handles off.[5]

Upon hearing the rumor, Milton claims he looked up Old John and offered him a pistol for the experiment. Selman subsequently laughed and denied the tale, or at least his part in it.

Milton later told J. Evetts Haley that John Selman was involved in numerous shakedowns of prostitutes[6] and that he and his deputy were plotting to kill him when as police chief he had caught on to their little game. While no one can deny that Old John's character and virtue could have stood some improvement, there is nothing in the records to indicate that there was any basis for such charges. This allegation of Milton's does, however, bring out an interesting aspect of Selman's character. In his earlier years the man had been not only ruthless and deadly, but unscrupulous—particularly in some of his cattle dealings. Yet when he left the outlaw trade and was elected to public office there is no evidence that he did anything other than a respectable job of running a clean and honest department.

The two men were actually a great deal alike, tough and shrewd, specialists in controlling other men by force, and at times absolutely without mercy. Had animosities ever reached the ignition stage, each would have maneuvered for an opportunity to kill the other. That never happened. Indeed, it looks as if the two gunmen got along quite well. Milton hired John Selman, Jr., as a city policeman (probably on the recommendation of Old John), and gave him the same beat as his father. In view of this gesture, it can only be assumed that if Milton and Selman were never the best of friends—neither were they the worst of enemies.

When the opportunity came, the constable and police chief worked hand in glove with each other. On the first of April, 1895, when John Selman was out of town (newspaper accounts indicate that he frequently made trips somewhere in Mexico), a police officer reported to Milton that Deputy Constable Schoonmaker was collecting unauthorized money from prostitutes. Milton replied that "it was scarcely probable as the justice court had no right to collect such fines."

The officer than handed Milton two receipts signed by J. N. Schoonmaker. They read as follows:[7]

El Paso, Texas. February 12, 1895. Received of Frankie Hamilton $6.50 for vagrancy for month of February in J. K. Lyon's court.

El Paso, Texas. February 27, 1895. Received of Frankie Hamilton $2.50 for fee on services for month of March in J. K. Lyon's court.

Instead of arresting the deputy, Milton decided to wait a day or so until John Selman returned and then "call him to assist in ferreting the thing out."

When Selman first saw the receipts, his reaction was the same as Milton's, puzzlement. The two men discussed strategy for a few minutes and then called in John Selman, Jr., who was acting constable while his father was away. The three then went to look for Selman's deputy, Jim Schoonmaker.

The deputy readily admitted his guilt, but said he had "collected the fines and turned them over to Justice of the Peace Lyon." [8]

The constable and police chief now walked swiftly down to Justice Lyon's court and asked to see the cases on the docket. Lyon complied with the request. However, there was no indication on the books that fines had been extracted from any of the prostitutes, nor was there any sign of a warrant or commitment paper to be found. When questioned, Lyon flatly denied Schoonmaker's allegations, swore he was not involved in the scandal in any way and did not know what the deputy was talking about. He also could think of no reason why he should be accused of such an offense.

Schoonmaker was insistent. He said Lyon had become very angry because receipts had been given and had called him a fool, screaming that if County Attorney Storms ever found out what was going on, he would "want his divy."

The deputy then went on to say that of the money collected, he took a dollar, John Selman, Jr., received a dollar and Justice Lyon swept in the rest. [9]

The extortion had been accomplished without difficulty because the girl had been plying her trade outside the Tenderloin and was understandably frightened when an officer showed up at her door with a badge on his shirt. Since she was a "free lance harlot," always hiding from the authorities, she had not amassed any wealth from her activities. She lived and worked outside the Tenderloin because even the ten-dollar fine was more than she could afford. The deputy realized this, and with pity playing a melody on his heart strings, he did not force her to pay the regular charge—he simply took all she had.

Both Selman and Milton left no doubt among the newspaper readers that they considered County Attorney Storms mixed up in the affair and Old John went on to remark that it was only upon the pleadings of Storms that he had accepted Schoonmaker as a deputy to begin with.[10]

"I do not intend to have any shaking down done in my name," John thundered to the newspapers, who were at this time describing him as an "honest, brave and frank old constable who was mad all over." He laid out his feelings on the matter for all to see. "No deputy of mine shall unlawfully hold up any person in El Paso and I intend to camp on this trail until every person mixed up in the affair is singled out and I want you to know that Schoonmaker is no longer my deputy." [11]

A day or two later, the entire matter was once again thrown into a turmoil when Justice Lyon committed suicide by taking a large dose of poison.[12] He left a note addressed to his son Horatio in which he said: "I expect to be within the presence of my God and Maker within thirty minutes; and I make this statement that I have not directly nor indirectly been connected with Jim Schoonmaker or any of his unlawful acts—so help me God as a Royal Arch Mason." [13]

The city was now divided into two camps, the largest of which felt bitter toward Schoonmaker, holding him responsible for Lyon's death. John Selman, as the man in the middle, quickly wound up his investigation and swore out a warrant against his former deputy, charging him with extortion in office. The penalty upon conviction was a fine of not less than $25 nor more than $100. Schoonmaker made bond for $200 and was released.

The case went to trial in the County Court of Law[14] with

Storms as the prosecuting attorney, even though he was directly involved as a result of Schoonmaker's earlier statements. Charlie Patterson and George E. Wallace, defense attorneys, were lawyers who had built themselves a lucrative practice by defending clients from the rougher end of town.

As the court's first witness John Selman stated that he was Constable of Precinct 1 and he knew Schoonmaker because the defendant had been his deputy.

Patterson then jumped up, gasping that he objected to Selman's testimony as proof of Schoonmaker's official capacity. He made it very plain that he intended to prove from the records that Schoonmaker had never properly filled out the correct papers to become a lawman and consequently, the accused man was never legally a deputy.

Now it was the prosecution's turn to howl. Mr. Harper, the assistant, came out of his chair yelling that it was preposterous that a man on trial for such a charge should attempt to dodge behind the subterfuge created by his own failure to comply with the law.

Though the wrangling went on for most of the afternoon, John Selman's testimony was finally allowed to stand. Others who gave their version of the matter were John Selman, Jr., Jeff Milton, Jim Schoonmaker and Frankie Hamilton. Storms also took the stand, but he confined his comments to the vagueness of Miss Hamilton's testimony on the stand compared to the fullness of her earlier admissions in his office.[15]

Jim Schoonmaker was found guilty as charged and fined twenty-five dollars.[16]

Why, we do not know, but John Selman, Jr., was not prosecuted as an accessory after the fact. He never made any published excuse for taking the dollar, except to say that he thought it was his share of the fees. The *Times* was also strangely silent about young John's participation in the extortion, although the feeling comes through that the newspaper

156

did not consider the boy an experienced law officer. The reasoning seems to have been that young Selman did not fully realize what was taking place, and had never completely understood the situation until approached by his father and Jeff Milton. To his credit, he never denied taking the money.

John Selman, Jr., was nineteen or twenty when he became a member of the police force, but in spite of his youth he was almost as well known around El Paso as his father. The newspapers frequently spoke well of him. Even Jeff Milton liked the youngster, commenting to Haley that "he was the best boy to have the sorriest daddy." [17]

Young John's road as a peace officer traveled through many a pitfall, however, and one of his first stumbles concerned a man named Boss Nelson who owned the Boss Saloon. The two men did not get along and presently they began wasting words on each other. Selman, smarting from the verbal lashing, decided to get instructions from Jeff Milton before he did anything rash.

The police chief changed color several times as he listened to the policeman's story. Then he called together the entire force, which consisted of seven or eight men[18] and roared that if he ever heard of another of his officers taking a cussing from someone who was not drunk, that he would discharge him.[19]

These instructions seemed pretty clear to young Selman and he returned to his beat. A few nights later he was walking up Overland Street and witnessed a crowd of hoboes gathered around the side door of the Boss Saloon. Several others were inside and the din was uproarious.

There are two stories about the events which followed, Selman's and Boss Nelson's. Young Selman's was that he interrupted the fun making and informed Nelson that unless his guests were less boisterous he would have to arrest them. Nelson then began cursing and ordered the police officer out of his saloon. Young Selman left, then walked angrily around the block and came up Overland on the other side of the street. Nelson, who was standing in the doorway of his saloon, saw the officer coming and motioned him over. Once more the swearing began, only this time Nelson went too far.

Lashing out with his fist, John, Jr., struck Nelson on the chin and sent him spinning to the floor. The saloon owner immediately got up, clawing for a derringer inside his shirt. Selman knocked it out of his hand, kicked it aside and in the brawl that followed bent his gun barrel on Nelson's head.[20]

Nelson's story was that young Selman entered his saloon and threatened to arrest a Negro fiddle player. The saloon owner objected to this and told the policeman that he had no authority to be in there unless he was called. Selman's reply was to hit Nelson a blow across the skull with his pistol.[21]

Nelson took a bad beating and was hauled off to the hospital where he almost died, lingering on the critical list for days.[22]

In less than a few minutes after the fight, young Selman was arrested by Captain Bob Ross of the police department. The matter was then referred to Jeff Milton for whatever action he wished to take.

Milton, who had promised he would give his men full support in any difficulty, now began to hedge. He finally squirmed out of the predicament by tossing the affair into the lap of the city council and asking that it be investigated.[23]

The council evidently approved of young Selman's actions, for no disciplinary action was ever taken.

The only rebuke John Selman, Jr., ever heard came from his father. A pistol, Old John angrily told the boy, was meant to shoot, and was not meant to be used as a club.[24]

16

JOHN WESLEY HARDIN

THE MOST FAMOUS gunfighter in the West, the estimated number of whose victims ranges from a low of twenty-three to a high of over forty, was now ready to bring his unique talents to the border city. John Wesley Hardin, named in honor of the founder of Methodism, was himself a preacher's son; yet he was a rebel, a wanted man at the age of fifteen. His adventures were legendary. But the El Paso Hardin was not the Hardin of twenty years before. The fires which had once blazed within his soul were now sinking into embers. Only a few coals remained, and these glowed only with the consumption of alcohol.

Hardin had begun his violent career in southeast Texas by shooting Reconstruction Negroes, had graduated to Union soldiers and had hit his peak as a gunman during the Taylor-Sutton feud.[1] In May of 1874 he shot down Deputy Sheriff Charles Webb of Brown County in a short but bloody exchange of gunfire which proved to be his undoing.[2] Three years later he was captured in Florida and sentenced to a long term in the Texas State Prison at Huntsville.

As the Huntsville prison gates slammed shut behind him, unexpected aspects of his nature began to appear. He read omnivorously. The Bible particularly interested him and he gave it a scholar's attention. Before long he became superintendent of the Sunday School and head of the debating team.

Next, he turned his abilities to the study of law, finally deciding to be an attorney instead of a minister of the gospel as he had planned. He penned letters by the ream to his wife and children, most of which have been saved and are in the hands of the Hardin descendants today. His correspondence indicates that he planned upon his release to take his family and reside in some small town while he practiced law. His plans came unraveled on November 6, 1892, when his wife died at the age of thirty-six. Had it not been for her untimely death, the life of John Wesley Hardin might have had a happier ending.

Two years later on February 14, 1894, Hardin walked out of prison, free for the first time in fifteen years. The following month he was granted a full pardon.

Hardin moved to Gonzales, Texas, where he passed the bar examination and should have settled down to a future of pleading in courtrooms. Instead he became involved in a race for sheriff, the man he backed lost and in bitterness Hardin packed his possessions and moved to the little brush-country community of Junction. There on January 8, 1895, he married teen-ager Callie Lewis, who left him a few days later. The age difference, from all accounts, was too great. She abandoned him on their honeymoon and refused to see or speak to him again.[3]

A call for help now came from a distant relative, "Killin' Jim" Miller of Pecos, Texas, this time himself the victim of a shooting. Miller, who had racked up a list of killings almost as impressive as Hardin's, had brought the trouble upon himself when he went looking for G. A. "Bud" Frazer. He had intended to talk loud with a shotgun, but Frazer saw him coming and spoke first. As a consequence, Miller was nearly killed and he appealed to Hardin to appear for the prosecution.

The case was transferred to El Paso on a change of venue and John Wesley Hardin followed it.

The El Paso court records do not mention Hardin, but he undoubtedly played some part in the trial, and it was in this courtroom that he probably made his first contact with John Selman when John brought a prisoner from the jail to take the witness stand. Rarely in the annals of bloodletting have two such cold, hard killers stood shoulder to shoulder, but it may be assumed that this meeting was amicable.[4]

The Frazer trial ended in a hung jury[5] but Hardin, impressed with the homicidal tendencies of the town, decided it could use another criminal lawyer and proceeded to hang out his shingle.

Had he known of the chain of events then beginning to shape in New Mexico, he might have chosen a more peaceful location to practice. These events began with Martin Morose, a man who fancied himself as a lady killer and desperado. In reality, he was no more than a small-time cattle and hog thief. For some odd reason, the name was spelled M'Rose by the early newspaper reporters in El Paso, who undoubtedly knew more Irishmen than Polanders. The strangest cowboy the West ever saw, he spoke a halting version of English, wore ill-fitting farm clothes and preferred clodhopper shoes to the more highly esteemed cowboy boots. He is said to have had a decided aversion to underclothing.[6] Nevertheless, he did have leadership abilities and at one time led a small assortment of insignificant hoodlums who operated with him around Eddy (Carlsbad), New Mexico. One of these, named Vic Queen, who became his partner, scared more men with his rough talk than with his six-shooter. But Vic was more polished than his slovenly companion. He was a cowboy and showed it in every detail of his dress.

Next to stealing, the boys' real love was the small sin town of Phenix, located on the outskirts of Eddy. Nobody knows how the town's name came to be rendered this way, but it is thought that whoever coined the name simply couldn't spell.[7] According to the United States post office, it was also spelled "Fenix" on occasions. Open twenty-four hours a day, the brothels, saloons, cockpits and other sources of diversion flourished almost entirely for the benefit of the lonesome cowboy. For the short time that it lasted, Phenix was a wild money-making success.

The bright lights of the town drew Morose and Queen as the rumor of a mother lode draws a gold miner. They spent more time in the bawdy houses than some of the girls, and it wasn't long before Morose was infatuated with a blond, blue-eyed prostitute called Helen Beulah. Her last name never seems to have been recorded. Quite superfluously, they married.[8] Beulah wasn't any help to Martin's luck, though this fact did not become apparent for some time. The trouble seemed to be the cattle-stealing business, which was just not prospering as of old. Rumblings of discontent were being heard from ranchers all over southern New Mexico—rumblings which alarmed Morose and Queen.

Both men hastily sold out their land and cattle holdings, and as reward posters went up all over the Southwest ($1000 for Morose; $500 for Queen), they headed for Mexico and did not stop until they splashed across the Rio Grande at Juarez.

New Mexico law enforcement officers, in close pursuit, entered a complaint in El Paso against the two men,[9] filed extradition papers with the Mexican authorities, then settled down to wait for their quarry to be brought across the river.

The plight of the outlaws became desperate. Mexican police picked up Queen on March 26, 1895, and Morose was captured a few days later, on April 6. The only question remaining was how long it would be before they were shoved across the border.

Beulah, with her share of Martin's money (reputed to have been several thousand dollars), went to El Paso and sought the services of an attorney who just happened to be John Wesley Hardin. Wes took one look at his bosomy visitor and made up his mind to take the case. Indications are, however, that he did not last long as the lawyer for Morose and Queen. His services were quickly terminated when he became more interested in the wife than in the client.

Dee Harkey says that General MacKenzie, a prominent cattleman in New Mexico, went to Juarez and gave Morose $4000. With this money Martin took out Mexican naturalization papers for himself and Queen.[10]

On Sunday, April 21, Hardin and an unidentified man crossed the river to Juarez, where they accidentally met Jeff Milton and Deputy United States Marshal George Scarborough. After a short chat in the street, all four of them retired to the rear of a saloon for a drink. Strolling through to the back, they found themselves face to face with five of Morose's friends in consultation with Beulah. It was too late for anyone to back out, so the Hardin party waved a salute and took seats.

The conversation between the two groups started off friendly enough, but it was not long before the name of Morose was mentioned and angry words began crackling through the air. Hardin, who was arguing with Tom Finnessey, became furious over something that was said and both men jumped to their feet. Wes, tight-lipped, stepped forward, slapped Finnessey and rammed his six-shooter into his belly. Tom would have died on the spot had not Jeff Milton seized Hardin's pistol and forced him to return it to his pocket.

Scarborough and the other member of the Hardin group now drew their guns and covered the Morose crowd. The situation looked grim, but Hardin had no desire to lessen tensions. He stepped up to a man named Lightfoot and nearly tore his head off with a whistling slap.

Milton now decided that events had gone far enough and might just as well be settled. So he put his back to the door and invited everyone to either fight or shut up. The Morose bunch was too badly shaken to pursue the matter any further and so refused to fight. It was just not the day for a killing.[11]

Shortly after this incident, Morose and Queen swore allegiance to Mexico and were released,[12] although they dared not go to El Paso. Martin's wife was also not making any more trips to Juarez. She was spending her nights in the arms of her husband's attorney and there appeared to be nothing the cuckolded Morose could do about it.

In the meantime the city of El Paso, after months of "clean" government, had absorbed about all the reform it could stand, and a new mayor was swept into office. Ed Fink, who had been fired from the police force when Milton took office, now became the new police chief and Milton found himself with idle time on his hands until Marshal Dick Ware appointed him a Deputy United States Marshal.[13] The only other federal deputy marshal in town was George Scarborough.

Milton and Scarborough now got their heads together and agreed that the Morose matter had drifted on long enough and he would have to be brought back from Mexico and taken into custody. Their concern was no doubt buttressed by the reward offered on the outlaw's head. Milton made certain the money was still there by telegraphing New Mexico authorities and obtaining the current figures on their man.[14]

The plot now becomes so sticky and involved that the truth of what actually happened may never be known. The only story which everyone seems to agree on says that George

Scarborough had been secretly meeting Martin Morose in Juarez for some time. Scarborough noted in an article published by the *Times* that Martin wanted the deputy to act as a go-between for himself and Beulah. Scarborough went along with this plan and carried messages back and forth between the two.[15]

John Selman was also employed at one time in this enterprise. He approached George Look, a saloon owner, shortly after Morose was released from jail in Juarez and tried to interest Look in permitting Morose and his wife to meet in a back room of Look's establishment.[16] Look wrote that he gave his permission, but did not know if the rendezvous ever took place. Selman remarked that Morose was a cattleman friend of his from New Mexico, and on this basis, plus the fact that if he was actually trying to get the couple to resolve their differences, it may make him the only honest broker in the lot. Why John's efforts failed, or why he dropped out of the picture in favor of Scarborough is unknown. A good guess is that Scarborough and Milton teamed up to convince Selman that they had a plan for the outlaw's capture, and John turned the job of luring Morose across the Rio Grande over to them. While relations between Selman and Milton may have been shaky, the feelings between Old John and George Scarborough were warm, and according to young Selman, George was one of their best friends in El Paso.[17] But John had already committed himself to some extent to bringing Morose across, and there is no reason to believe that he forgot about the situation after Scarborough took charge. The gunman, even though he continued to pound his beat and made very little ripple in the affairs of El Paso at this time, was undoubtedly still watching events closely from the sidelines.

The next move was for Scarborough to convince Morose that he should come to El Paso for a clandestine meeting with his wife. A good case also exists for the possibility that Morose was lured across in the hope of killing Hardin. The rustler at times was nearly wild with jealousy.

Late at night on June 21, 1895, Scarborough met Morose in the middle of the Mexican Central Railway bridge. Single file they crossed over, the deputy leading, and upon reaching the American side, the two were met by Deputy Marshal Milton and Texas Ranger Frank McMahon. Morose was subsequently killed in a wild barrage of gunfire which ended as the wanted man crashed heavily to the ground with eight pistol and shotgun slugs in him.

Investigating officers who rushed to the scene found the rustler's gun lying beside him, cocked, one shot fired. In his pocket was a sealed, blood-soaked letter addressed to Mrs. Helen Beulah Morose. No information has ever been released as to its contents.

Public opinion in El Paso strongly condemned the peace officers. It was not that anyone cared for the dead bandit; people simply felt that the rules of fair play had been violated.

Although the plans for the killing took place in utmost secrecy and the place of the death was apparently chosen carefully for its lack of potential observers, the event was witnessed by two Mexican smugglers. Vic Queen, in raging anger over what he considered to be outright murder, fired a letter across the river to the El Paso *Times.* In it, Queen accused Scarborough of a systematic course of deception to inviegle Martin Morose across the river on the pretense of getting a division of community property. Scarborough told Morose that his wife had nearly $1400 of their money left and was willing to effect a settlement. "Mr. Morose advised with some friends on the subject and they one and all told him not to trust Scarborough, but Scarborough had so worked on his confidence that at the last moment he slipped away and kept the ill fated appointment with his sacrificer."

Queen then went on to say that he had heard shooting across the river and he immediately went looking for Morose. Shortly after the firing stopped, two men came running across the bridge so badly frightened that they refused to talk when he accosted them. The next day, however, he located the same men again and was told that they were smugglers returning to Mexico when they witnessed three men conversing near the bridge. A tall slim man, otherwise unidentified, walked out on the bridge while the other two hid in the sunflowers alongside a dump. A half hour later the tall man came back, followed by a big, heavy man walking five or six steps behind. A cough, seemingly a signal, came from the tall man, and the guns from the two concealed men began to roar. Morose fell, flopped around momentarily and jumped back to his feet; then the tall man ran up and fired a shot directly into his breast. "Then the fat man with the long gun let fly . . . the big man fell but kept trying to get up. . . . The fat man put his foot on him and held him down until he died." [18]

The two Mexicans continued to watch as the killers picked up the dead man's pistol and placed it close to his hand. By this time, someone was coming with a light and the Mexicans swiftly crossed the river into Mexico.

Scarborough, Milton and McMahon were all charged with murder and ordered to stand trial. Deputy Marshal Scarborough was tried first, but his defense attorneys proved him to be a "quiet and peaceful man" and he was acquitted.[19] After that the trials of Milton and McMahon were mere formalities.[20]

Nobody cared enough for the corpse of Martin Morose to accompany it to the graveyard. The undertaker had to go out into the street and find four strangers to help lay Martin to rest. At Concordia Cemetery two mourners were the only people in evidence. They were Mrs. Helen Beulah Morose and her lover.[21]

17

FOUR SIXES TO BEAT

JOHN WESLEY HARDIN'S presence in El Paso was big news for some time. But while he occupied the forefront of the stage, other gunmen, including John Selman, continued to function as usual, though their place was in the wings.

We should know very little about Old John's activities, however, if it had not been for his son, John, Jr., who describes his father's movements, as well as his own, in an unpublished manuscript preserved by his descendants. Never one to belittle his father, young John shows him at this period as a sandhills Solomon who was capable of mixing a good deal of wisdom with his ordinary methods of settling problems.

There was, for instance, the night when the younger John was walking his beat on South El Paso Street and came upon a little Mexican boy, crying bitterly, who said in answer to John's question that his father was dead. He led the policeman to a miserable hut occupied by a half-starved woman and four untidy children. A dead man lay on the dirt floor. It was the woman's husband; she had stabbed him with a pocket knife.

He had been absent, she said, on a three-day drunk, had come home and found no food in the house—quite naturally, since he had spent all the money—and took that fact as an excuse to beat her up. After he had struck her several times, she seized the knife and used it. Now, full of remorse, she swore to the officer that she had never meant to kill him. The children substantiated the details of her story.

Young John knew that something had to be done, but he knew that if he arrested this pitiful, abused creature, he would have to take her away from her children. Unable to see the proper course of action, he sent for his father. Shortly thereafter the elder Selman appeared, bringing with him Deputy Wheat and Judge Farrell. After listening to the story, Selman put his arm about the judge's shoulders and suggested that they all go outside and have a consultation. A few minutes later they all came back, the judge looking very serious.

Turning to young John, he said in somber tones, "Tell her that we have talked it over and have come to the conclusion that her husband ran into the knife by accident. Something like a clear case of suicide." [1] Except for the funeral, the matter ended there.

The scene of another of Old John's demonstrations of intelligence was the old Monte Carlo dance hall on south Oregon Street, a famous dive which never closed its doors. By night it bounced to lively tunes and by day it was a bar. Customers were caught both coming and going. Probably this was El Paso's first nickel-a-dance establishment, and a popular girl could earn several dollars in an evening.

Once each week a masquerade party was held, a golden opportunity for the less attractive girls to earn money and have fun. All they had to show was a pair of lively legs and some personality.

One evening as John Selman, Jr., stood watching the merrymaking, his father strolled up and said he was looking for two Mexicans who, he suspected, were impersonating girls at the dance. The boy then called his attention to a young lady, the life of the party, on whom a soldier from Fort Bliss was spending money as if he had discovered the most wonderful thing in the world. At this particular time they were dancing.

"No woman ever had a pair of legs like that," John growled, and told his son to line them all up against the wall while he unmasked them.

When they got to her, the girl tried to run, but the old constable was too quick and tore the mask from her face. It wasn't the suspect he was looking for, but it was a man and a dance-hall bouncer at that. The soldier gasped in surprise, then struck the bouncer with his fist and probably would have tried to kill him had not the two police officers interfered. Frustrated, the victim turned and ran from the hall.[2]

While such things were taking place, Hardin was having his difficulties. His reputation as an attorney, meager to begin with, was slipping. Spending more and more time at the dice tables and less and less at the law office, he was doing very little to promote his own prestige. It was no secret that he now found the paying clients he liked best in the gambling rooms.

On the first of May, 1895, he took offense at the way a poker game was being played in the Acme Saloon. He was losing, so he took charge. He did it in such a friendly manner that no one objected; it was not even necessary to draw a gun. He simply scooped up the pot and walked off.[3]

On May 2 he was engaged in a crap game at the Gem Saloon and once again the chips were beginning to stack up, but not on his side of the table. The final indignity came when the dealer made a laughing comment about Hardin's playing ability. The gunfighter then gave the dealer a good look at the business end of a gun barrel and snapped, "Since you are trying to be so cute, I'll just take over the money I lost here." [4]

This second incident, unlike the first, aroused so much

unfavorable comment on the streets that he felt obliged to go to the newspapers and give a full account of his side of the controversy. In it he defended his "manliness," said he had been grossly insulted in a "hurrah manner," and since no one could take his money and hurrah him too he had demanded back the ninety-five dollars that the dealer had cheated him out of. He wrote, "I admire pluck, push and virtue wherever found and I condemn and despise a coward and assassin of character, whether he be a reporter, a journalist, or a gambler." In addition to the Gem Saloon, John Wesley plainly felt that the press was treating him unfairly.

In the final part of his letter he took advantage of the free publicity he was getting to announce that he had bought an interest in the Wigwam Saloon and cordially invited all those who "admire pluck and desire fair play" to come to "the big blowout on the evening of the fourth." [5]

On May 4, Hardin was arrested by Sheriff Simmons[6] and taken to the Thirty-fourth District Court, where a grand jury had indicted him for "unlawfully carrying a pistol." [6a] The district court then decided that it had no jurisdiction in the case and so trial was set for the county court. The trial records are not available here, but according to the *Times* Hardin went on trial on May 16. His defense, based on the testimony of several witnesses, was that his life was in danger from the remnants of the Morose faction and he had every reason to believe that they would kill him if the opportunity arose. He was then found guilty and fined twenty-five dollars.[6b]

Meanwhile, back on May 8, Hardin had also been indicted by the Thirty-fourth District Court on a charge of robbery. On this count the court decided that it had jurisdiction and trial was set for May 22. Wes, through his attorneys (Davis, Beall, Kemp and T. T. Toad) told the court that he was being swindled through the use of loaded dice, and he took back only what he had lost.

171

Among the numerous witnesses subpoenaed for the trial, John Selman's name appears. There is no record of what he testified to or if he was even called to the stand, but it is not beyond the reach of supposition that here hard feelings first began to sprout between the two men.

Perhaps this is one reason why Hardin swore that there existed in El Paso County "so great a prejudice against him that he could not get a fair and impartial trial." He requested a change of venue, which was denied. However, the proceedings did end in a mistrial and the case was rescheduled for the October term of court.[7]

As Hardin left the courtroom, Beulah was waiting to console him. What formerly had been a clandestine relationship had now bloomed so openly that the newspapers often referred to her as Mrs. J. W. Hardin, and she, after a day's remorse following the death of her husband, seemed content (most of the time) to be John Wesley Hardin's private property.

In addition to being wanton, she was wild and rowdy, and could, on occasion, be as much of a bottle punisher as any man. On August 2 she became completely inebriated while Wes was in New Mexico (Dee Harkey says Hardin spent a lot of time in Phenix, though living in El Paso).[8] Feeling reckless and carefree, looking for excitement, the blonde walked with irregular steps down San Antonio Street. About midnight she met officer John Selman, Jr., in front of Charlie's restaurant. Walking up to him she challenged the youth to a shooting match, though not specifying a target. She did not appear to be armed, but as John talked to her, he noticed the glint of metal in the folds of her parasol. He reached forward and removed the gun from its hiding place, which so infuriated her that she dressed him down in terms that made ordinary cursing sound like the Sunday sermon. Irked, he locked her up in jail and charged her with carrying a gun.[9]

172

The next morning Beulah went before the Recorder's Court[10] and paid a fine of fifty dollars. She told the judge that she was ashamed of herself and apologized to everyone, John Selman, Jr., in particular. In fact Mrs. Morose seemed so interested in getting young Selman's forgiveness that she waved and called to him from a buggy the next day and even offered him money if he would take a ride with her. According to John, Jr.'s, own statements, when she made this offer it created so much laughter among those near him that he began to run and didn't stop until he was out of her sight.[11]

When Hardin came back to town a day or so later, he appeared unconcerned about the arrest of his bed partner. Instead he began drinking heavily, so heavily that even the *Times* took notice and commented that Hardin was worried about something. "He expressed himself as not pleased with officer Scarborough and intimated that he would tell something about the killing of Morose." [12] The next morning Wes was sober enough to realize his indiscretion and apologized to Scarborough.

As for Mrs. Morose, she had gone out alone on Monday night, August 5, and did not say where she was going. This enraged Hardin. Perhaps it was a jealous anger; or maybe he was just taking out upon her his frustrations and fears in regard to other matters. It was now Tuesday and his hostility was compounded by drunkenness. They quarreled violently and Wes threatened to kill her and leave a note on her body explaining that she had committed suicide. Then he passed out on the bed and she and the landlady went to Justice Harvey's court where Annie Williams, the landlady, swore out a warrant for Hardin's arrest.[13] It was served by Captain Carr, officers Chaudoin and John Selman, Jr. They found their man deathly ill in the Acme Saloon, where he submitted meekly.

The next day in Justice Harvey's court John Wesley put

up a peace bond of $100. Court records also show that old John Selman collected a small sum at this trial for "Constable costs." [14]

John Wesley's troubles were by no means over. George Scarborough had been brooding about the remarks Hardin had made about him a few nights earlier. He collared Wes and steered him down to the El Paso *Times* where on August 11 the newspaper printed Hardin's humiliating public apology to the deputy: ". . . while under the influence of liquor, I made a talk against George Scarborough, stating that I had hired George Scarborough to kill Morose. I do not recollect making any such statement and if I did, the statement was absolutely false, and it was superinduced by drink and frenzy."

Jeff Milton claims that Hardin made the same remarks about him. According to his account, he forced Hardin to grovel like a dog,[15] but the newspapers missed this happy incident.

Hardin was now admitting in public that liquor was becoming a problem. His bad temper had become the talk of the town and even Beulah (she went back to him after he was put under peace bond) grew hopeless about their living together. She took a train west, as the newspapers worded it, to "grow up with the country." She sensed disaster hovering over Hardin's head, however, and wired from Deming, New Mexico, saying, "I feel you are in trouble and I'm coming back." [16] She did return, but the feeling between them was not warm and mellow. Shortly afterward she went to Phoenix, Arizona.

John Wesley Hardin was indeed in trouble. On the night of August 19, 1895, he wandered down to the Acme Saloon. There he and H. S. Brown, a grocer, began rolling dice for a quarter on the side. Hardin pitched and then remarked, "You have four sixes to beat." These were the last words he ever spoke, for at that instant John Selman stepped through the doors and with a blazing forty-five took Hardin's life.

As the blood spattered around the saloon, the patrons stormed the exits. The first shot struck Hardin in the head and as the gunfighter crashed to the floor, Old John fired again at his prostrate body. The second shot went astray and plowed through the floor when someone ran against him as the gun went off. Then, standing almost directly over the victim, he fired two more shots. One struck the right arm, the other penetrated the right breast, just missing the nipple. Possibly the firing would have continued had not young Selman rushed into the saloon, grabbed his father by the arm and cried, "Don't shoot him any more, he's dead." [17]

It did not take long for the saloon to refill, once the gunfire had stopped. The curious, coming from all over town, wanted to see the body of the slain gunman, and it lay there on the floor until everyone had a chance to view it. Then it was hauled off to the undertaker's where the dirt and gore were washed off to prepare it for the photographers. It was an exciting night for everyone but the deceased.

This is one of the famous killings of the wild old days in the West, and it has been described and analyzed a hundred times in the seventy years since it happened. There are two main versions of it. The commonly accepted one will be related first.

Version No. 1

When young John Selman arrested Hardin's mistress and caused her to be fined fifty dollars, Hardin was furious. He made several threats against the life of John, Jr., and when Old John stood up for his son, Hardin snapped that he would make the old gunfighter "[obscenity] like a wolf all around the block."

Selman replied, "My son only did his duty in arresting [his] whore," and challenged Hardin to a duel in the middle of the street.

To this challenge, Hardin replied, "I don't want to fight you—I'd rather fight your son." [18]

If the incident, as told by John Selman to Justice Howe at the inquest, ever actually took place, it is a safe bet that both men left the scene angrily gritting their teeth. It should be remembered, however, that one man was now dead, and the other was able to deny any story he disagreed with. The newspapers heaped praise on John Selman, but had he died in the dispute, Hardin might have fared better.

While Selman's story is the version usually accepted, it does have some glaring holes.

The biggest discrepancy is the unassailable fact that Beulah was arrested a full two weeks before the fatal showdown between the two men. Wes was not the kind of man to threaten for that long, and Selman was not the kind of man to wait for two weeks before taking matters into his own hands.

Moreover, young John in his memoirs indicates that Hardin was not angry at him for the arrest of Beulah. He was worried about the possible consequences and fretted for several days about what Hardin would say or do about it, but after passing the gunfighter peacefully at least twice in the street and in the park, he ceased to be concerned. Each time they met, Hardin greeted him very pleasantly and made no reference to the matter. Then young John suddenly decided that Hardin was in a towering rage over the incident and that his anger led to his death.[19]

Annie Williams, the inquisitive and talkative landlady who frequently questioned Hardin about his bloody career, remarked upon his death that he admired the elder Selman but hated the younger one as well as Officer Chaudoin.[20] This story would leave one to believe that Hardin's dislike for the boy resulted from his arrest for beating Beulah.

Another flaw in the accepted story is that Hardin seems to have had more important things on his mind during the two-week lapse than carrying out a vendetta against a mere youth. The Morose killing was evidently bothering him a great deal.

176

The newspaper indicated several times that he was angry at Scarborough and although its columns give fair coverage to his life in general during the days following the arrest of his woman, there is not so much as a whisper about his being sore at young John. If he was angry at the boy, furious enough to bring matters to a showdown, it was a circumstance kept secret from the *Times*.

Considering the trouble John Wesley and Beulah were having, it is not likely that Wes valued her virtue enough to kill a man over it. The story of their life together is one of brawls and drunkenness. Then too, she had left him for the wide open spaces before the trouble finally broke out.

Frank McMurray's testimony throws some light on this question. He testified before Judge Howe that he, John Selman, and John Wesley Hardin had all been rolling dice together in the evening before the killing at the Acme Saloon. "I left there about nine o'clock," the witness said. "Selman and Hardin had not been quarreling at all . . . seemed to be in perfectly good humor. Something was said between them about going down to the row [a line of sporting houses on El Paso's south side]." This witness, unless he was deliberately lying, was not aware of any hard feelings brewing at the hair-trigger level. Considering the reputations of these two, any hint of trouble between them would have spread all over town in minutes.

Of course, it is possible that Hardin was angry because Beulah had been arrested, but since two weeks had elapsed since the event, he could hardly have been in a homicidal rage about it. His supposed anger would, however, furnish an excellent excuse for killing him, provided his death was desired and would have to be explained.

These things having been weighed and considered, we come now to what may have been the real reason.

Hardin was killed because he did not split with John Selman the money which was taken from the body of Martin Morose.

In order for a man to appear prosperous and spend hard cash, he must have a source of income. John Wesley was one of those individuals everybody buys drinks for, but it was not beer money which enabled him to purchase an interest in the Wigwam Saloon. Though he often won at the gambling tables, his winnings probably no more than equaled his expenses. So where did his ready funds come from?

Beulah claimed in an interview that she advanced Hardin a considerable amount of cash, although she never said how much.[21] After this income dried up, another source of potential financing could have been the money Martin Morose had. To be sure, a great deal of Martin's money may have been spent in Mexico, but some of it he undoubtedly still had on his person when he died. No mention is made of his money after his death. So where did it go?

All the reliable stories, especially Vic Queen's letter to the *Times* after Martin's killing, indicate that Morose slipped out of town and left his partner Queen in Juarez on the night Morose was killed. Queen doesn't mention holding his currency. Consequently he may well have had his money on him when he crossed the river—and if so it probably was taken off his body after he was shot.

Keeping in mind that Hardin made some scurrilous remarks about hiring Scarborough (and possibly Milton) to kill Morose, it is time to find out what some other El Paso citizens have said and written about the affair.

In the files of Robert N. Mullin, distinguished Southwest historian and former resident of El Paso, are notations he made in interviews with one-time El Paso police officer Ed

Bryant and with Roy Barnum, who operated the Barnum Show Saloon. Both men flatly stated that Hardin arranged Morose's liquidation.[22] Unfortunately, they gave no details, but their opinion was evidently based upon facts.

Another man, George Look, also said he knew what happened and knew why. He occupied his niche in El Paso history as Selman, Hardin, County Attorney Storms and many others occupied theirs. He was a go-between who trod a difficult middle line between those who were bad and those who were worse. A saloon owner, an express guard, a wily politician, a man who corralled votes and delivered them for a price, Look either knew about or had his fingers in every bit of dishonest pie being cut in the community. For all these reasons he was the one person in a position to know the inside version of the Hardin and Morose killings. He had no reason to lie. This is his story.

After John Selman had approached Look for permission to use the rear of his saloon to bring Morose and his wife together, Scarborough talked the rustler into coming to El Paso to see Beulah. "On coming across the bridge with him, they met John Wesley Hardin, Milton and John Selman. Morose was killed by these men at the foot of the bridge. Then Hadin got to him first and took $3700 out of his pocket. The next day or two, John Wesley Hardin and Morose's wife [were] riding around town in a hack. John Selman came to me and told me that Wesley Hardin had quite a roll—in fact, had Morose's roll."

Hardin now began to hit the high spots in town. He held up the Gem and Acme Saloons, and also, according to Look, made several business trips. All of this was done to the chagrin of Selman.

The Gem holdup was the final straw for Old John. He went to Look and sputtered, "George, you people may stand for it, but I won't. He has to come across or I'll kill him." Now that he had started, Selman began to work himself up into a

179

murderous rage. "I believe he has cut with Scarborough," the old gunman snarled, "but he has not cut with any of the rest of us. What do you say—shall I get the son-of-a-bitch?"

George Look then acknowledged that things were in a bad way. The police either were in on the deal or were scared witless of Hardin. The only alternatives, as he saw them, were to let the matter rest—or to kill him. Old John chose the latter alternative, killing Hardin in the Acme Saloon "because he would not give him, Selman, his cut of the Morose money." [23]

Look's story has basically only one point wrong with it. Some of the names involved in his version of the Morose killing do not match the court records and newspaper articles. Perhaps this can be explained.

Morose was killed late at night in a deserted part of town and there is no positive evidence that anyone besides the killers witnessed the slaying. Even if the reports of the Mexican smugglers are correct, they did not recognize anyone. They spoke of the persons involved as the "fat man, tall man, thin man," etc. Thus two of the people they saw could have been Hardin and Selman. The smugglers would not have known the difference.

The trial records and newspapers say that there were three killers, while Look says there were four. He does not mention McMahon, perhaps not considering him important. It is possible for everyone, the smugglers, the courts, the newspapers, and Look, to be correct. Several men could have gone near the bridge, but remained in the background as lookouts. This is suggested by the smugglers who claimed to have seen someone bringing a lantern immediately after the shooting. Who could have been a better lookout than Selman? As constable, he could have turned anyone away from the scene. McMahon possibly served the same purpose. So could have Milton, but the evidence seems to show conclusively that he was at the bridge with Scarborough. The only one named as involved in this affair who would have aroused suspicion if he acted as a lookout was Hardin. His presence, if he was indeed there, must have been at the scene of the shooting.

So the drama, reconstructed, may have gone something like this. Scarborough, the thin man, crossed the Rio Grande railroad bridge after Morose. Hardin and Milton waited in ambush, and incidentally, since both were stout men, either one wearing any kind of bulky clothing could have passed for the smugglers' "fat man" that night. Then either Selman or McMahon picked up a light and started toward the bridge after the shooting stopped. Hardin grabbed the outlaw's money and left for town.

How did Frank McMahon, a Texas Ranger and former El Paso police officer, get mixed up in this, and who invited him in? The answer is that Scarborough and McMahon were brothers-in-law. Regardless of what the latter saw or knew, he could be counted on to keep his mouth shut.

These are the two possible explanations of John Wesley Hardin's death. Neither may be correct. At this late date, nothing is likely ever to be proved conclusively.

To Wesley Hardin himself, all arguments and speculations had ceased to be of interest. The preacher's son was placed in an expensive casket with the raised letters AT REST across the top. The El Paso *Herald* commented on August 20, that "The features were in good shape and he looked well." Burial was in El Paso's Concordia Cemetery, where he rests today in an unmarked [24] grave in an untended corner of the premises.

18

THE TRIAL

As JOHN SELMAN, JR., placed his father under arrest and led him from the saloon, the forces of truth and untruth, defense and prosecution were already beginning to line up for one of the most controversial trials in Western history. Even then, only hours after the killing, people could no more agree on whether it was murder or self-defense than present-day historians can.

Hardin had barely stretched out on the floor when the wheels of justice began to turn. Justice Howe and Recorder Patterson immediately began fighting over who had legal jurisdiction in the case. Within minutes after the shooting, Howe got there with a pen and paper and thus won the opening round when he started gathering up witnesses and securing their statements.

John Selman and his son readily gave signed affidavits written down by Howe. Others that night who gave versions of the death as they saw it were E. L. Shackelford, a broker[1] who at one time had employed John Selman; M. E. Ward, a railroad man and friend of the Selman family; Frank Patterson, the Acme bartender; and Henry S. Brown, the grocer.

Old John's story, as written by Howe and expanded somewhat by the *Herald*,[2] explained that he had been drinking and Shackelford had tried to get him to leave the Acme. He left, but only for a few minutes. "Hardin watched me very closely as we went [back] in," Selman said. "When he thought my eye was off him he made a break for his gun. . . . I shot him in the head first." John justified his fatal first shot by making reference to Hardin's alleged steel breastplate. The fabled vest, if it ever existed, was not being worn that night.

John Selman, Jr., told how Hardin had threatened to kill his father and how he had promised to "do up the whole police force." The boy had been instructed by his father to remain outside the saloon while the events were taking place inside. He left his post only at the sound of the first shots.

E. L. Shackelford's testimony smells of perjury. He remarked that he had heard threats made against Selman by the late gunfighter, that he had tried to get Selman to calm down and leave the saloon, then elbowed the old gunman outside where they talked together for a few minutes. They walked back inside the saloon, Shackelford in front and Selman following. Of the shooting which followed, Shackelford said, "I can't say who fired those shots and I did not see it. I did not turn around but left immediately."

It is worth noting, in view of Shackelford's remarkable candor, that he clearly implies that he knew Selman intended to kill Hardin and he (Shackelford) walked in ahead and probably gave a signal of some sort which triggered Old John into action.

Frank Patterson said that about eleven o'clock "Hardin was standing . . . with Brown and Mr. Selman walked in and shot him. Hardin was standing with his back to Mr. Selman. I did not see him face around before he fell or make any motion."

Grocer Brown testified the next afternoon and told how he and Hardin had been rolling dice. "I heard a shot fired . . . and Mr. Hardin fell at my feet at my left side. Hardin was adjacent the bar facing it . . . his back toward the direction the shot came from. [He made] no effort to get his six-shooter." Brown then finished his statement by saying he "had not the slightest idea that anyone was quarreling . . . from anything I heard."

Brown had finished testifying in Howe's courtroom and County Attorney Storms had started his cross-examination when Charlie B. Patterson, of the law firm of Patterson and Wallace, pushed his way into the courtroom and announced he was Selman's attorney. Blustering, Patterson objected that Brown was being asked leading questions and then said that he had issued a warrant for the arrest of John Selman.[3] It seems the attorney wanted the preliminary hearing transferred to Recorder Patterson's court.[4]

At this point John Selman left the courtroom and walked outside, where he was arrested by officer Chaudoin and taken to Judge Patterson's court at the city hall. There the Recorder took down as evidence the stories published by the *Times* on the day following Hardin's death. A copy of this edition no longer exists, and it is a good question how a court of law accepted a newspaper's version of the affair as evidence. The only explanation is that the newspaper had copied verbatim the statements of Judge Howe. Selman's bond was set at $10,-000.[5]

Howe was furious when everyone left his courtroom and went to Patterson's, but his anger was mild compared to the wrath he exhibited when he learned that John Selman was free on bond. Declaring bail to be illegal while a hearing was in progress, he instructed Sheriff Simmons to rearrest Selman. Simmons consulted his own attorney and was assured that John Selman could be legally jailed, but the lawyer advised against it on the grounds that "everybody knew Mr. Selman would never think of leaving the city." [6]

Full of indignation, Howe resumed calling witnesses and continued his investigation, even though the center of attraction was now being given a hearing in another court.

Shorty Anderson, a driver, testified that he, Selman, Hardin, Brown, Shackelford, Ed McDay and one or two other men were all together in the Acme at five minutes to eleven. He then left the group, picked up a drink at the bar and retired to the back room where he could see part, but not all, of the saloon. Selman and Shackelford had previously gone outside and the witness was idly watching John Wesley and Brown as they rolled dice when he saw the gunfighter, who had been leaning against the bar, straighten up. "I saw Hardin turn around and throw his hand on his hip—throw his coat back. Then I heard a pistol shot and he fell."

Other testimony was taken in Judge Howe's court, but unfortunately the transcripts are missing. R. B. Stevens, the proprietor of the Acme Saloon, was quoted by the *Herald* [7] as being in the back of the establishment where he could not see the actual shooting. He did, however, substantiate the story of Selman's drinking, the tales of trouble brewing between the two gunfighters, and Old John entering, then leaving the saloon before the fatal shots were fired. According to the witness, the bullet that passed through Hardin's head struck the big mirror frame which ran the length of the bar, glanced off and fell in front of the bar at the lower end.

Stevens' main complaint was that Hardin's body was blocking traffic inside his place of business, and after watching Police Captain Carr take two .41-caliber Colts off the body, he requested that the corpse be taken outside. Carr refused. He felt everyone had a right to see the body before the undertaker took charge.

On August 22 the *Herald* printed the testimony of Drs. G. S. Sherard, W. N. Vilas, and Alward White, who swore before Judge Howe that in their opinion the death bullet "entered near the base of the skull posteriorly and came out at the upper corner of the left eye."

In spite of Howe's attempts to exercise jurisdiction, Recorder Patterson still had the floor. On August 21 he called his crowded courtroom to order and asked County Attorney Storms to proceed with the investigation.

Storms, like Howe, had been thoroughly irked at the change in jurisdiction of the hearing. He stepped forward and announced that he was now only a spectator and did not wish to become involved.[8]

At this point Judge B. H. Davis and attorney Wyndham Kemp approached the bench and said their firm had been engaged to defend Selman.[9] Davis then took to the attack quickly. He railed at Storms, shouting that in all his forty years' experience before the bar he had never known a county attorney who refused to prosecute a case. Storms merely shrugged and leaned back in his chair. Judge Patterson then called the defense attorneys forward and after a short conference it was decided to dispense with the cross-examination and accept the testimony as written by Judge Howe.[10]

The hearing rolled merrily on with many El Paso citizens crowded inside the courtroom. The *Herald* noted that "The Recorder's Court was packed and the golden words of learned counsel were frequently punctuated by the cheerful splatter of tobacco juice on the bare floor, in sublime disregard of the cuspidores." [11]

Railroad man Frank McPherson took the stand and swore that Hardin had told him he was leaving El Paso soon

186

and he intended to kill John Selman before he left and "make young John break his neck running." According to McPherson the trouble started with the arrest of the Morose woman by policeman Selman.

After hearing McPherson's version of what Hardin had said previous to his death, attorney Davis told the court that the defense had another witness but saw no reason to take up any more time. He then requested that the hearing be closed and bail be reduced. The motions were granted and bond was reset at $1000. The only criticism came from John Selman, who grumbled that if Judge Buckler of the Thirty-fourth District Court had been on the bench, he would have released him on his own recognizance.[12]

At the following September, 1895, term of the District Court, the El Paso Grand Jury met, heard the evidence and wrote the following indictment. "John Selman . . . on or about the 19th day of August, 1895, in El Paso County did then and there unlawfully and with malice aforethought, kill John Wesley Hardin by shooting him, the said John Wesley Hardin, with a pistol." [13]

Selman was bound over to the Thirty-fourth District Court for trial and Judge Buckler set the bond at $5000. Trial was scheduled for the November term, but after a venire of a hundred jurymen had been called (and nearly as many witnesses) the case was continued until February, 1896, because of the State's inability to secure another witness.[14]

On February 5, 1896, the selection of a jury began[15] and when the trial commenced on the eighth, the indictment was read and John Selman answered in person that he was not guilty of murder.

The trial records do not contain any of the testimony which was given by the witnesses. Although subpoenas are stacked two inches thick in the file, it is probable that not all of those called to court actually testified. The records do not indicate that John Selman took the stand and the newspapers are silent on this point also.

The El Paso *Herald* practically ignored the trial. The *Times* gave adequate coverage to the first day's proceedings—then skipped over the rest of it.

According to the *Times,* E. Krause took the stand first to exhibit and explain a scale diagram showing the interior of the Acme Saloon.

Henry Brown testified substantially as he did before Justice Howe. Dr. S. G. Sherrard did likewise. The newspapers made no mention of Drs. White and Vilas at the trial.

The bartender, Frank Patterson, who was a witness for the prosecution, stuck pretty much to his original story, expanding it a little by admitting that Hardin and Brown had several disputes over the dice and asked him to referee. He also claimed that "Hardin was leaning with his left elbow on the counter when Selman entered the door and taking two or three steps forward . . . fired." Patterson said that he did not know where Hardin's right hand was when the shot was fired, but then reversed himself in the next sentence and said, "Hardin's hands were on the counter when the shot was fired."

Several other witnesses of minor importance (so the *Times* reported) were called and then the State rested its case.

Shorty Anderson was the first witness for the defense and he described how he was in another room and could not see Selman, but could view Hardin perfectly. Wes, according to Anderson, suddenly threw his right hand to his pistol and started to turn around an instant before he was shot.

Captain Carr, the night police captain, explained that he was the first to take hold of the dead man, "that Hardin's right hand was resting near the handle of his pistol, which had been partly drawn out, but was caught fast in the tight waistband of the dead man's trousers."

It remained for an obscure witness, Mr. J. A. Brock,[16] to

188

startle everyone. He testified that he "had examined Hardin's wound, and believed the ball had entered his eye and came out through the back of his head." Brock's expert qualifications for making this diagnosis were not established.

Brock was by no means the only one in town with this belief, although he is the only one recorded as having so testified. Actually a great many people thought the same thing, including a Mr. Burge who had photographed Hardin's body and sold pictures of it. The El Paso *Herald* commented that Burge had made numerous examinations of gunshot wounds and "he declares that Hardin was shot directly in the face and not in the back of the head." Burge gave as his reasons the fact that "if the bullet had entered the back of the head, it would have torn the eyeball and environment from its exit, whereas the bullet hole in the left eye is . . . clean and well defined." [17]

Selman himself repeatedly told the press and everyone he could get to listen (which was a great many), that he had looked Wesley Hardin in the eye and shot him there. The witnesses themselves were divided over how the shooting took place.

Unfortunately, no one ever rolled the body over and photographed it from the rear, but a front photo has been shown by the author of this book to numerous physicians, police officers and ballistic experts and they state positively and without exception that in their opinion the bullet holes as shown in the photographed body of John Wesley Hardin were entrances and not exits. A letter which represents quite clearly the opinions of the various experts was written by Mr. Fred R. Rymer, Supervisor, Firearms Section, Texas Department of Public Safety, Austin. Mr. Rymer understandably hedged a bit by saying that the photography of that period left a great deal to be desired; nevertheless: "I would say that the hole in the eye area and arm are entrance holes." He also felt that the chest wound was the result of a frontal shot, but due to the poor quality of the picture he could not be sure. Concentrating most of his remarks on the eye hole, Rymer felt that the photo indicated that the bullet was spinning as it entered, causing the area where it slipped through to be dark as the lead "wiped" the skin.

He also expressed doubt that the bullet could go completely through the skull if fired from behind: "There is also the question as to whether or not a .45 Colt bullet using black powder would penetrate the head—entering from the back and passing out the front—it is possible but I feel somewhat unlikely." [18]

All of this brings to a focus an issue of major importance. Heretofore, few have questioned the view that Hardin was shot in the back of the head. But now a considerable body of evidence and expert opinion indicates that John Wesley Hardin and John Selman were truly facing each other that night in the Acme Saloon—at least for one breathless second.

The last point of controversy is the part played by Albert Bacon Fall in the Selman murder trial. Many have scoffed at the story which claims he was present, but again the evidence departs from the view generally accepted and points conclusively to the fact that Fall was not only there but played an important part in the proceedings.

To begin with, both El Paso newspapers and the Las Cruces *Rio Grande Republican* cite numerous instances of Fall's visits to El Paso shortly before and after the trial, thus firmly establishing his presence in the area at that time.

Fall, a trial lawyer and politician, enjoyed a good reputation in his home town of Las Cruces, New Mexico (about forty miles north of El Paso), but he was little known among the average citizens of Texas and other parts of the nation. His appointment as Secretary of the Interior in President Harding's Cabinet and his date with disgrace during the Teapot Dome scandal were still years away. Also his two most famous murder cases—the 1899 trial of Oliver Lee at Hillsboro for the murder of Albert J. Fountain and his nine-year-old son[19] and the trial of Wayne Brazel at Las Cruces in 1908 for the killing of Pat Garrett—were still in the future.

Nevertheless, Mrs. C. C. Chase (A. B. Fall's daughter, now living in Alamogordo, New Mexico) has told in two separate interviews[20] how John Selman asked her father to represent him. It seems that Selman's attorneys had almost despaired of getting him to change his story about shooting Hardin in the eye. They told Old John repeatedly that the prosecution had Hardin's hat and with it they could prove that death struck the gunfighter from behind. Just how the State's lawyers hoped to do this has never been established, nor is there any evidence that the hat was ever introduced in court.

John Selman stood firm. Being familiar with Fall from his days of punching cattle in New Mexico, John suggested that the Las Cruces attorney be brought in to assist. So Fall was approached by one of Selman's lawyers who hoped that the young barrister could get the old gunman to change his story.

It took only one interview with Selman to convince A. B. Fall that John was telling the truth or what he believed to be the truth and that further efforts to change his mind would be useless. Fall then went to the Acme Saloon to reconstruct the shooting and there he developed a theory of what actually happened.

Old John, ever since the Bass Outlaw gun battle, had never been able to see perfectly even during daylight hours. After dark, according to his son, he was nearly blind. On the night of the slaying he had been drinking, perhaps heavily. Add to this a high degree of agitation, a dim saloon, a bar mirror, a deadly opponent, and the recipe is complete. It was Fall's opinion that if Selman did not shoot his man in the eye as he claimed, then he saw his reflection in the bar mirror and

191

for an instant thought he was staring directly into the face of his adversary.

The face in the barroom mirror is not, of course, as pat an argument as it may appear at the outset. A diagram of the old Acme Saloon is in existence, and if Hardin was standing against the bar near the front, where *most* witnesses indicate he was; and if Selman fired his pistol immediately after entering the front door, as *most* witnesses say that he did, then it would have been impossible for the two men to have seen each other in the mirror at this time. If Selman went several steps farther into the saloon, however, it would have been possible to view Hardin's reflection—and equally possible to have honestly thought he was standing gunbarrel to gunbarrel with his opponent.

Another hypothesis is that Hardin, looking into the mirror, was warned by the expression on another man's face farther down the bar. He may have then started reaching for his gun, turning around just in time to catch a bullet in the face. Evidence for this point of view can be somewhat substantiated by the fact that some witnesses claimed to have seen Hardin attempt to draw a weapon.

It undoubtedly mattered not to Fall how Hardin was killed, but he wanted to bet at least some of his chips on the face in the mirror. This, hopefully, would satisfy everyone and it had the added beauty of making Selman a more sympathetic defendant.

A. B. Fall's grandson, M. T. Everhart, of the Hachet Ranch in Hachita, New Mexico, remembers hearing his grandfather speak about the case. Mr. Fall told him that "he had wasted time saving Selman in the Hardin affair, as he had succeeded in getting himself killed anyway in fairly short order." [21]

The El Paso newspapers substantiate the statements of Mrs. Chase and Mr. Everhart, particularly about A. B. Fall's presence at the trial. On February 6, the El Paso *Times* reported "Davis, Beall and Kemp for the defense, assisted by Judge Fall." The El Paso *Herald* on the same day wrote "Messrs Davis, Beall and Kemp are defending Selman." Then on February 12, after the conclusion of the trial, the *Herald* noted that "In addressing the Selman jury, A. B. Fall, counsel for the defense, stated that for the past twenty years Texas juries had made law by declaring that when an officer or citizen killed a man like J. W. Hardin who sought a reputation for deluging the earth with gore, he should be acquitted."

The *Times* also made one other interesting comment which may have had something to do with the trial. On September 20, 1895, "Captain John Selman returned yesterday from Las Cruces." This remark came after the shooting of Hardin, but before the trial. It could be that Selman went to New Mexico to consult with Fall.

As the proceedings came to a close, Judge Buckler furnished the jury with an awesome set of instructions (a copy of which is still in the court records) on the basis of which the members were to find the defendant innocent or guilty. The charge occupies ten legal pages, much of it typewritten and single-spaced. It defines thirteen different types of murder with malice and describes the punishment therefor. It then explains several different aspects of second-degree murder and notes the punishment of each. The concluding pages are handwritten instructions covering justifiable homicide.[22]

The jury took the document of February 10 and on the 12th announced they were unable to reach a verdict. The judge polled the jury, decided it was truly hung, and rescheduled the case for the next term of court.[23]

The newspapers reported that the jury stood ten to two for acquittal.[24]

19

A HIGHER COURT

THE FUNERAL of John Wesley Hardin was not a large one. Only two carriages and two buggies followed the narrow, rutted road to Concordia Cemetery where he was placed one grave over from Martin Morose.[1]

As the procession filed past the squat adobe buildings of downtown El Paso, it passed John Selman standing on a street corner, his hat tilted back, hands folded across his chest. He, along with the others, was watching the mourners file by. John's light blue eyes never changed expression. A *Herald* reporter caught him standing there and during the interview Selman dwelt for a few minutes on the rumor that Hardin had sworn to have the lives of three men before he left town. Old John had no doubt that his name headed the select list.[2]

Then, straightening up from his slouching position, Selman said it had come to his certain knowledge that Hardin and "a number of pals had planned to make a descent on the State National Bank with Winchesters and six-shooters and get out of the country with the plunder before the local authorities could attack them." [3]

Although this story never received any wide circulation, another was soon going about everywhere. This was the rumor that someone was in town to kill the man with a big notch on his pistol. Newly arriving strangers were closely watched and the *Times* warned those who had a custom of carrying their hands in their hip pocket to abolish the habit at once. The papers even jokingly recommended that visitors send their photographs to the city in advance so the newspapers could give the matter publicity. [4]

Selman was accompanied by one or both of his sons [5] everywhere he went, especially at night. Young John writes that for a reason he cannot explain, he expected trouble from Mannen Clements, a cousin of Hardin's and a noted killer in his own right. [6] As an added precaution the boy cut the barrel of his father's forty-five off short, so Old John could carry the weapon in a rear pocket during his trial. [7]

On one occasion Constable Selman became so angry at a drunk patron in Billie Ritchie's restaurant, that startled customers expected blood to flow again. Evidently the man was upset over Hardin's slaying and was telling just how he felt about it. John, who was busily engaged eating hog's head and hominy, tried to ignore the situation but finally became so enraged that he arose, jerked the stranger around and challenged him to back up his words with bullets. This the man was not prepared to do. John then told the agitated fellow a few things about himself and his relatives. As an afterthought he pulled his own gun and gave the man a good smell of the barrel. The gentleman paid his bill and left hurriedly. [8]

But John had other problems besides people who wanted to kill him or merely criticize his actions in shooting Hardin. John Wesley's death brought him no peace of mind. Although he may possibly have desired the dubious distinction of killing

195

the West's most notorious gunman, he was poorly equipped to handle his fame. He had spent so much of his life trying to stay out of the limelight that now when the crown had passed to his head he did not know what to do with it. He was a champion, but one frightened by the roar of the crowd. He responded by glowering and drinking, and whisky soon became his master. Although up to now he had been known affectionately by nearly everyone as "Uncle John," his surly temper and argumentative nature made him the bane of El Paso. Only occasionally did some flashes of good humor peep through his gloomy exterior. Once, in a hurry to see a circus, he dashed into the Big Top just as the elephants began to parade around in a circle. John collided heavily with one of the big fellows, a pachyderm who was completely unimpressed with the old gunman's fearsome reputation. Selman suddenly found himself sprawled in the dirt looking up as the elephant, quite unconcerned, stared down at him. To his credit, Uncle John took it all good-naturedly enough;[9] amid the roar of the spectators he jumped up, laughed, dusted himself off and took a seat in the stands.[10]

Poker still interested Selman, and his son tells the story about how he, Judge Roy Bean, Pat Garrett, El Paso Judge Farrel and a man known only as Jim Sherman were playing for high stakes in the Ruby Saloon. Sherman, who was drunk, finally drew what looked like a good hand and he opened the pot with fifty dollars. This caused Selman and Garrett to drop out. The game then began in earnest. Judge Bean asked for one card. Judge Farrel said, "I will play these."

Sherman took two and passed. Bean bet fifty dollars more and Farrel called and raised fifty. This scared Sherman, who held three aces, and he decided to withdraw. The two master players now continued to raise each other until all their money was lying in the middle of the table.

When the cards were displayed, Judge Farrel had only a

196

bobtailed flush and Bean picked up the money with a grin. He flipped two trays out on the table.

The badly bluffed Jim Sherman, seeing all the money he was not destined to pocket, became so angry that he started breaking up saloon furniture. Constable Selman finally had to threaten him with jail if he didn't behave.[11]

In addition to participating in and policing poker games, Selman made life for confidence men such a burden that many familiar faces literally disappeared from the streets of El Paso.[12] He worked just as well drunk as he did sober and though he spent considerable time punishing the bottle, he managed to show up for duty even during the period of his trial. On August 24, less than a week after Hardin's death, he woke up the town with a booming barrage of gunfire. The *Times* explained that the constable had been killing a mad dog for a neighbor.

All the while something was happening to the old man's mind. He lost confidence in himself and seemed to feel that he must convince others of his bravery and his efficiency with a six-shooter. When drinking heavily, he would corner the nearest person and pathetically try to prove that he was really a great gunman. Selman was a daily visitor to the office of Lawyer Sweeney, where he made numerous demonstrations of how quick he was with a revolver. The attorney used to relate that Uncle John examined the cartridges every night, kept the gun carefully oiled, and lined his holster with chamois skin—to facilitate the fast draw.[13]

The event that was the beginning of the end occurred in the spring of 1896. On April 2, John Selman, Jr., was in trouble. The fifteen-year-old daughter of José Maria Ruiz, a prominent El Paso grocery owner, according to the boy, and the former Mexican consular official in El Paso, according to the newspapers, had informed the youthful policeman that her father had been appointed Mexican consular officer in San Salvador and was about to leave El Paso. So young John and the girl pedaled bicycles to Juarez, Mexico, and disappeared. Supposedly they intended to get married, but, unable to find someone to perform the ceremony, they retired to a hotel for the night.

It was not long before the girl's mother heard the news and solicited the assistance of the Juarez mayor to track the errant couple down. The mayor and two policemen immediately got on the trail. Sometime after midnight they located them and nearly beat down the door of the house where the two lovebirds were staying. Young John was promptly transported from the delights of a warm bed to the meager comforts of the Juarez jail. He was charged with abduction. By the next day the situation looked bad for the ex-police officer (Chief Fink fired the boy as soon as he learned of the incident) and some people were even predicting a five-year stay for the youth in the Chihuahua penitentiary.[13a]

On the afternoon of April 4, Old John Selman visited his son in jail. They talked for a while and when the elder Selman left, he remarked that he would get George Scarborough and return the next day. In spite of the fact that he and George had recently had their differences, particularly concerning the Morose money, Scarborough was the only one Old John felt that he could count on to help free his boy. However, the jail appointment was never kept. By the next day Uncle John lay mortally wounded—by bullets fired from the pistol of his friend George Scarborough.

On April 5, Easter Sunday, at nearly four o'clock in the morning, Old John Selman, blind drunk, accosted Deputy United States Marshal George Scarborough coming downstairs from the gambling room in the Wigwam Saloon. One of them wanted to speak to the other in private and so together they walked into the alley.

A few minutes later four gunshots lit up the early-

198

morning darkness and when curious citizens rushed to the scene, they found George Scarborough with a smoking pistol in his hand. John Selman was down, moaning in agony, eyes glazed, struggling to rise. He had been shot four times; he had a flesh wound in the back of the neck which ran from left to right; a flesh wound in the right hip; a serious wound in the side which paralyzed him from the waist down; and a bullet hole in the left knee, the slug having gone completely through the leg. Selman's revolver was missing.

Old John was in such pain that he could not make a coherent statement. The newspapers did quote him as gasping, "Boys, you know I am not afraid of any man; but I never drew my gun." [14]

By this time Dr. White had rushed to the scene and at first could find only the neck wound. He then put the wounded man on a stretcher and sent him home to Sonora Street, where a more thorough examination could be made. [15]

George Scarborough was taken to jail. Justice Howe set bond for $500 and took a statement, which has since disappeared. The El Paso *Times* and *Herald* published confusing and contradictory versions of the story, which in substance claimed that Selman met Scarborough at the foot of the Wigwam stairs and invited him into the alley. There John fidgeted with his gun and asked the marshal to go with him to Juarez in the morning and help get his son out of jail. Scarborough agreed to go and then Selman wanted to buy him a drink, an offer which was declined. George, making reference to an offense Selman's second son Bud had recently committed in Juarez, said, "There must be no more plays like [that] . . . as they do harm."

Selman then snarled, "You damn son of a bitch, I think I will kill you."

The marshal, still talking for the benefit of Judge Howe and the newspaper reporters, said, "I grabbed my .45 [and] tried to shoot him through the head. . . . He fell with the first shot and got up and I fired three more shots. . . ."[16]

John Graham, a resident of Doña Ana County, New Mexico, and the only one close to being an actual eyewitness, testified before Judge Howe that he, Selman and Scarborough had been drinking earlier in the Wigwam Saloon and Uncle John had been telling them about a Mexican whom he had struck over the head with his cane because the man had "given him some slack." The talk among the three men had been friendly. Later Selman left the saloon and returned in a few hours to meet the same two men. This time as both lawmen walked into the alley, Graham turned and was starting down the street when he heard someone scream, "Don't try to kill me like that." Graham was unable to identify the voice, and the shout was immediately followed by four shots.[17]

John Selman's condition continued to worsen during the day. The following morning, April 6, Dr. White turned his patient over to Dr. Thompson, who, along with Drs. Turner and Dooley, made the decision to transfer the suffering man to Sisters Hospital and probe for the bullet which was pressing on his spine. The operation was successful and the slug was removed, but the patient died. The *Times* remarked that just as Selman's bullet had transferred Hardin's case to a higher court, so now his own was pending there also.[18]

On April 11, 1896, George Scarborough resigned as Deputy United States Marshal and on June 19 he went on trial in Thirty-fourth District Court for murder.[19]

Once again court records give only scant details about the trial itself. The newspapers quote Scarborough as saying that Selman threatened to kill him because he (Scarborough) would not take a drink with him, and not because of remarks allegedly made by him about young John's imprisonment in Juarez. George told of "a previous quarrel he had with Selman

200

over a game of cards and that he had been warned by Sheriff Simmons, Chief Fink, and Captain J. D. Milton that Selman would kill him." [20]

Jim Burns, the man whom Selman had stood by when the city took steps to close his Red Light dance hall, was the only person recorded by the newspapers as rising to John Selman's defense. He told how he had called on his friend at eight o'clock on the morning after the shooting. John told him he was dying and Jim asked how it happened. "George Scarborough came downstairs [from the Wigwam] and we spoke friendly together," Selman groaned, according to Burns. "He put his arm around my neck and said 'Uncle John, I want to see you'; and he led me out to the alley and before I knew [it] he had shot me in the neck and I fell. I said, 'My God, George, do you intend to kill me this way.' I reached for my pistol but didn't have it. . . ." [21]

The missing pistol turned up in the hands of a young tough named Cole Belmont, *alias* Kid, *alias* Kid Clark. When he began boasting in Pecos, Texas, that he had the Selman gun, the local authorities placed him under arrest and he was brought back to El Paso. There, Bud Selman positively identified the revolver as belonging to his father. [22]

Belmont testified at Scarborough's trial that he had been employed as a bouncer at the Bonanza dance hall in El Paso, but was in the Wigwam watching the antics of a drunken woman when the shots were fired which killed Selman. He immediately ran outside to where Old John was lying and his foot struck something which turned out to be the victim's pistol, fully loaded and cocked. He took the gun and left town. [23]

After Belmont's testimony, the case went to the jury. It took them only a few minutes to pronounce the defendant, George Scarborough, not guilty of murder.

Belmont was then charged with theft of property under

the value of fifty dollars and tried in the El Paso County Court of Law. He pleaded innocent, but was found guilty and sentenced to sixty days in jail.[24]

With the exception of Jim Burns, no one stepped forward during the trial to hint that George Scarborough might actually have been guilty of murder. It appears that justice was not only blind—but bound and gagged. There was plenty of evidence if anyone had wanted to present it.

Probably the most damning evidence of deliberate murder was the order of the shots and in particular the angle of the first one. Everyone, including the doctor, John Selman and George Scarborough agreed that the first shot had been in the neck. Police Captain Carr was quoted by the *Times* on April 5 as saying the wound was in the back of the neck. Dr. White said the wound was in the back of the neck, leaving a slash from left to right.[25] If these allegations are correct, and there is no evidence to prove otherwise, then the only way John could have received that first bullet was to have had his back to Scarborough or turned sideways to him with more of his back exposed than the front. The first shot, grazing the rear of his neck, could not possibly have been fired while John was facing the marshal. And if the two men were not facing each other, this was certainly a peculiar position for an old experienced gunfighter like Selman to be caught in, especially when he was allegedly threatening to kill a man.

Furthermore, John Graham, who testified at the inquest before Justice Howe, heard someone say before the shots rang out, "Don't try to kill me like that." Selman afterward claimed to have said words to this effect and no one ever disputed him. It seems likely that a man saying these words would be the victim and not the killer.

A study of the known facts and circumstances—and at this late date, admittedly, the whole truth will never be known

202

—suggests that George Scarborough deliberately murdered John Selman. The question remains: *Why?*

George Look may have the answer. Continuing his version of the Hardin killing, Look says that after the death of John Wesley, Selman made some talk around town about how Scarborough and Hardin had split the Morose money. For this Scarborough called Selman into an alley and killed him.[26]

After the trial George Scarborough went to New Mexico and began working as a detective for a cattle raisers' association. Somehow he got involved in a chase after train robbers and he and another man named Birchfield were fired upon by what was probably a remnant of the Butch Cassidy gang. The weather was bitter cold on April 5, 1900, when he and Birchfield entered a canyon in eastern Arizona in close pursuit of the bandits. A few minutes later a .30-40 bullet slammed into his leg, driving on through and killing his horse. Night came. Birchfield rode to San Simon for a wagon. Scarborough was carried to the railroad and taken to Deming, New Mexico, where his leg was amputated. He died either on the operating table or shortly afterward. The date was April 6, 1900, exactly four years to the day after John Selman died in El Paso.

John Selman, Jr., a few days after his father's death, broke out of the Juarez jail. He returned to El Paso, but the town was not the same. His father was dead, and the girl he planned to marry had been sent away. He never saw her again. He too left El Paso within weeks.

The whole town turned out for John Selman's funeral.[27] He was laid to rest by the Catholic Church in Concordia Cemetery on April 8, 1896, probably near the graves of Bass Outlaw, Martin Morose and John Wesley Hardin. Trotting behind the hearse came John's horse—an empty saddle on its back— empty boots tied to the pommel.[28]

EPILOGUE

JOHN SELMAN lacked the qualities which make legends. Unlike Hardin he never created his own press, and unlike Billy the Kid and others he never had admirers dedicated enough to do it for him. He always seemed somewhere in the middle, a step short of fame and a step shy of oblivion. Almost any book dealing with Western hardcases will mention his name—the irony is that it is nearly always misspelled.

Selman's name is big enough to stand alone in the annals of the West, but for some reason his name has always been tied in with Hardin's, thus automatically relegating him to a secondary position. He has been treated like a poor relation in the family of Western gunfighters—sometimes even placed in the same class with John McCall and Bob Ford.*

It was his misfortune that he grew old. Nearly all the well known *pistoleros* were dead by the time they reached middle age, but Old John was just beginning to hit his stride. His age should have been a tribute to his effectiveness as a gunfighter

* John McCall killed Wild Bill Hickok. Bob Ford shot Jesse James.

and of course it did make him unique, but it added nothing to his fame. An old gunman is embarrassing to have around; people try to ignore him.

Nevertheless, John Selman was the last of the old-time gunfighters. With his passing, none of any stature was left. This fact, if he had known it, might have brightened his final months, but men of his type do not philosophize about their situations or wonder about their place in history. They live for the moment and die the same way.

John Selman would be astonished and incredulous if he could know that he helped to write the history of a transitional era when the old lawless ways were being swept out and new ways were being ushered in. He had no intention of attracting anybody's notice. Publicity was bad for his business. And until his very last years he covered his tracks so well that even now we can't be completely sure of all that he did or exactly what kind of man he was.

Perhaps that is why no tombstone marks his grave today. Nobody knows just what to put on it.

NOTES

CHAPTER 1

1. John Selman's last name has been spelled at least five different ways (Silliaman, Sillman, Silman, Sellman and Selman). He himself signed his name Selman.

2. File designation, John Selman, Co. B, 22 Texas Cavalry, CSA—General Services Administration, National Archives and Records Service, Washington, D.C.

3. John Selman, Jr., "John Selman," *All Western Magazine*, Oct. 1935, p. 45; Edna Selman Haines to LCM, Dec. 13, 1963.

4. Census, 1840, Madison County, Ark. This gave the age and sex of children but not names.

5. Mrs. R. C. Hardie to LCM, May 26, 1964 (Mrs. Hardie is the daughter of John Selman's sister Lucinda).

6. Jeremiah Selman's English nationality on authority of Mrs. Hardie; 1840 census did not show place of birth.

7. Mrs. R. C. Hardie to LCM, Mar. 19, 1964.

8. Ruins of Ft. Washita lie in Bryan Co., Okla, a few miles east of Lake Texoma.

9. Mrs. Manon B. Atkins (Librarian, Research Lib., Okla. Historical Society, Okla. City) to LCM, Apr. 13, 1964.

10. The horse was valued at $125, the rigging at $25.

11. W. R. Cruger to John B. Jones, July 2, 1880, Adj. Gen.'s File, Texas State Lib., Austin. Hereafter cited AGF.

12. The 22nd Regiment, Texas Cavalry, was organized Jan. 16, 1862, and reorganized June 30, 1862, with ten companies, A to K. It was known at various times as the 1st Indian Regiment, Texas Cavalry; Merrick's Regiment, Texas Dismounted Cavalry; Taylor's Regiment, Texas Cavalry; Taylor's Regiment, Texas Mounted Rifles; Stevens' Regiment, Texas Cavalry; Stone's Battalion, Texas Cavalry; and Merrick's Battalion, Texas Infantry or Dismounted Cavalry.

CHAPTER 2

1. This should not be confused with the present Fort Davis, located in the Davis Mts. of west Texas.

2. Shackelford Co. was not organized until 1874.

3. Ben O. Grant, *Early History of Shackelford County,* master's thesis 1936, Hardin-Simmons U. Lib., Abilene, Texas; 29-30.

4. John Selman, Jr., *John Selman of El Paso,* typed MS. in possession of Edna Selman Haines, California. Hereafter cited *John Selman of El Paso.*

5. Northern officers were George H. Thomas, I. N. Palmer, George Stoneman and K. Garrard. Confederates: Lee, W. L. Hardee, Earl Van Horn, E. Kirby Smith and John B. Hood. Carl Coke Rister, *Fort Griffin on the Texas Frontier,* U. of Okla. Press, Norman, 1956; p. 32. Hereafter cited Rister.

6. *Ibid.,* 20-32.

7. *Ibid.,* 30-31.

8. Ben O. Grant, "Early Hist. . . ." (See note 3, *supra*), 29-30.

9. The lower fort was probably either Ft. Hubbard or Ft. Owl Head. Interview with Mrs. Joan Farmer, Sec., Shackelford Co. Hist. Survey Com., Albany, Tex., May 12, 1964.

10. Both Samuel Newcomb and his wife, Susan E. Newcomb, kept diaries. MS. secured and typed under supervision of J. Evetts Haley, El Paso, 1936. Copy in possession of Robert Nail, Albany, Tex.

11. Newcomb's musings proved prophetic for himself: he died of the German measles a few years later.

12. Sam Newcomb, 50-51.

13. *Ibid.,* 19.
14. *Ibid.,* 26.
15. Mrs. L. E. Farmer, "Fort Davis on the Clear Fork of the Brazos," *West Texas Hist. Ass'n Yearbook,* XXXIII (Oct. 1957), 117-126.
16. Sam Newcomb, 26; *Rister,* 46.
17. The Rev. Mr. Slaughter did stop when his infant son was accidentally shot with a pistol; the wound did not prove fatal but Slaughter turned to other pursuits, and became a prosperious rancher.
18. Susan Newcomb, 39.
19. Mrs. Hardie to LCM, Mar. 19, 1964.
20. *Ibid.* Lucinda, a few years later, married Owen Donnelly at Ft. Griffin.
21. Susan Newcomb, 40.

CHAPTER 3

1. Men could avoid conscription by holding public office, overseeing slaves, or hiring a substitute. Rupert N. Richardson, *Frontiers of Northwest Texas, 1846-1876,* The Arthur H. Clarke Co., Glendale, 1963; p. 243. Hereafter cited Richardson.
2. Sam Newcomb, 93.
3. *Ibid.,* 8.
4. *Ibid.,* 23.
5. *Ibid.,* 13. Newcomb's fears were unfounded: no serious Indian attack was made on the fort, and the Jayhawkers apparently had enough action to satisfy them in Kansas and Missouri.
6. Thomas P. deGraffenreid, *History of the deGraffenreid Family, 1191-1925,* Vail-Ballou Press, N.Y., 1925. Jasper received some mention in this but Edna was overlooked.
7. Census Records, Colfax Co., N.M., 1870.
8. Susan Newcomb, 63.
9. Sallie Reynolds Matthews, *Interwoven,* Texas Western College Press, El Paso, 1958; 40.
10. Interview with Mrs. Joan Farmer, May 12, 1964. Also see Joan Farmer, "Sandstone Sentinels," *West Texas Hist. Ass'n Yearbook,* XXXIV (Oct. 1958), 112-127.
11. Thomas P. deGranffenreid, *op. cit.,* 155-156. The author makes no mention of John Selman and family on this trip; however, the deGraf-

fenreids and Selmans were related, lived together in Texas, and showed up together at the same time in New Mexico, so it is safe to assume they made the journey together.

CHAPTER 4

1. Throckmorton Co. was not actually organized till 1879.
2. Matthews, *op. cit.*, 139-141.
3. *John Selman of El Paso*, Chap. 1, 4.
4. Rister, 65-67.
5. *Ibid.*, 84. Satanta was released in 1873 but soon was taken back into custody for violating parole. He then committed suicide.
6. *John Selman of El Paso*, Chap. 2, 4-5.
7. *Ibid.*
8. J. R. Webb, "Chapters from the Frontier Life of Phin W. Reynolds," *West Texas Hist. Ass'n Yearbook*, XXX (Oct. 1945), 112; *Richardson*, 133; *John Selman of El Paso*, Chap. 1, 4-6.
9. Matthews, *op. cit.*, 141, 142, 149. Describing the house as it was after she and her husband moved into it, Mrs. Matthews comments that one of the support posts bore panther's teeth marks. She makes no mention of the Selmans. The house was blown down by a tornado in 1903.
10. A *comanchero* was any Mexican or American who traded, lived and intermarried with the Comanches.
11. Rister, 154. Rister refers to the members of the mob as "Low Boys" and indicates they and the Vigilantes were one and the same group.
12. Matthews, *op. cit.*, 136-138.
13. Grant, "Early Hist. . . ." (See note 3, chap. 2), 86.

CHAPTER 5

1. C. L. Sonnichsen, *I'll Die Before I'll Run*, Devin-Adair, N.Y., 1962; 150. Hereafter cited Sonnichsen.
2. Rister, 125-129.
3. J. R. Webb, "Henry Herron, Pioneer and Peace Officer," *West Texas Hist. Ass'n Yearbook*, XX (Oct. 1944); 23.

4. Ben O. Grant, "Life in Old Fort Griffin," *West Texas Hist. Ass'n Yearbook,* X (Oct. 1934); 41.

5. The term "flint hide" derived from the flintlike hardness of the cured buffalo hides.

6. Rister, 192-193.

7. Harry Sinclair Drago, *Great American Cattle Trails,* Dodd, Mead, N.Y., 1965, 193.

8. Grant, "Early Hist. . . ." (See note 3, chap. 2), 83-84.

9. *Ibid.*

10. Many people in Shackelford Co. do not think the man's name was actually John Larn. Some have slurred the surname in speech, rendering it as "Loren" or "Laren." Interview with Watt Matthews, May 12, 1964; Robert Nail to LCM, Jan. 8, 1964. Shackelford County court documents and other official records spell the name Larn.

11. Henry Griswold Comstock, *Some of My Experiences and Observations on the Southwestern Plains During the Summers of 1871 and 1872,* unpub'd typeset work, copy in possession of LCM. Hereafter cited Comstock.

12. Comstock, 3.

13. Walter Prescott Webb, *The Texas Rangers,* Houghton Mifflin Co., N.Y. and Boston, 1935; 322.

14. Comstock is the only source of information about this drive. He reports that Larn killed three Mexicans on two different occasions. Two of the bodies were thrown into the Pecos "to feed the catfish." The trail drivers were embroiled in many arguments and brawls and one fatal shoot-out. "Stray" cattle were picked up along the way and one of Larn's crew stole a horse before he left Griffin. When near the Pacos, the herd was overhauled by twelve Negro cavalrymen from Ft. Concho, with the evident intention of taking the herd back to the fort for tallying. Larn led the soldiers into a trap and threatened to kill them all. They decided to forget it and returned to their post.

15. P. W. Reynolds to J. R. Webb, 1945; Newton J. Jones to J. R. Webb, Mar. 15, 1947. John C. Irvin to J. R. Webb, 1934. Among other items that deal with Shackelford Co., these are part of the Webb Papers in the R. N. Richardson Collection, Hardin-Simmons U. Lib., Abilene, Texas, Mrs. Mabel B. Willoughby, Director; hereafter cited Webb Papers. Also see Comstock, 5.

16. Only one man escaped the massacre: Charlie Wilson, who had stayed behind with his new bride and intended to catch up the next

day. The killings were over before he left but his wife figured he still was in danger. She buckled on a six-shooter and rode in to see Lt. Turner at the fort, warned him that if anyone touched her Charlie she would kill him, then drew her pistol, fired it in the air and cantered away. No one bothered Charlie. Comstock, 5.

17. The book *Interwoven* was so named by Sallie Reynolds Matthews because of the intertwining of the Reynolds and Matthews families; it gives an interesting and valuable account of the area and the times.

18. The author of a never-completed MS titled "Once Only," a lady with an active imagination, lived at the Camp Cooper ranch after Larn's death. She claimed to have found secret places in the house where Larn lucked with dirks and bowie knives; skeletons were dug up in the yard; she accused Larn of poisoning one of his infant children; she saw Larn's ghost everywhere.

19. Alias Capias to Presidio and El Paso counties, J. R. Fleming, county judge, to Jack ―――― (last name not recorded), May 20, 1879. Shackelford Co. Clerk's Office, Albany, Tex.

20. Amos Quitter was a young cowboy who went north on a cattle drive and drowned while fording a stream. The Ft. Griffin *Echo* noted: "A large number of his relatives reside in Fort Griffin and vicinity and we can only wish that the whole family had gone to Kansas with the cowboy and been whizzed into eternity by the raging waters of the Arkansas." Random notes from Webb Papers.

CHAPTER 6

1. Sonnichsen, 155.
2. Don Biggers, *Shackelford County Sketches*, Albany News office, 1908; 35. Hereafter cited Biggers. For some reason Biggers mentioned names charily but usually left no doubt of whom he was referring to.
3. Caruthers to Jones, June 28, 1880, AGF.
4. Undated, unsigned paper in AGF. Identical note in Webb Papers identifies John Selman as the writer.
5. Mrs. Joan Farmer and Mrs. Watt Matthews, interview with LCM, May 12, 1964. There is no mention of a George Matthews in *Interwoven* or in the *Pictorial Supplement to Interwoven*, Albany, Tex., 1908.

6. Memoirs of Skelton Glenn, typewritten, n.d. Copy courtesy of Mr. Rod Moss, Lawrence, Kas.

7. *John Selman of El Paso,* Chap. 2, 7.

8. Biggers, 36.

9. Bond Record Book, 78. Shackelford Co. Court House, Albany, Tex.

10. *Ibid.,* 56.

11. J. R. Webb, "Henry Herron . . ." (see note 3, Chap. V.), 23; Edgar Rye, *The Quirt and the Spur,* B. N. Conkey Co., Chicago, 1909, 100 (hereafter cited Rye).

12. Skelton Glenn said it was the Matthews ranch.

13. Rister, 156. The note is an example of the grim humor of the vigilantes. Other notices designed for undesirables were posted around town; one read "The presence of Long Kate, Big Billy, Ellen Gentry, Minnie Gray, and Sally Watson, prostitutes; and Pony Spencer and Tom Riley, general rustlers, have overstayed their welcome in Griffin." Skull, crossbones and black hand added a macabre touch.

14. Skelton Glenn MS.

15. Edgar Rye was a justice of the peace in Albany during this time so was in a position to know whether John Selman actually was a deputy or not.

16. Skelton Glenn MS.

17. W. H. ("Bill") Selman to LCM, Jan. 21, 1964.

18. *Ibid.,* June 6, 1964. Mr. Selman is a treasure hunter by hobby and has more than a passing interest in the money.

19. Rye, 104-105; Ed Bartholomew, *Kill or Be Killed,* Frontier Press, Houston, 1953; 75-76.

20. Biggers, 35.

21. J. Evetts Haley to LCM, Feb. 8, 1965. Haley interviewed John Meadows in 1935 and obtained this story.

22. Deed Record Book, Vol. C, 2-3, County Clerk's office, Albany, Tex.

23. Milus McComb, interview with LCM, June 25, 1964.

24. Deed Record Book, Vol. C, 514.

25. Minutes 34th District Court, Albany, Tex., Book A.

26. *Ibid.*

27. Frontier *Echo,* Apr. 28, 1876; Sonnichsen, 155.

28. Frontier *Echo,* Apr. 18, June 16, 1876.

29. *Ibid.,* June 9, 1876; Austin *Weekly Statesman,* June 22, 1876.

30. Grant, "Early Hist. . . ." (See note 3, chap. 2), 89.

31. Skelton Glenn MS.

32. The governor was also referring to the recent hangings in Springtown, Parker County. "The home of a certain widow was said to be a place of prostitution and gathering of horse thieves. Some warning was received by the widow and the oldest daughter, fearing mob action, fled. She was pursued by a mob, caught fifty miles away and hanged. A few days later the mob took two sisters from the house and hanged them. A few days later they burned the home, overtook the fleeing mother and two daughters and hanged them. Six women hanged in just a few days." Ben O. Grant, "Citizen Law Enforcement Bodies, The Vigilantes," *West Texas Hist. Ass'n Yearbook*, XXXIX (Oct. 1963), 157-158.

33. See also Galveston *News*, Dec. 12, 1876.

CHAPTER 7

1. *John Selman of El Paso*, Chap. 2, 3.

2. John Selman, Jr., claimed both men used the same brand—the Four of Clubs. The Shackelford County records, however, show that Larn used an H.A.H. brand and an ear notch. John Selman registered only an ear notch, different from Larn's. Brand Book, 3, 4, 7.

3. Galveston *News*, July 13, 1878.

4. *Ibid.*

5. Edgar Rye was probably the most credible authority who claimed that Larn and Selman were good lawmen at one time and went bad later. See Rye, 104.

6. Newton J. Jones to J. R. Webb, Mar. 15, 1947, Webb Papers.

7. *Ibid.* J. R. Webb, "Chapters from the Frontier Life of Phin W. Reynolds," *West Texas Hist. Ass'n Year Book*, XXI (Oct. 1945), 127. Rister, 151-153. Jones also told Webb that several years later Reed killed a man named Dumas in a saloon in Ogalala, Neb., and was hanged by a mob.

8. Minutes of Commissioners Court, Albany, Tex., Vol. 1, 67, 112.

9. Mrs. Clark, interview with C. L. Sonnichsen, June 6, 1944.

10. Newton J. Jones to J. R. Webb, Mar. 15, 1947, Webb Papers.

11. *Ibid.*

12. Records of Official Bonds, Book B, 54-63.

13. Mrs. Ed Brewster, interview with LCM, June 25, 1964. Mrs. Brewster is secretary to the Sheriff of Shackelford Co.

14. J. Evetts Haley to LCM, Feb. 8, 1965.

15. Minutes 34th District Court, Albany, Tex., Book A, No. 24, p. 97.

CHAPTER 8

1. Newton J. Jones to J. R. Webb, Webb Papers. Jones indicated that Arrington had resigned but W. P. Webb (*The Texas Rangers*, 412-413) says he was transferred to the Panhandle to fight an Indian uprising.

2. John C. Irvin to J. R. Webb, 1934, Webb Papers. There is no evidence that Sheriff Cruger was with the posse.

3. Newton J. Jones to J. R. Webb, Mar. 15, 1947, Webb Papers.

4. John C. Irvin to J. R. Webb, 1934, Webb Papers.

5. Lt. G. W. Campbell to Maj. John B. Jones, Feb. 26, 1878, AGF.

6. Fred Smalley, interview with LCM, May 10, 1964. Smalley is a former resident of Albany, Tex.

7. Newton J. Jones to J. R. Webb, Mar. 15, 1947, Webb Papers.

8. Lt. G. W. Campbell to Maj. John B. Jones, Feb. 26, 1878, AGF; Galveston *News*, July 13, 1878.

9. Campbell to Jones, June 16, 1878, Walter Prescott Webb Ranger Reports, Library Archives, Texas, U. of Austin. Hereafter cited U. of Tex. Archives.

10. Harry Sinclair Drago, *op. cit.*, 165-168.

11. Campbell to Jones, Apr. 3, 1878, U. of Tex. Archives.

12. Skelton Glenn MS.

13. Letters were frequently opened and the juicier bits of information posted for all to chuckle at. See Van Riper to Jones, June 15, 1878, U. of Tex. Archives.

14. J. R. Fleming to Gov. R. B. Hubbard, May 1, 1878, U. of Tex. Archives.

15. Gen. Steele was Adjutant in command of Ranger forces in Texas.

16. Maj. John B. Jones to Gen. William Steele, May 20, 1878, U. of Tex. Archives. The original letter to Campbell has been lost; a copy was sent to Steele.

17. Campbell to Jones, June 16, 1878, U. of Tex. Archives. Campbell had to plead with Jones to correct the rumors.

18. *Ibid.*

CHAPTER 9

1. Campbell to Jones, June 16, 1878; Van Riper to Jones, June 15, 1878; U. of Tex. Archives.
2. Many of the stone fences around Selman's and Larn's ranches are still standing and in good condition.
3. Galveston *News,* July 13, 1878.
4. Van Riper to Jones, June 15, 1878, U. of Tex. Archives.
5. *John Selman of El Paso,* Chap. 2, 10.
6. Galveston *News,* July 13, 1878.
7. Newton J. Jones to J. R. Webb, Mar. 15, 1947, Webb Papers.
8. Rye, 107.
9. Dave Richards, interview with Mrs. Joan Farmer and LCM, May 13, 1964. Treadwell was Richards' grandfather.
10. Skelton Glenn MS.
11. John Selman, Jr., tells a slightly different version: John Selman had gone to Weatherford to sell a wagonload of buffalo hides and was returning two weeks later when he met a messenger 20 miles out of Ft. Griffin; upon hearing the news he took the messenger's horse and rode for Larn's ranch. *John Selman of El Paso,* Chap. 3, 2-3.
12. Robert Nail to LCM, Jan. 8, 1964. Mr. Nail is Chairman of the Shackelford Co. Hist. Survey Committee.
13. George Reynolds and John Larn both married daughters of Joe Matthews. Ben Reynolds married a niece of Joseph Beck Matthews. Thomas Lindsay Blanton, *Pictorial Supplement to Interwoven,* John H. McGaughey's Albany News, Albany, 1953; 1-6.
14. P. W. Reynolds to J. R. Webb, 1944-45, Webb Papers; Newton J. Jones to Webb, Mar. 15, 1947. Webb Papers.
15 Reynolds and Hawsley both had married Matthews girls. Blanton, *op. cit.,* 3.
16. P. W. Reynolds to J. R. Webb, 1944-45, Webb Papers.
17. Rye, 108.
18. Newton J. Jones to Webb, Mar. 15, 1947, Webb Papers.
19. *Ibid.*
20. Galveston *News,* July 13, 1878.
21. J. R. Webb, "Henry Herron . . ." (see Note 3, Chap. V), 32.
22. John Poe went on to achieve fame by being with Pat Garrett when Garrett killed Billy the Kid.

23. Mollie W. Godbold, "Comanche and the Hardin Gang," *Southwest Hist. Rev.*, LXVII (Oct. 1963), 247-277.

24. P. W. Reynolds to J. R. Webb, 1945, Webb Papers ("Bill Hawsley told me there was nine men in the bunch that killed Larn and he was one of them. He said the leader was a tall man and I said, 'I guess he was Tom Merrill who worked for the Horseshoes on the Double Mountain Fork.' He said, 'No, it was not him,' and left the impression it was one of my brothers.").

25. Mrs. Larn later remarried and had several children. Will Larn, John's only son except the one who died in infancy, became a wheelchair invalid in his youth and died at an early age; he never married. Watt Matthews, interview with LCM, May 13, 1964.

CHAPTER 10

1. Rye, 112.
2. P. W. Reynolds to J. R. Webb, 1945; Newton J. Jones to J. R. Webb, Mar. 15, 1947—both Webb Papers; Robert Nail to LCM, Jan. 1, 1964.
3. Newton J. Jones to J. R. Webb, Mar. 15, 1947, Webb Papers.
4. Case Nos. 138, 140, 141, 142, 143, 144, 145, 147, 148; 34th District Court, Albany, Tex.
5. Case Nos. 145, 148, 149.
6. J. R. Fleming was a county judge in Albany; who "Jack" was is unknown.
7. *John Selman of El Paso*, Chap. 3, 5-7.
8. *Ibid.;* Charles Siringo, *Riata and Spurs*, rev. ed., Houghton Mifflin Co., Boston, 1931, 171-174.
9. Skelton Glenn MS. Glenn has the incident happening in 1879 but it actually took place in 1878. R. N. Mullin has put everything in its proper order; see "Robert Mullin, Noted Authority of Period, Gives His Version of Selman's Early Life," *The Southwesterner*, Vol. III (June 1964), 3. Hereafter cited as Mullin.

CHAPTER 11

1. Robert N. Mullin was a close friend of the late Maurice Garland Fulton, had access to his papers and has been commissioned to complete Fulton's unfinished *History of Lincoln County*.

2. George Coe, *Frontier Fighter*, U. of N. M. Press, Albuquerque, 1934, 106-107.

3. *Ibid.*

4. R. N. Mullin to LCM, Sept. 15, 1964.

5. Philip J. Rasch and Lee Myers, "The Tragedy of the Beckwiths," The English Westerners' *Brand Book*, V (July 1963), 4-5.

6. Mullin, 3.

7. *Ibid.*

8. This letter, believed to have been written in March 1879, describes some of the territory and hiding places for stolen cattle. Lew Wallace Collection, William Henry Smith Memorial Library, Indianapolis, Ind. Hereafter cited Lew Wallace Collection.

9. Mullin, 3.

10. *Ibid.;* Lew Wallace to Capt. Carroll, Mar. 12, 1879, Lew Wallace Collection.

11. Col. Dudley to Asst. Adt. Gen. of New Mexico, Sept. 29, 1878, National Archives.

12. Sanchez led the Mounted Rifles in a hot but futile pursuit of Jesse Evans after Evans broke prison at Ft. Stanton in March 1879.

13. Col. Dudley to Asst. Adt. Gen. of N.M, Sept. 28-29, National Archives; Mullin, 5

14. Mullin, 5.

15. Col. Dudley (see Note 13).

16. Mullin, 5.

17. Mullin to LCM, Dec. 4, 1963. Mullin says Gildea used the name "Selman Scouts" in a letter he wrote to Col. Fulton.

18. Col. Dudley (see Note 11).

19. *Ibid.*

20. *Ibid.*

21. *Ibid.*

22. Mullin, 5.

23. Lew Wallace, *Statements by Kid Made Saturday Night, March 23, 1879,* Lew Wallace Collection.

24. Mullin, 5.

25. *Ibid.*

26. Unsigned, incomplete letter in Lew Wallace Collection (Mar. 1879?).

27. Mrs. Eve Ball, Hollywood, N.M., interview with LCM, Oct. 20, 1964.

28. Lew Wallace, *Statements by Kid* . . . , Lew Wallace Collection.

218

29. William A. Keleher, *Violence in Lincoln County, 1869-1881*, U. of N. M. Press, Albuquerque, 1957, 162-182. Also see Philip J. Rasch, "Exit Axtell, Enter Wallace," *N. M. Hist. Rev.*, XXXII (July 1957), 231-245.

30. Keleher, *op. cit.*, 183-203.

31. Lew Wallace to Captain Carroll, Mar. 11-12, 1879, Lew Wallace Collection.

32. This edition has been lost or destroyed; the only reference to it is in the editorial printed in the Mesilla *Independent*.

33. Mesilla *Independent*, May 24, 1879.

34. Moses Wiley (County Attorney of Wheeler Co., Tex.) to Maj. John B. Jones, July 1, 1879, U. of Tex. Archives.

35. *Ibid.*

36. Mullin to LCM, July 16, 1964, Keleher, *op. cit.*, 228.

37. Keleher, *op. cit.*, 232; Frazier Hunt, *The Tragic Days of Billy the Kid*, Hastings House, N.Y., 1956, 91-94. Hunt says Long experienced heavy rifle fire after he left the McSween house and had to dive into a privy ditch for safety, remaining there until night rescued him.

38. James McIntire, sworn statement to Moses Riley, June 30, 1879. Affidavit in Webb's Texas Ranger files, U. of Tex. Archives.

39. Moses Wiley to Maj. John B. Jones, July 1, 1879, U. of Tex. Archives.

40. J. Evetts Haley, *Charles Goodnight*, U. of Okla. Press, Norman, 1949, 335.

CHAPTER 12

1. *John Selman of El Paso*, Chap. 3, 10.

2. *Ibid.* John Selman, Jr., is the primary authority that his father operated a butcher shop in Ft. Davis. No one questions this, but there is some uncertainty as to what name he used while running the business. Selman Jr. does not say. R. N. Mullin thinks he used the *alias* "John Gunter." So do some others. However, since it is unlikely that Selman used two different names in one place, the Texas Ranger reports that refer to him as "Captain Tyson" will be accepted.

3. Caruthers to Jones, June 14, 1880, AGF.

4. Barry Scobee, *Fort Davis, Texas, 1583-1960*, Hill Pub. Co., El Paso, 1963, 132. Hereafter cited Scobee.

5. Jno. W. Dean to Gov. Roberts, May 21, 1880, AGF; Frazier to Roberts, May 24, 1880, AGF.

6. G. W. Frazier, Bates and others to Roberts, June 16, 1880, AGF.

7. Caruthers to Jones, June 14, 1880, AGF.

8. Scobee, 145.

9. Caruthers to Jones, June 14, 1880, AGF.

10. Caruthers to Nevill, June 8, 1880, AGF.

11. Sieker to Jones, June 15, 1880; Caruthers to Nevill, June 8, 1880, AGF.

12. Caruthers to Jones, June 14, 1880, AGF.

13. *Ibid.*

14. Caruthers to Jones, June 28, 1880, AGF; R. N. Mullin to Robert McCubbin, Mar. 15, 1961.

15. John Selman's confinement did not prevent him from collecting $27 from the county for ten days' services rendered as jailor. The money was paid to him under his alias of John Tyson, Aug. 10, 1880. Commissioners Court Minutes, Vol. 1, 133, Marfa, Tex.

16. Caruthers to Jones, June 28, 1880, AGF.

17. Marriage License Records, Marfa, Tex., Vol. 1, 102.

18. Ed Bartholomew, *Jesse Evans,* Frontier Press, Houston, 1955, 51-53. For another account of the life of Evans, see Philip J. Rasch, "The Story of Jesse Evans," *Panhandle Plains Hist. Rev.,* XXXIII (1960), 108-122.

19. Carlyle Raht, *The Romance of the Davis Mountains and Big Bend Country,* Odessa, Tex., 1963, 255-257.

20. Sieker to Jones (letter), July 12, 1880; Sieker to Jones (telegram), July 12, 1880; Caruthers to Jones, July 12, 1880. AGF.

21. *Ibid.*

22. Nevill to Jones, Aug. 8, 1880, AGF.

23. Nevill to Jones, Sept. 5, 28, 1880, AGF.

24. Case Nos. 94, 107, Minutes District Court, Vol. 1, 283, 289, Marfa, Tex.

25. Case No. 108, Minutes District Court, Vol. 1, 289, Marfa, Tex.

26. Caruthers to Jones, June 28, 1880, AGF.

27. Cruger to Jones, July 2, 1880, AGF.

28. Comanche *Chief,* Aug. 21, 1880.

29. P. W. Reynolds to J. R. Webb, 1945, Webb Papers; J. R. Webb, "Henry Herron . . ." (see Note 3, Chap. 5), 21-50; Sonnichsen, 165.

30. Mrs. Ruby Moore, County Clerk, Shackelford Co., letter to LCM, Dec. 12, 1964.

31. Deed Records, Vol. M-C, 632-633, Throckmorton, Tex.
32. *Ibid.*, also see Deed Records, Vol. 1, 1-6 and Vol. 4, 23.
33. *John Selman of El Paso,* Chap. IV, 6-8; also interview with Edna Selman Haines, El Paso, Dec. 15, 1964.
34. *Ibid.*
35. *Ibid.*, Chap. IV, 11 and Chap. V, 7.
36. *Ibid.*, Chap. V, 3-4.
37. *Ibid.*, Chaps. V, VI.
38. Paso del Norte, later called Juarez, lay on the Mexican side of the Rio Grande, directly across from El Paso.
39. Some authorities have referred to El Paso as "Franklin." This is an error. The city has never been known by any name other than El Paso. Franklin was a small settlement nearby.
40. *John Selman of El Paso,* Chap. VI, 2-7.
41. *Ibid.*
42. P. W. Reynolds to J. R. Webb, 1945, Webb Papers.
43. Skelton Glenn MS.
44. Minutes 34th District Court, Vol. B, 268, Albany, Tex.

CHAPTER 13

1. Clyde Wise, "The Effects of the Railroads on El Paso," *Password,* July, 1960; El Paso City Directory, 1895-1896.
2. W. W. Bridgers, "Just Chatting," El Paso *World News,* June 13, 1934.
3. George Millan, El Paso *Times,* Dec. 13, 1964.
4. John Selman, Jr., in *All Western Magazine,* Oct. 1935, 50; *John Selman of El Paso,* Chap. VI, 9-10.
5. Siringo, 171-174.
6. No city marshal ever was slain in line of duty in El Paso. Dallas Stoudenmire had resigned his city marshal's job and was serving as a deputy U. S. marshal when he was killed.
7. The volumes of the El Paso city council's minutes are replete with charges accusing almost all the officials of having their hands in the public till at one time or another. Most of this has obvious political overtones.
8. Albert Scasta, employment officer, American Smelting & Refining Company, interview with LCM, July 3, 1964.

9. The Hueco Tanks water holes are protected by clusters of huge rocks lying on the desert floor near the Hueco Mts., about 35 miles east of El Paso.

10. El Paso *Times,* Oct. 22-23, 1891.

11. *Ibid.*

12. *Times,* Nov. 5, 1891.

13. *Ibid.*

14. *Ibid.*

15. *John Selman of El Paso,* Chap. VIII, 5-6. No mention is made here of John Gilan.

16. Frank Collinson, *Life in the Saddle,* U. of Okla. Press, Norman, 1963; 97. Hereafter cited Collinson.

17. E. L. Shackelford, testimony taken by Judge Howe as to the killing of Hardin by Selman, Aug. 21, 1895.

18. For the most comprehensive account of this struggle, see C. L. Sonnichsen, *Tularosa,* Devin-Adair, N.Y., 1961.

19. *Ibid.;* also see A. M. Gibson, *The Life and Death of Colonel Albert Jennings Fountain,* U. of Okla. Press, Norman, 1965; 212-231.

20. *John Selman of El Paso,* Chap. VIII, 10-11.

21. *Times,* Nov. 9, 1892.

22. *John Selman of El Paso,* Chap. X, 4-5.

23. *Times,* Nov. 9, 1892.

24. *Herald,* Oct. 26, 1892.

25. Record of Election Returns, Book 1, 22. On Nov. 6, 1894, Selman ran for re-election against F. E. Archer and won by 97 votes out of 1503 cast.

26. Judicial Court Record, Vol. III, 257 & 271.

CHAPTER 14

1. The local jail had been under heavy fire for years from the El Paso *Times,* which called it a "bat cave." It charged that the one means of ventilation was a little barred window on one side, "and the stench even with the doors thrown open is simply stifling. It is an outrage on public decency that humanity should be forced to inhale the noxious gasses arising from the filthy atmosphere." June 23, 1884.

2. *Times,* Dec. 27, 1892.

3. Jim Thompson was repeatedly charged with assault, threatening peo-

ple's lives, personal injury, carrying a pistol, extortion, etc. Justice Docket, Criminal, El Paso County, March 1892-1895 and 1895-1899, Case Nos. 1140, 1141, 1142, 2121, 2123, 2124, 2125, 2126.

4. Case No. 1414, 34th District Court, El Paso. A crude diagram of the Red Light Saloon is included with the court records.

5. *Times,* Apr. 27, 1893.

6. Case No. 1414, *supra,* testimony of John Selman. John's account of events seemed to be slanted to put Burns in a good light; he ignored some of the more damaging incidents, especially those concerning the shooting.

7. *Ibid.; Times,* Apr. 27-28, 1893.

8. *Times,* Apr. 28, 1893.

9. *Times,* Apr. 27-28, May 2, 3, 4, 7, 24, 1893.

10. Leases and Deed Records, Book 19, 604. On Dec. 7, 1892, John Selman purchased one-half interest in the property from Jim Burns for $21. There is no hint of what use Selman and Burns put the land to, if any.

11. El Paso Marriage License Records, Book 3, 58.

12. Case Nos. 1847, 1848, 34th District Court, El Paso.

13. Miss Granadino, born in Case Grande, Mexico, was of Italian and Spanish descent. She died Feb. 6, 1934, and is buried at Deming, N.M. After John's death she was married to three other men, being widowed twice more. She was an attractive woman, and well educated. She bore four children, all by her last three husbands. After John's death she moved to Deming, where she became known as the "six-shooter woman," because of her habit of shooting through the door when drunken cowboys came to call. Mrs. Rosebelle Moore, daughter of Romula Granadino, interview with LCM, Dec. 13, 1964.

14. El Paso *Times* and *Herald,* Aug. 24, 1893.

15. Mrs. Edna Selman Haines and Mrs. Rosebelle Moore, interview with LCM, Dec. 13, 1964.

16. W. H. "Bill" Selman, "Hardin Had Four Sixes to Beat," *The Southwesterner,* June 1964, 17.

17. Justice Docket, Criminal, June 1893 through 1894, Case Nos. 2188 through 2600. This does not cover all the Selman arrest cases but it has most of them.

18. Mrs. Ann Jensen to LCM, Feb. 28, 1964. Mrs. Jensen is the daughter of Ranger Alonzo Oden, who was a close friend of Bass Outlaw.

19. *Ibid.*

20. Alonzo Oden, *Texas Ranger Diary and Scrapbook,* ed. by Ann

Jensen, The Kaleidograph Press, Dallas, 1936; 40. Hereafter cited Oden.

21. *Times,* Apr. 7, 1894.

22. *Ibid.,* Apr. 6, 1894. Case No. 1485, 34th District Court. The court record is missing from the file.

23. Dr. Rex Strickland, quoting from interview with Mrs. O. L. Shipman in interview with LCM, Jan. 6, 1965.

24. *Times,* Apr. 7, 1894.

25. *Ibid.,* Apr. 6-7, 1894; Oden, 40; Collinson, 98.

26. Oden, 40.

27. Capt. John R. Hughes to Gen W. H Mabry, Apr 6, 1894, AGF.

28. *Ibid.; Times,* Apr. 6, 7, 12, 1894; Oden, 40; Collinson, 98.

29. El Paso *Times,* Apr. 12, 1894; W. H. Bridgers, "Just Chatting," El Paso *World News,* June 29, 1934.

30. *Times,* Apr. 6, 13, 17, 1894; Selman, *All Western Magazine, op. cit.,* 52; *John Selman of El Paso,* Chap. X, 1-4.

31. Case No. 1753, 34th District Court, El Paso.

CHAPTER 15

1. The district began on the south side of E. Overland St. at the intersection of Oregon, ran east to Utah St. (now Mesa Ave.), south to Third St., west to Oregon, North to Overland, El Paso City Council Minutes, Book F, Part I, 212 (El Paso Public Library).

2. The girls once organized and petitioned the city council for a reduction in fines from $10 to $5 a month, claiming the high cost constituted an undue hardship on their profession. The matter was tabled and forgotten. City Council Minutes, Book H, Part II, 295.

3. The gambling ban was one in name only. Occasional flurries of reform activity would drive the gamblers underground for a few days, then they would come back as strong as ever.

4. City Council Minutes, Book H, Part II, 348.

5. J. Evetts Haley, *Jeff Milton: Good Man With a Gun,* U. of Okla. Press, Norman, 1948, 217.

6. *Ibid.,* 218.

7. El Paso *Times,* Apr. 19, 1895.

8. *Ibid.*

9. *Ibid.,* May 9, 1895.

10. Case Nos. 1224, 1238, 34th District Court, El Paso. Jim Schoonmaker went on trial in January 1891, charged with burglary. Case file missing, no record of conviction. Still one wonders where he got his qualifications for acting as Selman's deputy.
11. *Times,* Apr. 19, 1895.
12. The newspapers indicate El Paso had a surprising number of suicides, sometimes as many as three a week. The prostitutes departed frequently in this manner, and poison was the most popular means.
13. *Times,* Apr. 21, 1895.
14. Case No. 1140, Minutes of County Court, Book 4, 581-582. The minutes do not give any of the testimony.
15. *Times,* May 9, 1895.
16. Case No. 1140, *supra.*
17. Haley, *Jeff Milton, op. cit.,* 222.
18. Cleofas Calleros, *El Paso: Then and Now,* American Printing Co., El Paso, 1954, 21.
19. Haley, *Jeff Milton,* 223.
20. *Times,* Mar. 16, 1895; *John Selman of El Paso,* Chap. XI, 1-3.
21. El Paso *Times,* Mar. 16, 1895.
22. *Ibid.*
23. City Council Minutes, Book H, Part II, 570.
24. *John Selman of El Paso,* Chap. XI, 2-3.

CHAPTER 16

1. For the full story of the Taylor-Sutton feud, see C. L. Sonnichsen, *I'll Die Before I'll Run,* 35-115.
2. For two versions of this controversial slaying, see John Wesley Hardin, *The Life of John Wesley Hardin, as written by himself,* U. of Okla. Press, Norman, 1961, and Mollie M. Godbold, "Comanche and the Hardin Gang," *Southwest Hist. Qu.,* LXVII (July 1963), 55-57.
3. After Hardin's death, Annie Williams, his landlady, stated in a newspaper interview: "He [Hardin] laughed gleefully as he told me how he frightened his young bride into returning home and telling her parents that it was all her fault; that she did not love him any more." El Paso *Times,* Aug. 23, 1895.
4. Case Nos. 1789, 1790, 34th District Court, El Paso. There is no indication of which side the witness testified for.

5. The story of Frazer and Miller is a long series of shooting incidents, finally ending in Toyah, Texas, when Miller blew Frazer's head off with a shotgun. Not long afterward Miller was hanged by a mob in Ada, Okla. C. L. Sonnichsen's *Ten Texas Feuds*, 200-210, has a complete rundown on Miller's career.

6. Haley, *Jeff Milton*, 229.

7. See Lee Myers, "Frontier Sin Spot," *New Mexico*, XLI (Mar. 1963), 36-37.

8. Haley says Morose met the blonde in Midland and "married her at the Sheriff's whore house in Eddy." *Jeff Milton*, 232.

9. Case No. 1832, 34th District Court, El Paso. The file shows that Morose was charged with bringing stolen property to El Paso but the case never was brought to trial.

10. Dee Harkey, *Mean As Hell*, U. of N. M. Press, Albuquerque, 1948, 132.

11. El Paso *Times*, Apr. 24, 1895.

12. *Ibid.*, June 30, 1895. On July 2, 1895, the *Times* printed a statement by the Mexican government saying that Morose was not a Mexican citizen and never had applied for citizenship. Morose was dead by this time, of course.

13. *Ibid.*, June 8, 1895.

14. *Ibid.*, July 2, 1895.

15. *Ibid.*, June 30, 1895.

16. George Look, letter to party unknown, June 13, 1909. The George Look memoirs are quoted through the courtesy of Wyndham White, El Paso attorney; the MS. is part of the collection of the late Maury Kemp.

17. *John Selman of El Paso*, Chap. XIII, 5.

18. *Times*, July 2, 1895.

19. Case No. 1902, 34th District Court, El Paso. No recorded testimony enclosed.

20. Case Nos. 1903, 1904.

21. *Times*, July 2, 1895.

CHAPTER 17

1. *John Selman of El Paso*, Chap. XIV, 9-10.
2. *Ibid.*, Chap. XV, 2-3.
3. El Paso *Times*, May 2, 4, 1895.

4. *Ibid.*

5. *Ibid.* There is no record of how big an interest Hardin purchased in the Wigwam, nor how much he paid for it.

6. *Ibid.*, May 10, 1895.

6a. Case No. 1814, 34th District Court, El Paso.

6b. El Paso *Times*, May 16-17, 1895.

7. Case No. 1815. On Oct. 1, 1895, the state's attorneys said they could no longer prosecute the case because of the defendant's death.

8. Dee Harkey, *op. cit.*, 100-106.

9. El Paso *Times*, Aug. 2, 1895.

10. The Recorder's Court was similar to the present-day Corporation Court. The records of this court have not been located.

11. El Paso *Times*, Aug. 3, 1895; John Selman, Jr., *All Western Magazine, op. cit.*, 55-56; *John Selman of El Paso*, Chap. XVII, 3-6.

12. El Paso *Times*, Aug. 7, 1895.

13. The court record shows that Annie Williams swore out the warrant. Beulah was the main witness, testifying that Hardin meant to kill her.

14. Case No. 1599, Justice Docket, Criminal 1882-1895, 136.

15. Haley, *Jeff Milton*, 245.

16. John Middagh, *Frontier Newspaper, The El Paso Times*, Texas Western College Press, El Paso, 1958, 76; El Paso *Times*, Aug. 15, 1895.

17. Selman, *All Western Magazine, op. cit.*, 56; *John Selman of El Paso*, Chap. XVII, 6; El Paso *Herald*, Aug. 20, 1895.

18. The testimony was written down by Judge Howe and signed by John Selman.

19. *John Selman of El Paso*, Chap. XVII, 1-8.

20. El Paso *Times*, Aug. 23, 1895.

21. *Ibid.*, Aug. 27, 1895.

22. Robert N. Mullin to LCM, Nov. 4, 1964.

23. George Look MS.

24. The Hardin family marked the grave in late 1965.

CHAPTER 18

1. The term "broker" was then applied to many men who were more or less opportunists.

2. El Paso *Herald*, Aug. 20, 1895.

3. El Paso *Times*, Aug. 21, 1895.

4. Attorney Patterson and Recorder Patterson quite possibly were one and the same.

5. *Times*, Aug. 21, 1895.

6. *Ibid.*

7. *Herald*, Aug. 20, 1895.

8. *Times*, Aug. 22, 1895.

9. *Ibid.*

10. *Ibid.*

11. *Herald*, Aug. 22, 1895.

12. *Times,* Aug. 22, 1895.

13. Case No. 1874, 34th District Court, El Paso.

14. *Ibid.;* El Paso *Times*, Nov. 19, Dec. 3, 1895.

15. According to the newspapers the members of the jury were E. L. Worden, C. F. White, C. N. Swisher, C. D. Adams, W. H. Kelley, C. H. Purtell, Carl Schmidt, I. M. Lawrence, F. A. Low, M. Counerton, G. M. Grant and G. G. Briggs.

16. The El Paso City Directory, 1896-97, lists a J. A. Brock as a live-stock, land and mine commission merchant with offices in El Paso.

17. El Paso *Herald*, Aug. 21, 1895.

18. Fred R. Rymer to LCM, Oct. 8, 15, 1964.

19. A. M. Gibson's fine book, *op. cit.*, gives an excellent account, although perhaps one-sided, of the Oliver Lee trial. While making no mention of Selman, Gibson makes repeated references to Fall's defense of noted gunmen.

20. Mrs. C. C. Chase, interview with C. L. Sonnichsen, Jan. 15, 1964; interview with LCM, Sept. 18, 1964.

21. M. T. Everhart to LCM, Nov. 20, 1964.

22. Case No. 1874, 34th District Court, El Paso.

23. *Ibid.*

24. El Paso *Times,* Feb. 12, 1896. The *Times* went to press a few hours before the jury announced itself hung.

CHAPTER 19

1. El Paso *Herald,* Aug. 21, 1895.

2. *Ibid.; Times*, Aug. 23, 1895.

3. *Herald,* Aug. 22, 1895. Selman did not give his source of information but the *Herald* remarked "the Constable is not given to making wild, unsubstantiated charges."

4. *Times,* Aug. 24, 1895.

5. William "Bud" Selman, older brother of John, Jr., worked as a guard for the AT&SF railroad, and also as a streetcar conductor between El Paso and Juarez. El Paso Directory, 1896-97; William H. Selman to LCM, Jan. 11, 21, Apr. 11, 18, Sept. 8, 1964.

6. Clements made no attempt to avenge Hardin's death. He was himself shot and killed Dec. 29, 1908, in El Paso's Coney Island Saloon; his slayer never was apprehended. Middagh, *Frontier Newspaper, op. cit.,* 126-127.

7. *John Selman of El Paso,* Chap. XIX, 5.

8. *Ibid.,* 3-5.

9. Selman evidently changed his mind later, bringing suit against the Great Syndicate Show. No details available; case dismissed at cost to John Selman, Case No. 1647, Book 5, Minutes County Court, 71, Nov. 5, 1895.

10. Mrs. Alward White, interview with LCM, Jan. 18, 1964. Mrs. White witnessed the incident.

11. *John Selman of El Paso,* Chap. XIX, 1-3.

12. *Times,* Apr. 1; *Herald,* Apr. 2, 1896.

13. W. W. Bridgers, "Just Chatting," *op. cit.*

13a. For the story of young John's imprisonment and subsequent bizarre escape, see Leon C. Metz, "Why Old John Selman Died," *Frontier Times,* Nov. 1965, 30-65.

14. *Times,* Apr. 7, 1896.

15. *Ibid.,* Apr. 5, *Herald,* Apr. 7, 1896.

16. *Times,* Apr. 5, 7, *Herald,* Apr. 6, 7, 1896.

17. *Ibid.*

18. *Times,* Apr. 7, 1896.

19. Case No. 1945, 34th District Court, El Paso.

20. Scarborough and Fink may not have been as good friends as this remark might imply. Chief Fink once made some derogatory remarks about Scarborough, who met Fink in the street and called him a liar. Fink walked away saying he was going to have Scarborough arrested. George then gave himself up to Officer Chipman and went to the Recorder's Court, where it was held that he could not very well be tried on a charge that had not been made. El Paso *Times,* Sept. 7, 1895.

21. *Ibid.,* June 20, 1896.

22. *Ibid.,* May 2, 1896.
23. *Ibid.*
24. Case No. 1305, Vol. 5, 233, Minutes County Court, El Paso.
25. El Paso *Herald,* Apr. 7, 1896.
26. George Look MS.
27. The members of the John C. Camp Confederate Veterans, assisted by members of the Emmett Crawford Post of the G.A.R., took charge of the funeral. Pallbearers were Judge Wyndham Kemp, Dr. W. M. Yandell, W. T. Kitchens, Mr. McConnaughey and Frank Tusten. Union and C.S.A. veterans were honorary pallbearers.
28. Mrs. Rosebelle Moore, interview with LCM, Dec. 13, 1964.

ACKNOWLEDGMENTS

My first and foremost thanks must go to my good friend C. L. Sonnichsen, Dean of the Graduate Division of Texas Western College in El Paso. Without his help, cooperation, and patience, this book would never have developed beyond an idea. He graciously gave many hours of his time in working with me and reading and editing the manuscript. His advice and suggestions raised it from a faltering work to its present form.

Next I wish to thank Mr. Robert N. Mullin, formerly of El Paso, now living in South Laguna, California. Mr. Mullin, a valued personal friend, opened his files of New Mexicana and gave freely of knowledge and advice that was available from no other source.

Mrs. Edna Selman Haines of California, daughter of John Selman, Jr., graciously consented to spend a week in my home during December, 1964. She also furnished a valuable, unpublished photograph of her grandfather, along with an unpublished manuscript of his life as written by her father.

Mr. William H. "Bill" Selman of Texas, also a personal friend and son of the late William "Bud" Selman, graciously invited me into his home and we spent several enjoyable evenings discussing the different aspects of John Selman's life.

Mrs. Joan Farmer of Albany, Texas, introduced me to Mr. and

231

Mrs. Putnam (present owners of the Larn home), with whom we made a tour of the Shackelford County countryside, visiting the scene of much of the conflict of the 1870s, including the ruins of the old Selman ranches. With Mrs. Farmer I also visited the ranch home of Mr. Watt Matthews and spent a pleasant hour or so chatting about the history of the area.

My thanks also go to the El Paso Public Library, particularly to the reference section. Mrs. Rosemary Corcoran, head of the reference department, Mrs. Marcelle Hamer, head of the Southwest Room, and Mrs. Virginia Hoke, reference clerk, were generous with their time and services.

The staff of the Texas Western College Library also opened up their facilities. Mr. Baxter Polk, Director of the Library, made available several obscure items not ordinarily on display. Also, Mr. Frank Scott, head of the periodical department and Mr. James Cleveland, assistant, were readily available with time and assistance.

Mr. J. Evetts Haley of Canyon, Texas, opened his files of personal interviews and gave generously of his Selman material.

Mr. Robert Nail, playwright, Albany, Texas, first opened the door to the possibility of untapped Selman material in Shackelford County.

Mrs. Caroline Dunn, Librarian, William Henry Smith Memorial Library, Indianapolis, made available the Lew Wallace collection.

Mr. Bill Johnson, District Clerk of El Paso, and Earl Forsyth, Deputy District Clerk, plus all the assistants, made available the maze of court records in their charge and through their knowledge helped me narrow down my search.

Mr. Wally Fields, County Clerk of El Paso, and Mrs. Maxine Lindop, secretary, opened up records pertaining to Selman which had never been used before.

Dr. Rupert Norval Richardson, Head of the Department of History at Hardin-Simmons University, made available the Richardson Collection containing the late J. R. Webb's personal papers dealing with the Shackelford County feud. Without the start given by these papers, much of the new information available in this book would never have been collected.

Mabel E. Willoughby, Director of the Library at Hardin-Simmons, generously allowed me to continue studying the papers even though the library was closed and has since answered numerous questions about data I overlooked.

Mrs. Ruby Moore, District and County Clerk of Shackelford

County, and her assistant, Mrs. Lucy Matthews, gave generous amounts of their time and energy in locating records which no one dreamed existed.

Mr. Chester V. Kielman, Archivist of the University of Texas, made available the W. P. Webb Ranger letters and reports.

Mr. James Day, Director of the Texas State Library, sent me many documents from his files and opened his office to me in Austin. A friendly man of great patience, he answered all my questions when I was beginning to feel my way in the book.

Mr. Ed Bartholomew, author and publisher, now living in Toyah, Texas, took time out from his busy schedule to help clear up a few points about Selman's history.

Mr. Wyndham White, attorney in El Paso, furnished me with the memoirs of the late Maury Kemp, invaluable in dealing with early-day El Paso.

Norman Rosen, also an El Paso attorney, gave considerable time to showing me through the various court-house offices, a chore which made research much easier.

Mrs. Ann Jensen of Dallas, Texas, daughter of Texas Ranger Alonzo Oden, furnished valuable information about Bass Outlaw and her father.

Mrs. R. C. Hardin of San Diego, furnished data about John Selman's early life, particularly about his father and mother.

Mr. Rod B. Moss of Lawrence, Kansas, donated the Skelton Glenn manuscript which helped fill in information about little known Selman adventures.

Mrs. Frank Skidmore of El Paso made available the book *History of the deGraffenreid Family*, a personal family possession, and thus opened up another avenue of Selman's life.

Mrs. C. C. Chase of Alamogordo, New Mexico, filled in many details concerning her father, the late Albert B. Fall.

Mr. Robert G. McCubbin, formerly of El Paso and now of Gallup, New Mexico, welcomed me into his home and allowed me to browse at will through one of the greatest collections of rare Western books in America.

Mr. Barry Scobee of Fort Davis, Texas, helped with some of his deep insight into the history of that area.

Mr. G. A. Feather of Las Cruces, New Mexico, gave me several hours of his time as we discussed New Mexico history.

Mr. William S. Wallace, Librarian, New Mexico Highlands University at Las Vegas, New Mexico, sent several New Mexico census records and contributed other bits of information.

Mr. Emory Christian, Chairman of the Grayson County Historical Society, came up with nothing I could use in the book, but a man never worked harder.

Mr. Fred R. Rymer, Supervisor, Firearms Section, Texas Department of Public Safety, put all his facilities to work in an attempt to find out if John Wesley Hardin was shot in the face or in the back of the head.

Mrs. Elizabeth Tucker, Assistant Librarian of Stephen F. Austin State College, and Sue Massey, Nacogdoches County Clerk, made a gallant try to locate John Selman descendants in that part of Texas.

Mrs. Eve Ball of Hollywood, New Mexico, author and historical researcher, welcomed me into her home and gave me a fascinating discourse on local history.

Mr. George Shalkhauser of El Paso is the craftsman who reproduced the fine-quality pictures for this book.

To Mrs. Joyce Wilson of El Paso, who typed the manuscript, goes a debt of gratitude which surpasses my ability to express it.

Others who contributed in some measure to this book are: Lee Myers, Carlsbad, New Mexico; Ed Syers, Ingram, Texas; Fella Kerr, El Paso; Father Stanley, Pep, Texas; William A. Keleher, Albuquerque; Kittie C. Swetnam, Santa Fe; Mr. Jan Oskam, Ziest, Holland; Mollie M. Godbold, Dallas; Mr. Beale Stewart, Clovis, New Mexico; Carl B. Mayfield, Dallas; Mrs. Nanon B. Atkins, Assistant Librarian, Oklahoma Historical Society; Mrs. Walter Humber, Librarian, Albany High School; William V. Morrison, El Paso; and Bobby Henry, great grandson of John Selman, Altus, Oklahoma.

And finally, a special note of thanks to Jose Cisneros, who made the map of John Selman's Wanderings.

BIBLIOGRAPHY

BOOKS AND ARTICLES

Bartholomew, Ed. *Jesse Evans: A Texas Hide Burner*. Houston: Frontier Press of Texas, 1955.

————. *Kill Or Be Killed*. Houston: Frontier Press of Texas, 1953.

Biggers, Don H. *Shackelford County Sketches*. Albany, Texas: Albany News Office, 1908.

Blanton, Thomas Lindsay. *Pictorical Supplement to Interwoven*. Albany, Texas: Albany News Office, 1953.

Calleros, Cleofas. *El Paso: Then and Now* (Volume VII). El Paso: American Printing Company, 1954.

Coe, George. *Frontier Fighter*. Albuquerque: University of New Mexico Press, 1934.

Collinson, Frank. *Life In the Saddle*. Norman: University of Oklahoma Press, 1963.

deGraffenreid, Thomas P. *History of the deGraffenreid Family: 1191 AD to 1925*. New York: The Vail-Ballow Press, 1924.

Drago, Harry Sinclair. *Great American Cattle Trails*. New York: Dodd, Mead and Company, 1965.

Farmer, Joan. "Fort Davis on the Clear Fork of the Brazos." *West*

Texas Historical Association Year Book (October, 1957), XXXIII, 117-126.

————. "Sandstone Sentinels." *West Texas Historical Association Year Book* (October, 1958), XXXIV, 112-127.

Gibson, A. M. *The Life and Death of Colonel Albert Jennings Fountain.* Norman: University of Oklahoma Press, 1965.

Godbold, Mollie M. "Comanche and the Hardin Gang." *Southwest Historical Quarterly* (July, 1963), LXVII; (October, 1963), LXVII, 247-266.

Grant, Ben O. "Life In Old Fort Griffin." *West Texas Historical Association Year Book* (October, 1934), X, 32-41.

————. "Citizen Law Enforcement Bodies: The Vigilantes." *West Texas Historical Association Year Book* (October, 1963), XXXIX, 155-165.

Haley, J. Evetts. *Jeff Milton: A Good Man With A Gun.* Norman: University of Oklahoma Press, 1948.

————. *Charles Goodnight: Cowman of the Plains.* Norman: University of Oklahoma Press, 1949.

Hardin, John Wesley. *The Life of John Wesley Hardin* (with an introduction by Robert G. McCubbin). Norman: University of Oklahoma Press, 1961.

Harkey, Dee. *Mean As Hell.* Albuquerque: University of New Mexico Press, 1948.

Hunt, Frazier. *The Tragic Days of Billy the Kid.* New York: Hastings House, 1956.

Keleher, William A. *Violence in Lincoln County: 1869-1881.* Albuquerque: University of New Mexico Press, 1957.

Matthews, Sallie Reynolds. *Interwoven* (reprint). El Paso: Texas Western College Press, 1958.

Metz, Leon C. "Why Old John Selman Died." *Frontier Times,* November, 1965, 30-65.

Middagh, John. *Frontier Newspaper: The El Paso Times.* El Paso: Texas Western College Press, 1958.

Myers, Lee. "Frontier Sin Spot." *New Mexico* (March, 1963), XXXXI, 36-37.

Oden, Alonzo Van. *Texas Ranger Diary and Scrapbook,* ed. by Ann Jensen. Dallas: The Kaleidograph Press, 1936.

Raht, Carlysle Graham. *The Romance of the Davis Mountains and Big Bend Country.* Odessa, Texas: The Rahtbooks Company, 1963.

236

Rasch, Philip J. and Lee Myers. "The Tragedy of the Beckwiths." *The English Westerners Brand Book* (July, 1963), V, 1-6.

Rasch, Philip J. "Exit Axtel: Enter Wallace." *New Mexico Historical Review* (July, 1957), XXXII, 231-245.

———. "The Story of Jesse J. Evans." *Panhandle Plains Historical Review* (1960), XXXIII, 108-122.

Richardson, Rupert N. *Frontier of Northwest Texas.* Glendale: The Arthur H. Clark Company, 1957.

Rister, Carl Coke. *Fort Griffin On the Texas Frontier.* Norman: University of Oklahoma Press, 1956.

Rye, Edgar. *The Quirt and the Spur.* Chicago: The W. B. Conkey Company, 1909.

Scobee, Barry. *Fort Davis, Texas: 1583-1960.* El Paso: Hill Printing Company, 1963.

Selman, John, Jr. "John Selman," (as told to Franklin Reynolds). *All Western* (October, 1935), 44-61.

Siringo, Charles A. *Riata and Spurs,* revised edition. Boston and New York: Houghton Mifflin Company, 1931.

Sonnichsen, C. L. and William V. Morrison. *Alias Billy the Kid.* Albuquerque: University of New Mexico Press, 1955.

Sonnichsen, C. L. *I'll Die Before I'll Run.* New York: The Devin-Adair Company, 1962.

———. *Ten Texas Feuds.* Albuquerque: The University of New Mexico Press, 1957.

———. *Tularosa: Last of the Frontier West.* New York: Devin-Adair Company, 1963.

Webb, J. R. "Henry Herron, Pioneer and Peace Officer During Fort Griffin Days." *West Texas Historical Association Year Book* (October, 1944), XX, 21-50.

———. "Chapters From the Frontier Life of Phin W. Reynolds." *West Texas Historical Association Year Book* (October, 1945), XXI, 110-143.

Webb, Walter Prescott. *The Texas Rangers: A Century of Frontier Defense.* New York: Houghton Mifflin Company, 1935.

Wise, Clyde. "The Effects of the Railroads on El Paso." *Password* (July, 1960), III, 91-101.

237

UNPUBLISHED MANUSCRIPT MATERIAL

Anonymous Author. *Once Only.* Typescript of a book preface. The book, never published, was supposed to cover the period from 1882 to 1943. The author, evidently a woman, describes her experiences while living in the John Larn home after his death. Copy obtained by LCM from Mrs. Joan Farmer, Albany, Texas.

Comstock, Henry Griswold. *Some Of My Experiences And Observations on The South Plains During the Summers of 1871 and 1872.* Typescript. Copy obtained by LCM from Mrs. Joan Farmer, Albany, Texas.

Glenn, Skelton. This typescript has no title, being simply the observations of an old buffalo hunter in the late 1800s. Copy on microfilm at Texas Western College. Original in possession of Mr. Rod Moss, Lawrence, Kansas.

Grant, Ben O. *The Early History of Shackelford County.* Typescript thesis for a Master's Degree, 1936, Hardin-Simmons University, Abilene, Texas.

Howe, W. S. (Justice of the Peace in El Paso). Depositions written by himself in longhand and completed on the 21st day of May, 1895. They relate to the killing of John Wesley Hardin by John Selman, and are signed individually by Selman and witnesses to the slaying. Copy in possession of LCM.

Look, George. Typescript in the files of the late Maury Kemp, attorney in El Paso. Copy in possession of LCM, courtesy Wyndham White, attorney in El Paso.

Newcomb, Samuel P. and Susan E. *Newcomb Diaries.* The diary of Sam Newcomb runs from January 1, 1865, to August 21, 1866. Susan's goes from August 1, 1865, to May 1869; then from January 1, 1871, to June 4, 1873. The Newcombs were schoolteachers living at Fort Davis on the Clear Fork of the Brazos River. Copies secured and typed under the supervision of J. Evetts Haley in El Paso in 1936. Copy on microfilm at Texas Western College, courtesy of Robert Nail, Albany, Texas.

Selman, John. *John Selman of El Paso.* Unpublished book manuscript in type, July 16, 1934. Original in possession of Edna Selman Haines, California.

Wallace, Lew. The Lew Wallace papers are on file in the William

Henry Smith Memorial Library, Indiana Historical Society, Indianapolis, Indiana.

Webb, J. R. The R. N. Richardson collection at Hardin-Simmons University includes the Webb papers dealing with the Shackelford County feud of the 1870's. Some of it is typescript and some longhand.

NEWSPAPERS

Austin *Weekly Statesman.*
Comanche *Chief.*
El Paso *Herald.*
El Paso *Times.*
El Paso *World News.*
Frontier Echo.
Galveston *News.*
Mesilla *Valley Independent.*
Rio Grande Republican.
Southwesterner.

DOCUMENTS

Shackelford County Courthouse, Albany, Texas.
Brand Book, Throckmorton County, Texas. (Why this is filed in Shackelford County is not known.)
Deed Record Book, Volume C.
Minutes of Commissions Court, volume 1.
Minutes of 34th District Court, Book A, volume 1.
Records of Official Bonds, Book B.
Case Nos. 138, 140, 141, 142, 143, 144, 145, 147, 148. 34th District Court. (John and Tom Selman charged with rustling.)
Presidio County Courthouse, Marfa, Texas.
Marriage License Records, volume 1.
Commissioners Court Minutes, volume 1.
Case No. 94 & 95. 34th District Court. Jesse Evans, robbery.
Case No. 95 & 96. 34th District Court. Ace Carr, robbery.

Case No. 97 & 98. 34th District Court. Charles Graham, robbery.

Case No. 107. 34th District Court. Jesse Evans, murder.

Case No. 108. 34th District Court. John Gunter, murder.

Throckmorton County Courthouse, Throckmorton, Texas.

Deed Record Book, volume M-3. (Letter to LCM from Don Chandler, County and District Clerk, Throckmorton, Texas).

Deed Record Book, volume 4. (Letter to LCM from Don Chandler, County and District Clerk, Throckmorton, Texas).

El Paso City-County Building, El Paso, Texas.

Case No. 1224 and 1238. 34th District Court. (Jim Schoonmaker charged with burglary.)

Case No. 1414, 34th District Court. (Jim Burns charged with aggravated assault.)

Case No. 1485, 34th District Court. (Unspecified charge against Bass Outlaw.)

Case No. 1753, 34th District Court. (John Selman's trial for killing Bass Outlaw.)

Case No. 1789 and 1790, 34th District Court. (Trial of G. A. "Bud" Frazer for shooting Jim Miller.)

Case No. 1832, 34th District Court. (Martin Morose charged with bringing stolen property to El Paso.)

Case No. 1847 and 1848, 34th District Court. (W. H. Wheat charged with rape and seduction.)

Case No. 1885, 34th District Court. (J. W. Hardin charged with robbery of Gem Saloon.)

Case No. 1874, 34th District Court. (John Selman's trial for killing John Wesley Hardin.)

Case No. 1902, 34th District Court. (George Scarborough's trial for killing Martin Morose.)

Case No. 1903, 34th District Court. (Jeff Milton's trial for killing Martin Morose.)

Case No. 1904, 34th District Court. (Frank McMahon's trial for killing Martin Morose.)

Case No. 1945, 34th District Court. (George Scarborough charged with murder of John Selman.)

Case No. 1140, Minutes County Court, Book 4. (Jim Schoonmaker's trial for shaking down prostitutes.)

240

Case No. 1305, Minutes County Court, volume 5, p. 233. (Cole Belmont charged with stealing property below value of fifty dollars.)

Case No. 1467, Minutes County Court, Book 5, p. 71. (John Selman files charges against Great Syndicate Show.)

Case No. 1140 & 1141, Justice Docket, Criminal, 1892-1895. (Jim Thompson charged with simple assault.)

Case No. 1142, Justice Docket, Criminal, 1892-1895. (Jim Thompson charged with simple assault against Jim Burns.)

Case No. 1507, Justice Docket, Criminal, 1895-1899. (W. H. Wheat charged with seduction.)

Case No. 1525, Justice Docket, Criminal, 1895-1899. (Jim Burns charged with gambling and betting.)

Case No. 1599, Justice Docket, Criminal, 1882-1895. (Annie Williams and Beulah Morose place John Wesley Hardin under a peace bond.)

Case No. 2100, Justice Docket, Criminal, March 1892-June 1893. (Jim Burns charged with assault and battery.)

Case No. 2188 through 2600, Justice Docket, Criminal, June 1893-1894. (This is the book which has the most Selman arrest cases.)

Deed Record Book, Quit claim deeds, Book 19, page 604, County Clerk's office. (John Selman buys land from Jim Burns: complete description of land given.)

Judicial Court Record, volume 3, page 207, County Clerk's office. (John Selman makes bond for Constable: 1892 and 1894.)

Marriage License Records, Book 3, page 358, County Clerk's office. (John Selman's marriage to Miss Romula Granadino and W. H. Wheat's written permission for her marriage.)

Record of Election Returns, Book 1, page 22 and 27. (Results of elections for Constable in 1892 and 1894.)

City Council Minutes, typescript, unpublished, El Paso Public Library.

Book C, part 1, p. 30. (Office of City Recorder is created.)

Book F, part 1, p. 212. (Ordinance locating houses of ill fame.)

Book F, part 1, p. 250. (William Allen wants location of houses of ill fame changed so as not to include his residence.)

Book H, part 2, p. 295. (Petition from prostitutes asking monthly fines be reduced from $10 to $5.)

Book H, part 2, p. 348. (Jeff Milton sworn in as Chief of Police.)

Book H, part 2, 570. (Milton asks Council to investigate complaint that John Selman, Jr. assaulted H. Nelson.)

Miscellaneous documentary material.

El Paso City Directory: 1895-1896. Frank J. McDevitt. El Paso Steam Printing Company.

El Paso City Directory: 1896-1897. Evans and Worley: Dallas.

Census Records. 1840, Madison County, Arkansas.

Census Records. 1860, Grayson County, Texas.

Census Records. 1870, Colfax County, New Mexico.

Adjutant General's Files, Texas State Archives, State Library and Archives Building, Austin, Texas.

W. P. Webb Collection of Ranger Reports, Texas University Archives, Austin.

Military Service Record, John Selman; also letters from Dudley to Asst. Adgt. General of New Mexico, September 28-29, 1878.

United States Department of Archives, National Archives and Records Service, Washington, D.C.

PERSONAL INTERVIEWS

DURING THE PAST two years I have had numerous conversations in El Paso with the following people: C. L. Sonnichsen, Rex Strickland, and Robert N. Mullin. Others who have kindly consented to interviews have been: Edna Selman Haines, El Paso, December 15, 1964; W. H. "Bill" Selman, Belton, Texas, June 24, 1964; Cleofas Calleros, El Paso, January 7, 1963; Mrs. Alward White, El Paso, January 18, 1964; Wyndham White, El Paso, January 10, 1964; Norman Rosen, El Paso, December 10, 1963; Fred Smally, El Paso, May 10, 1964; Albert Scasta, El Paso, July 3, 1964; Ann Jensen, El Paso, June 19, 1964; Mrs. C. C. Chase, Alamogordo, New Mexico, September 18, 1964; Joan Farmer, Albany, Texas, May 13, June 25, 1964; Robert Nail, Albany, June 25, 1964; Watt Matthews, Albany, May 13, 1964; Mr. and Mrs. Carol Putnam, Albany, May 13, 1964; Milus McComb, Albany, June 25, 1964; Mrs. Ed Brewster, Albany, June 25, 1964;

Ruby Moore, Albany, May 13, June 25, 1964; Mrs. Lucy Matthews, Albany, May 13, June 25, 1964; Dave Richards, Albany, May 13, 1964; Barry Scobee, Fort Davis, December 7, 1964; Eve Ball, Hollywood, New Mexico, October 20, 1964; Mrs. Rosabelle W. Moore, El Paso, December 13, 1964, January 8, 1965.

INDEX

Davis, B. H., 186, 187
Davis, Jefferson, 25
deGraffenreid, Edna: *See* Selman, Edna deGraffenreid
deGraffenreid, Elizabeth Selman (Mrs. Jasper N.), 21, 25, 32, 34
deGraffenreid, Jasper N., 26, 34, 40, 93, 209
Dirt farmers, 76
Dolan, Jimmy, 98
Dolan-Riley faction, 97, 98
Dooley (doctor), 200
Draper, James, 57
Dudley (Army colonel), 103, 105
Duke, Francis (Frank), 118
Dwyer (Dyer), William, 101, 104

E

Earp, Wyatt, 62
Ellis, Isaac, 103
Ellison, Dewees and Bishop ranch, 59
El Paso, 16, 129-38, 139, 151, 155, 164
El Paso *Herald*, 131, 138, 181, 183, 185, 186, 188, 189, 190, 192, 193, 194, 199
El Paso *Times*, 131, 134, 137, 141, 143, 156, 165, 166, 173, 174, 177, 178, 184, 188, 190, 192, 193, 195, 199, 200, 202
Evans, Jesse, 62, 98, 99, 103, 108, 114, 115, 118, 119, 120, 218
Everhart, M. T., 192

F

Fall, Albert Bacon, 136, 190, 191, 192, 193, 228
Farrell (judge), 169, 196
Faught, Houston, 65
Fink, Ed, 164, 198, 201, 229
Finnessey, Tom, 163
Fisch (lawyer), 47
Flats, The, 48, 49
Fleming, J. R., 80, 93
Floyd, Hank, 59, 60, 65, 75
Ford, Bob, 204
Fort Davis, 25, 27, 28, 30, 31-32, 37, 39, 113
Fort Griffin, 15, 41-47, 48-56, 73
Fort Griffin Vigilance Committee, 15, 57, 58, 59-60, 65-66, 70, 72, 78, 88, 92
Fountain, Albert J., 136, 191
Frazer, G. A. (Bud), 161, 226
French, Jim, 108
Fritz, Emil, 97
Frontier *Echo*, 65, 67

G

Galveston *News*, 123
Gambling, 151, 224
Garrett, Pat, 62, 98, 99, 191, 196
Gem Saloon, 137, 170, 171, 179
Gilan, John (French John), 133, 134, 135
Gildea, Gus, 104, 108
Gillett, James, 131
Gilson, William, 60, 86

247

H

I

J

McSween, Alex, 97, 98, 110, 219

Mackenzie (Army colonel), 43

MacKenzie (cattleman), 163

Marcy Trail, 22

Marshal, Andrew Jackson (Jocko), 30

Martin, Hurricane Minnie, 55, 64, 79, 85, 93

Martin, William A. (Hurricane Bill), 74, 79, 80, 89

Masterson, Bat, 62

Matthews, George, 57, 212

Matthews, Joseph Beck, 54, 69, 70, 73, 85, 122; family, 57, 86, 212, 216

Matthews, Mary: *See* Larn, Mary Matthews

Matthews, Sallie Reynolds, 40, 212

Maulding, T. F., 38

Maxwell, Lucien, 40

Maxwell Land Grant, 40

Meadows, John, 63-64, 73

Merrill, Tom, 61, 127

Mescalero Apache Indian Reservation, 97

Mesilla *Independent*, 108

Mesilla *News*, 108

Mexican Central Railroad, 135

Meyers (Cavalry lieutenant), 71

Miller, Jim, 62

Miller, "Killin' Jim," 160, 226

Millet (rancher), 64

Millet, Alonzo, 72

Milton, J. D., 201

Milton, Jeff, 151-58, 163, 164-67, 174, 178, 179, 180, 181

Montague County Minute Men, 41

Monte Carlo dance hall, 169

Morose, Helen Beulah, 162, 163, 164, 166, 167, 172-73, 174, 176, 177, 178, 179, 187, 227

Morose, Martin, 161-67, 176, 178, 179, 180, 181, 203

Mullin, Robert N., 102, 178

Murphy, G. L., 104

Mussleman, Chas., 65

N

Neal, Doc, 60, 66

Nelson, Boss, 157

Nelson, John, 101, 104

Nesmith, George, 105

Nesters, 76

Newcomb, John, 100

Newcomb, Samuel P., 28, 30, 31, 32, 36, 37, 38, 39

Newcomb, Susan, 30, 31, 33

New Mexico Mounted Rifles, 102, 218

O

Oden, Alonzo, 146, 223

Old Law Mob (OLM), 45-47, 57

Outlaw, Bass, 139-50, 203, 223

Owens, Jake, 101, 104

P

Palo Duro Canyon, 43

Patron, Juan, 106

251

marshal, 131; capabilities, 23; cattle brand, 214; cattle stealing, 75-78; children, 40, 43, 44, 124; Confederate Army, 19, 21-24, 38; death, 198, 200; Deputy Inspector of Hides and Animals, 72-73; elected constable, 136; family, 20-21, 25, 31-33; Fort Davis, 27-28, 31-32, 39; Fort Griffin Vigilance Committee, 57-60; funeral, 203, 230; killings, 14-15, 62, 63, 102, 149, 174; Lincoln County War, 96-108; marriages, 39, 118, 144; Old Law Mob, 45-47; partial blindness, 149, 191; Rock Ranch, 45; runs for sheriff, 30, 31; scouting, 36-38; Seven Rivers Warriors, 100-04; silver mining, 126; smallpox, 112; Stockton Ranch, 40; Texas State Troops, 35-38; Tonkawa Indians, 49, 51

Selman, John Marion (John Jr.) (John's son), 44, 58, 90, 94, 124, 125, 127, 128, 131, 132, 135, 137, 145, 165, 175, 176, 207, 208; as city policeman, 153, 154, 156, 157-58, 168-169, 172, 173, 182, 183, 187, 195; elopement and imprisonment, 197-98, 199, 203

Selman, Lucinda (John's sister): *See* Willet, Lucinda Selman

Selman, Margaretta (John's daughter), 43, 124, 125

Selman, Mary Ann (John's sister), 21, 25, 32, 34

Selman, Niconora Zarate (John's

second wife), 112, 118, 124, 127, 128

Selman, Romula Granadino (John's third wife), 144, 223

Selman, Tom (John's brother), 21, 25, 33-34, 41, 70, 72, 76, 77, 91, 93, 94, 99, 100, 101, 104, 106, 108, 109, 122

Selman, William (Bud) (John's son), 40, 44, 124, 125, 126, 127, 132, 145, 199, 201, 229

Selman's Scouts 104, 105

Sender and Siebenborn store, 115

Seven Rivers Warriors, 97, 98, 100, 105, 107

Shackelford, E. L., 135, 182, 183, 185

Shackelford County, 49, 56, 57-61, 75, 120

Sherard, G. S., 186, 188

Sherman, Jim, 196

Shields (Shailes), George, 123

Sieker (Ranger sergeant), 115, 116, 118, 123

Simmons (sheriff), 171, 185, 201

Siringo, Charlie, 94

Slack, R. A., 88

Slaughter, John, 106

Slaughter, Rev. Mr. 33, 34, 209

Smith, Buck, 109

Smith, Jack, 91

Snow, Charlie, 101, 104

Sonnichsen, C. L., 48, 57, 210

Speakes, Robert, 101, 104, 106, 108

Stevens, R. B., 185

Stevens County Company of Texas State Troops, 35-36

252

253

Willet, Tod, 30, 31, 34, 39
Williams, Annie, 173, 176, 225, 227
Wilson (sheriff), 117
Wilson, Charlie, 211
Wilson, John B., 101
Wise, Lola, 105
Woosley (Woolsey), Ed and Frank, 46-47

Wray, John W., 88
Wrestlers, 103

Z

Zarate, Guadalupe, 112
Zarate, Niconora: *See* Selman, Niconora Zarate